DANGEROUS GOD

A DEFENSE OF TRANSCENDENT TRUTH

DANGEROUS GOD

A DEFENSE OF
TRANSCENDENT TRUTH

Albert Norton, Jr.

Published by New English Review Press
a subsidiary of World Encounter Institute
PO Box 158397
Nashville, Tennessee 37215
&
27 Old Gloucester Street
London, England, WC1N 3AX

Cover Art and Design by Kendra Mallock

ISBN: 978-1-943003-49-5

First Edition

NEW ENGLISH REVIEW PRESS
newenglishreview.org

Do your best to present yourself to God as one approved, a worker who has no need to be ashamed, rightly handling the word of truth.

—2nd Timothy 2:15.

Contents

Introduction

THERE IS A SICKNESS at the heart of Western civilization. It is worse than racism, sexism, xenophobia, injustice, incivility, loneliness, isolation, or inequality. We are anxious about these things but not about what underlies them all. We're like a person with both a hangnail and terminal cancer, obsessed with the hangnail because the pain is more immediate. The more lethal sickness, which we too often ignore, is the collapse of belief in objective goodness and truth. From transcendent truth springs the metanarrative of faith we have inherited but which we are on the way to destroying. The metanarrative that built civilization should be mended, not levelled. The sickness is curable, but only if we see it for what it is.

In his seminal work, *A Secular Age*, Charles Taylor wrote of "the buffered self," to describe the various ways by which we mediate our experience of God, if we believe in God. That is, between us and God are all manner of perturbations in the atmosphere that attenuate our experience of him. We can think of those as things like church practice, theological dispute, secular philosophical speculation, busyness, exasperation, skepticism in general and as applied to religion, and preoccupation with little decisions about everyday living.

The "buffered self" is conceptually valid outside the religious context, too, and it goes a long way toward explaining why Christians and atheists are so nearly indistinguishable despite their fathomless differences in worldview. Christians are "buffered" against the reality of how they say they see the world, by various irreligious cultural considerations. At the same time, atheists are "buffered" against theirs, not seeing its inescapable pointlessness, wherein life is about seeking pleasure and avoiding pain, and then we die.

Existentialism was a response to the problem of meaninglessness in a Godless world. Philosophical pragmatists imagined away God, too, but they bootstrapped meaning from social activism. Truth in pragmatism is socially located, rather than subjectively (as with existentialists) or objectively (as with theists). Existentialism and pragmatism came together and had a Frankenstein baby called postmodernism. Postmodernism holds that there is no objective truth, much less a transcendent Source for objective truth. With a postmodern outlook, we no longer debate what is true. We internally conceive truth, and attempt to make it socially operative. This means never-ending ideological war, as we see with critical social theory. This puts the big problem of meaning at a little remove from us in our everyday lives, which is another way of saying it puts the bottomless pit of meaninglessness just out of sight—we are buffered, perhaps for another generation or so, but perhaps less, from the meaninglessness to which the postmodern view of reality inevitably takes us.

The theist worldview by contrast means there is too much meaning to life. More than we humans can manage. God is dangerous. So we mediate our relationship to him with all manner of churchy stupidity. We're like Moses in the cleft of the rock, trying to peer out at the blinding light after God has passed by. But we don't live in the fullness of that reality, in this life. We couldn't possibly. We can't look upon God and live. Instead we're caught in the day-to-day struggle for bread, and then ambition for prestige, honor, possessions, legacy, and so on, just like our peers who have already written off God. The culture wraps around us like a thick fog, limiting our vision to about the same scope as our Godless contemporaries. That thick fog includes (perhaps especially) church culture. Christians' view of reality is buffered, too, just as it is with those who've thrown over any ambition to seek God.

The net result is this: There is a bottomless chasm between the light-flooded reality of Christianity, and the Stygian reality imagined by secular agnostics or atheists. If we lived openly in reality without buffering self-delusion, we might see that bottomless chasm all the time. But we don't. Our perceptions of reality are buffered, on both sides. So much so that in this life we see almost no difference between one who says he is a Christian—and therefore ought to have the expanded version of reality—and one who is agnostic or atheist. The zone of buffering overlaps, you might say. Or the fog intermingles. Everyone, Christian and atheist and shoulder-shrugging agnostic alike, is wandering around in the fog.

We want a lightness of being: the pagan feeling of ease and freedom and openness that seems to attend a godless reality. But that doesn't sat-

isfy, so at the same time we want the opposite—the feeling of seriousness and significance that attends a consciousness of God's presence. We
need to feel that what we do matters. And so we vacillate between these
ways of feeling inside a narrow band well removed from the extremes of
meaning and meaninglessness, because both extremes are emotionally
problematic. Utter meaninglessness (or total lightness) makes suicide
just as valid an option as continuing to live. Utter meaning (or total
seriousness) indurates the soul with fear. The way through is reconciliation with God, the Source of meaning. God is too dangerous to simply
ignore.

Among the purposes of this book are to show how God imparts
meaning to the cosmos, and how we corrupt it, and how we can find
our way back. We find, if we look, meaning embedded in the binary
structures of physical reality and transcendent ideals. Semantic meaning, reducible to words. All of reality and rational thought exists in binary oppositions, dualisms which create meaning, as Heraclitus observed
long ago. We think in binary terms because the universe presents to us
in binary terms. Truth and ideals and value derive from this meaningful
structure, which is to say that meaning builds upon meaning, hierarchically, into a system of ever more refined ideals. God draws this system
of ideals up to himself; we don't build it from the ground up. We make
things ever harder for ourselves, however, becoming confused by the
postmodernist attempt to destroy claims to objective and transcendent
truth, and objective right and wrong.

God is at the apex of ideals and of meaning and is the absolute to
which all absolutes point, including especially absolute truth. The idea
that truth is an objective "out there" phenomenon has been discarded
in recent years by trendy postmodern philosophical developments that
take us ever further from ultimate truth, and the Author of it. We can be
rescued from these misconceptions by bringing the reality of God back
into sharp relief. The goal here is to show he is not merely a fearsome
idea in the heads of some people, but is present in the warp and woof, so
to speak, of all of our daily existence. We can't run from him and we can't
reshape reality to make him less dangerous and less demanding. It is imperative that we understand, rather than ignore, the intellectual trends
which delude minds and hearts to stray from the Lover of their souls.

We are being dumbed-down in our thinking by eschewing oppositions. We live an "either/or" existence whether we like it or not. Dualist
binary oppositions exist and comprise physical reality, and our interior
rationality, and our conception of the God who is. These oppositions

can be blurred or collapsed with the result that we grope blindly within systems of thought devised for polemical ends beginning with rejection of God. The religious/secular divide is non-overlapping; there's a bottomless chasm between, and everything important about our existence hinges on getting on the right side of it. We should understand how we can be misled away from God, from truth, and from our best selves.

Meaning is derived from discerning distinctions in things and ideas, in ever finer gradations. It emerges from the oppositions of this thing or concept, and that thing or concept. Ever more abstract values develop, such as virtues of honesty, courage, loyalty, and so on, each in contradistinction to their opposites: dishonesty, cowardice, disloyalty. These include values necessary to good governance, such as equality, justice, community, and their opposites. From these values, and contrasted opposites, a hierarchy of values emerges. These comprise the system of values to which we subscribe, individually and collectively. This is the way people think, and the way communal values have historically developed. This process depends on the existence of objective truth as distinguished from falsity; objective good as distinguished from evil; beauty as distinguished from ugliness. Removal of the good, the true, and the beautiful as objective realities, locating them instead in individual feeling or socially-located consensus, means collapse of the system of values that depends on them. We should be attuned to developments in our ways of thinking that threaten this collapse. One thesis of this book is that postmodernism presents such a threat.

For theists, the Source of objective truth and goodness is God. Abstract truth is understood to be ontologically original in God, who radiates it into the world for us to apply to our understanding of purpose, of meaning, and the development of individual virtue and societies maximizing the resulting values. Truth and goodness are transcendent. Even among those who are atheist or ambivalent about the existence of One who is the originator of our hierarchy of values, there may be a sense that these abstractions of truth and goodness are nonetheless objective; that is, real, "out-there" phenomena in reality, there to be discovered rather than created by us.

To start from the bottom and work our way up, we begin in chapter 1 with the binary structure of material and conceptual reality, and how it gives rise to meaning. That meaning, we see in chapter 2, does not merely reside subjectively with us, but is extant in the universe. It builds upon itself into ideals (chapter 3). Likewise information, also a pervasive and real but immaterial constituent of reality, pervasive for us like water is for fish, will be developed in chapter 4. Then in chapter 5 we consider living in a meaning-full reality, and our ways of attempting to escape the tension that inheres in colliding binary oppositions. These five chapters can be considered the foundation for understanding the source of meaning and purpose in our lives.

From this foundation, we move to secular philosophies in recent history that have brought us to this pass. Thus we follow, in chapters 6-15, developments of modern through postmodern secular philosophy on these subjects: individualism and collectivism; the social element derived from the intersubjectivity of consciousness; the nature of truth; and postmodernism as desperate search for meaning. The result of this philosophical superstructure is to take us inexorably to mechanistic materialism, as we will see in chapters 16-18.

On purely rational grounds (that is, discounting instinct), why suppose there is a God at all? The purpose starting in chapter 19 is to clear the air of fine-graded philosophy and return to the foundational reason for intuiting two-layered metaphysics: the fact that there is something rather than nothing. The difficulty of conceiving of "nothing" diverts attention from the insoluble problem of somethingness. The opposition to God and his creation brings us (chapter 20) to an expression of the mutual exclusivity of the worldviews in a binary opposition. Subjectively, we may substitute Nothing with a "nothing-as-such" which is a buzz of angst or tension that reformulates in our imaginations as an ill-defined something, upon which we construct man-made, but false, philosophies of freedom. This is equivalent to the pagan tendency which secular philosophies feed.

We can see this play out in the legal realm (chapter 21): How the evolution of secular philosophy is reflected in the law in the twentieth century. The false neutrality imagined in the jurisprudence clears the public square of religious perspectives, in favor of the irreligious philosophies jostling for ideological dominance. This is not all the fault of secularists bent on destroying Christianity, however. In chapter 22 we critique the inadequate response of Christian institutions in the twentieth century, including causes of failing to see the principalities and powers arrayed against it. A corrective to this is to first be honest about what constitutes knowledge and belief (chapter 23). We don't all have Damascus road experiences. Religious truth is subject to rational understanding just like anything else. It is not true that religion is irrational like postmodernism. Because Christians look to the Bible for what "belief" is, what does it say? (chapter 24). It does not demand fideism, in fact it exists as an extended argument from evidence. Nor does it mean mere intellectual assent to some form of truthiness of the narrative.

In the final chapter, we end on themes carried throughout the book: the theistic and materialistic worldviews are non-overlapping, irreconcilable conceptions of reality; that our intuition of significance is warranted; virtues and values and hierarchies of value and systems of logic resulting in higher-order reasoning are real, extant, "out-there" features of the universe. They originate in, reside in, and are shared with us by God, who is dangerous because he won't stay in any cage we devise for him, and he requires something of us.

CHAPTER ONE

Binary Reality

THERE IS A BINARY REALITY to the cosmos. There is a corresponding binary reality to our ability to perceive it. Physical things exist and are understandable in binary terms. There is something, or there is nothing. Existence/non-existence; presence/absence; good/evil; light/dark; truth/falsity; beauty/ugliness. Each of these dualisms is defined in terms of its opposite. God cannot both exist and not exist. The Biblical assertion by God, "I am," is either true or it is false. There is no in-between, but we are capable of living as if there were, in an ongoing state of hesitation to avoid this inevitable and ultimate binary opposition.

Binary thinking is a necessary component of the obvious fact that we are time-bound creatures with agency. The temporal dimension means that we live and move and have our being in a series of choices we make, some moral and consequential, some frivolous and less so. But every time we make any choice in life, we are deciding against all the other choices we might have made. Our life unspools in a continuous stream of this-not-that decisions. Each is necessitated by binary opposition, even when there are a near-infinite number of not-taken choices. Because we make choices continually all day every day, we are operating on binary decision-making, whether we are aware of it or not, and whether we like it or not.

We perceive external, objective things over the interval of our subjective consciousness. We rely on a correspondence between our internal subjective discernment of objective things and the fact of those things externally and objectively. Through innumerable verifications, we can know that reliance is well-placed. We are not mere brains in jars, re-

15

ceiving stimuli that evoke false perceptions. Our internal perception of reality also consists in binary oppositions. We make sense of the world because we make binary distinctions continually. In our visual field, we expect the sky above and the distinct ground below because they exist in opposition and re-present themselves to us continually and consistently. In every moment and in every situation, binary thinking makes the world comprehensible, instead of presenting as undifferentiated sludge. We distinguish thing A from thing B and idea X from idea Y by mentally setting them in opposition each to the other. This takes place subjectively in the mind, which receives and discriminates among stimuli on the basis of oppositions. The external world we perceive is objectively comprised of these oppositions, too, in that everything about it is reducible to them, beginning with existence and non-existence.

In this way, dualisms naturally arise and we naturally employ them. They are a necessary corollary to the law of non-contradiction: contradictory propositions cannot be true in the same sense at the same time. According to Aristotle, without the principle of non-contradiction we could not know anything that we do know. We would have no way of distinguishing between subject matters and properties. The inability to draw distinctions in general would make rational discussion impossible. The oppositional nature of things (and ideas and ideals) presupposes that identical things are indiscernible (that is, not opposed) and any two things which do not share all properties are thereby discernible; that is, subject to at least some form of dualism.[1] This is consonant with (perhaps equivalent to) Aristotle's principle of the excluded middle, which holds that for any proposition, either the proposition is true or its negation is true.

Dualism means division of a thing or concept into two, with the two parts comprising all the possibilities for the thing or concept being divided. It means dividing phenomena by two opposing principles, for example, night and day; up and down; alive and dead; right and wrong; present and absent; existent and non-existent. The opposing principles are intended to be the universe of possibilities relating to the subject matter. There is only day and night, for example, as long as we're talking about our experience of light and darkness in the atmosphere. We make this dualistic distinction because it is helpful to understanding states or activities like waking and sleeping and the circumstances in which we expect to encounter others around us. The two parts to the dualism are

---

1 See, e.g., "Leibniz's Law," attributed to Gottfried Wilhelm Leibniz.

in opposition if each excludes the other, and is yet defined by the other. Presence and absence constitute an oppositional dualism because a thing is one or the other. Same with night and day; up and down; alive and dead; right and wrong.

An oppositional dualism is not invalidated as such simply because one can imagine an in-between state. For example, twilight is neither day nor night, but day and night remain in opposition because twilight is a transition between one state and the other, not a new state altogether that eliminates the binary opposition of day and night. To the contrary, the binary opposition must remain if we are to make sense of twilight. Day is not-night and night is not-day. The two states remain oppositional such that each necessitates the other. Similarly, hot and cold remain in binary opposition and are employed in our thinking as such when we procure tepid water. Each state in opposition defines—and is defined by—its opposite.

We might suppose that binary oppositions do not inhere in things that present as an array, or on a spectrum, but they do. There is binary opposition in play even when we distinguish one thing from a group of many like things. The recognition of the one thing results from binary distinctions. If you distinguish your sister in a crowd, binary oppositions in play include sister/not-sister; choosing/not-choosing; crowd/solitude. In the case of amino acid combinations of DNA, each position exists in the state of both (1) one among the finite number of alternatives; and (2) not the other alternatives. Binary opposition exists even when there are more than two combinations possible.

Generally when we think in dualistic terms, we are thinking in terms of properties that present in binary opposition, precisely because their binary and oppositional nature makes the dualism helpful to our thinking. The parts to a dualism are in opposition if each is definable in terms of the other. Evil is incomprehensible except in contrast to good, for example. One might try to think of the colors blue and green as a dualism, perhaps, but why, given that they're not in opposition? If a thing is not blue, that does not mean it's green. It is the oppositional feature of a conceptual dualism that creates tension and thereby produces meaning. The opposition enables us to make distinctions necessary for ordinary rational thinking.

It is important to recognize certain specific dualisms; to be clear we're speaking of dualism more generally. In theology, "dualism" also refers to the distinction between body and soul, or body and spirit. It is sometimes used to set good and evil off each against the other. A dualist philosophy of religion, for example, would suppose divinity as comprised of two equal and opposing forces of good and evil in constant tension, as is understood in Zoroastrianism, and gnostic heresies, perhaps in a Star Wars sense of "the Force." This kind of dualism is decidedly not orthodox Christianity, because God is not comprised of two forces locked in combat, nor does he have an equal opponent. Rather, God is supreme. He creates all, including mankind with moral agency, which means mankind has the capacity for evil. In the philosophy of mind, dualism refers to theories by which mind and body are regarded as distinct kinds of substances or natures, as René Descartes concluded. These dualisms are put under the microscope from time to time in philosophy and theology, but for our purposes they are but specifics of the general mental process by which we look at opposed and contrasted aspects of a thing or an idea, to draw meaning from their differentiation. Here we address dualisms in the general sense.

The universe around us is comprehensible on the basis of observations we make on a binary basis. But does that mean the universe and the mind are structured in a binary way? Much speculation goes into whether the human brain is fundamentally binary in nature. In one sense, it doesn't matter, because the mind certainly operates this way in making things comprehensible, regardless of the brain's structure. That we make ever finer differentiations in setting off "this" from "that" does not mean, necessarily, that the entirety of the human brain is given over to binary constitution. That qualification made, it is certainly of interest whether the brain itself has a binary structure. Many have reached that conclusion based on the intuition that the bilateral symmetry of the body, including the brain, suggests it. Elementary investigations into brain functioning suggest different emphases in left brain hemisphere as opposed to right. This is suggestive of binary brain operation. At a minimum, we know neurons in the brain either fire, or they don't, and in this limited way, there is necessarily a binary structure to brain functioning.

There's much more to the brain, however, so much so that it's difficult to conclude one way or the other whether the brain is fundamentally binary or not. The levels of complexity to brain functioning overtake the simplicity of the binary model. It's true that neurons fire or they don't, but they fire in differing frequencies and sometimes different intensities. In the synapses in-between neurons, there are evidently chemical functions imposing a gradient governing whether to fire or not fire the next neuron. There are parallel functions in the brain so that merely following a single series of neurons as if in linear fashion is incomplete, in attempting to explain the physical component of thought. The brain apparently has analog functions, therefore, in addition to digital binary functions.

In addition to all this, in speaking of binary or any other functioning, we must remember we are speaking of time-bound processes. At some level of detail, the binary digital model breaks down. Let's think of lightning by analogy to a neuron firing. We see lightning and it appears as a flash, brightening the sky for less than a second. We think of it as "on" for the briefest of moments, and then "off:" a binary phenomenon. But if we perceived it on a much slower scale, as by extreme slow motion, we would perceive a more gradual build-up and fall-off of light. If the lightness were charted graphically, the "shoulders" of the graph would be more rounded than the flash we perceive in real time. At some sufficiently short span of time, even a neuron firing is something more fluid than an on/off binary. This is among the features of the brain which suggest it may be too complex to function or be structured in a strictly binary way.

This does not defeat the dualist paradigm, however. The dualism of light and dark in that lightning flash is still a fundamental in our thinking. Light and dark are opposites and understandable, each in relation to the other. Setting light and dark off against each other in binary fashion is what produces meaning concerning the presence (or absence) and quality of both light and darkness. As with the flash of light following a lightning strike, so with the firing of a brain neuron. The mind is oriented to perceiving and thinking in binary opposition, regardless of whether the brain is physically structured and functioning in a binary way.

Computers certainly are binary, because we made them that way. They are inevitably analogized to the brain, and this tends to reinforce the idea of a binary brain.[2] The computer analogy comes into play even though mind created computers, and not the other way around, because mathematical knowledge produced computers, and mathematical knowledge includes the binary theory which is the basis of computer operations. Gottfried Leibniz (1646-1716), among others, contributed to the development of the binary number system, upon which almost all modern technology, including computers, depends. Leibniz found confirmation for his ideas concerning a "universal characteristic" of mathematics in the Eastern concept of the yin and yang, from the Chinese *Book of Changes*, dating to at least the third century BC. He incorporat-

2 John von Neumann, *The Computer and the Brain*, 1958.

ed this into his view that the Biblical principle of creation—something from nothing—supported a binary numerical structure in the universe. His paper, "Explanation of Binary Arithmetic," was published in 1703. His work included a conceptual computer, based entirely on a binary number system, which described in its essentials what would become the modern computer.[3]

Anyone with a passing familiarity with computers will understand they operate on a binary system. Even quantum computers do so, because in a given logic gate only one outcome, excluding others, is possible. Human beings impose a binary system on computers because binary reality is the common experience. Using a computer analogy, all of reality is reducible to a series of 1's and 0's. Our undertaking is to understand reality, first by distinguishing between 1's and 0's, and then by decoding the message they convey.

That there is order to the universe rather than chaos suggests there are patterns to the oppositional dualisms of the universe.[4] The pattern produces meaning. The mathematical concepts, including oppositional dualisms, are not self-contained inventions of the human mind, but have independent significance. They are ideals, transcending the tangible physical reality we observe. The distinction between permanent and unchanging ideals, on the one hand, and that which is confined to space and time, on the other, is among the dualisms by which we discover meaning. These dualisms exist in reality, not just in human minds. That human minds can make sense of them attests not to their being a human invention, but rather to a match between the dualisms extant in the universe bringing order, and the human mind's ability to invoke them in discerning that order.

Thinking in accord with binary oppositions thus makes intellectual discernment possible, but we sometimes use the phrase "binary thinking" pejoratively, confusedly associating it with the tendency to force matters into broad categories, with the result of blunting intellectual discernment.[5] "He sees everything in black or white," we might say, to

---

3   Lande, Daniel R. (2014) "Development of the Binary Number System and the Foundations of Computer Science," *The Mathematics Enthusiast*: Vol. 11 : No. 3 , Article 6. Available at: https://scholarworks.umt.edu/tme/vol11/iss3/6.

4   For a discussion based on this concept, see Davies, Paul, *The Mind of God/The Scientific Basis for a Rational World*, especially pp. 140 – 161 (chapter 6). Davies finds the Platonist view more compelling in large part because of Gödel's Incompleteness Theorem of 1931.

5   See for example, Mark Baer, "When Binary Thinking is Involved, Polarization Follows," *Psychology Today* online, January 27, 2017. This is a name-calling exercise where-

suggest a failure to grasp nuance. But actually binary thinking is precisely the mechanism by which nuance becomes apparent. Ever greater nuance results from repeatedly invoking the ability to identify and then distinguish between opposites, in ever greater refinement. Indeed, one can consider an otherwise intractable opposition to be resolved, or transcended, by doubling down on the oppositional concept, finding still more oppositional features to offset, in more sophisticated analysis, to generate ever deeper and more nuanced meaning. As Jack Denfeld Wood and Gianpiero Petriglieri put it:

> One could argue that the development of our minds from childhood follows a pattern of increasing differentiation in our thinking. With increasing differentiation comes a need to structure, that is, to organize, classify, order, and regulate the objects, processes, and concepts that have been first articulated by "this and "that." Intelligence may essentially be the general measure of our capacity to make numerous, ever-finer, multidimensional distinctions of the reality around us, and within—to transcend "binary thinking" and our elementary tendency toward dualism.[6]

Thus, more binary thinking in ever finer distinctions is a means to transcend polarizing "binary thinking" —in quote marks to identify the phrase in the popular misconception. More sophisticated binary thinking is the cure, not the disease. The placement of objects (or people, or ideas) into opposing camps is how we always think, all the time. If we don't engage in this activity, we won't make sense of our world. It will present to us as a muddled, undifferentiated gray.

It might be useful to shift to another medium of understanding, visual art, to illustrate these ideas. There's a concept in painting called "value," referring to degree of brightness, you might say, or tone or depth of color. A deep red and a deep blue could have the same value, though they're different colors. Values are harder to discern in color, but easier in black and white. Imagine a color painting, suddenly switched to black and white. You would then easily see whether there is an aesthetically-pleasing balance of values, or a purposeful concentration of them. This is one reason why black-and-white photography can seem more artistically suited for a given subject.

---

in binary thinking is confused with prejudice.

6   Jack Denfeld Wood and Gianpiero Petriglieri, "Transcending Polarization: Beyond Binary Thinking," published in *Transactional Analysis Journal*, Vol. 35, No. 1, January, 2005, p. 33.

A color value is not significant unto itself. It is only significant in contrast with other color values. Think of a favorite black-and-white photo. Perhaps an Ansel Adams print of a scene in Yosemite. A reductionist account of that photo would be an accumulation of many shades of gray. Each by itself has limited aesthetic value. You might choose one to paint your wall. By itself a particular shade is meaningless, which is to say it imparts no semantic message to the viewer. Each gray shade in the photo acquires meaning only in relation to those surrounding it. The tension among relatively lower and higher values in the picture produces meaning.

In the same way, abstract ideas on the "canvas" of our minds would be meaningless without their opposites, with which they move in tension. It makes no sense to speak of evil, for example, without a concept of moral good, which is why it's nonsense to say there can't be a God because there's evil in the world. Why did God create a world with evil in it? Because he created a world with good in it. We know evil only because we know good. God made us with moral agency, the ability to choose good and to choose evil, and evil exists because we create it. It is nonsense to say the world might have existed with good but not with evil, because good and evil comprise an oppositional dualism in which each defines, and requires, the other.

In painting, a dark value like phthalo blue takes on meaning as a shadow if placed next to something with higher color value, by the painter who intends to impart a particular meaning. But by itself, it's just a color, period; it means nothing. With something else, placed where it is by the painter, it does mean something. In this example, a shadow, which by its placement in opposition to the lighter value object, communicates light and a direction of light source as one element of the over-all meaning of a painting. The darker value acquires semantic content only by virtue of its opposition with the lighter value. The opposition gives the painting meaning reducible to words.

In that way, dualisms are like the DNA of living things or the mathematical constants of the universe. They are meaning-full, which is to say they have and convey information. They contribute to the word extant in the universe—the logos. Divine reason: creative order expressible in words. "In the beginning was the Word, and the Word was with God, and the Word was God,"[7] as we read in the first line of the Gospel of John. The logos implies a transcendent source of meaning, spoken

---

7 John 1:1.

into the world. This centrality of the word in our understanding of anything is logocentrism. Logocentrism is an ineradicable feature of our existence, and we should be glad for it, not attempt to "deconstruct" it because we don't like it pointing inexorably to God.

Imagine again the black and white Yosemite photo. A high level of meaning is created by the intricate placement of varying intensities of gray, creating innumerable oppositions in value. If we collapse those oppositions, or some of them, what are we left with? Instead of a valley, a stream, cliff walls, and trees, all presented in detailed and pleasing perspective, we get a dumbed-down collection of hues that may or may not resemble a landscape. Or worse, one muddled gray replacing the innumerable variety and hierarchy of values. The Yosemite photo is an accurate representation of an objective and real place. The collapse or partial collapse of the oppositions contained in it yield a muddle that doesn't really exist anywhere. We're left to argue over what it means, if it means anything at all.

Our culture carries a strain of thought that binary oppositions have a divisive and stratifying effect, preserving outmoded categories that inhibit free thinking about our relations with others and how we receive the world in general. We should push back against this impression because it's backwards. In reality, we only make sense of the world by setting thoughts and sense impressions in opposition. We are doing this now in contrasting the concept of binary opposition against a monist conception of reality. Thinking in binary opposition is necessary for science. It is also how we make distinctions in philosophy and theology and metaphysics. We necessarily employ binary oppositions like good and evil, right and wrong, justice and mercy, man and woman, heaven and hell. Rejection or "deconstruction" of ordinary dualisms of thought is a philosophical category error. It means distortion of our mental picture of the world.

A denial of duality or of opposing distinctions in some sphere is monism. So if one were to take a monist position on the nature of mind and body, for example, it would be to say that they are in substance the same thing. Another example: body and soul are one and the same thing. Monism on a particular subject means finding one unifying principle, rather than making antagonistic dualistic distinctions. Much of Eastern religion, for example, we might regard as monistic, in comparison to the Christianity of the West. We might look to someone like influencer Deepak Chopra as an example of monistic thinking, in particular with regard to the nature of God:

[T]he God hypothesis is unique and can only be interpreted by standards applicable to monism. Monism refers to wholeness and the qualities of wholeness. . . .God is monistic, not as a humanoid figure sitting above the clouds but as the basis of consciousness. Nothing can be conscious without a basis or source in consciousness; therefore, religious monism states that God is the source of all mind, and mind is the source of the universe. [8]

A monist conception of God, as with pantheists and panentheists, involves some form of harmonious spiritual continuity between God and the self, such that there is less reason to think dualistically of a far-off God up there, and a me down here getting through life in the world. God on this understanding is not an entity to be (in dualistic terms) embraced or rejected in the same way a monotheist would.

Reductionist materialists are monists, too. All of reality is reducible to matter in motion, in the materialist view, which is to say everything is of one substance; there is no immaterial spiritual realm. "Naturalism" is the philosophical view of this form of monism, meaning there is no God, no heaven, no spirit, no hell, and no soul. In some past philosophical usages, "naturalism" did not necessarily mean there was no God, but those outlooks were more accurately monist, taking the spiritual and the physical to be all of one essence. "Naturalism" still means monism, but now monism is reductionist materialism, a point of view that excludes any spiritual reality, and of course God or gods within it. Monism is the essential outlook of some religious schools of thought which reject the natural/spiritual dualism of Augustine and the Bible. For a time in the nineteenth century, "necessarianism" had traction with some Christian thinkers,[9] though it was essentially reductionist materialism, emphasizing its resulting determinism, and was therefore also monist.

Monism certainly affects the cultures in which it is found, but it doesn't result in wholesale monistic thinking about all of reality. It is necessary to make dualistic distinctions in one's day-to-day thinking, regardless whether the inclination to monism obtains in some spheres of thinking, like the religious. A person who embraces a monistic vision of God will nonetheless drive on the correct side of the road.

If you're of a philosophical bent, you might recognize some of the

---

8   Blog at deepakchopra.com, April 16, 2018, "As We Evolve, Do We Need God?" by Deepak Chopra, MD and Anoop Kumar, MD.

9   Rée, Jonathan, *Witcraft: The Invention of Philosophy in English*, UK: Allen Lane, 2019, p. 216.

concepts here in thinkers as diverse as Heraclitus, Aristotle (in his analysis of logic), and modern structuralists like Ferdinand de Saussure and Claude Levi-Strauss. Structuralists sought to identify structural context for linguistics and social interaction, by identifying binary oppositions. Post-structuralists like Michel Foucault and Jacques Derrida seized upon binary oppositions to demonstrate what they regarded as hidden injustices and oppressions inhering in absent or weaker partners in oppositions. That is, deconstructionists imputed to each side of the dualism value or hierarchy judgments, to show resulting inequities. About the deconstructionists, more later. For now, we hew to the dualist foundation of rational thought.

Joseph Campbell, a well-known professor and student of myths who thought they all converged by metaphor to universal truth, was interviewed in a widely-viewed series called *Joseph Campbell and the Power of Myth*, aired on public television in 1988 after Campbell's death. In them, Campbell pointed out, based on the Bible, that Western mythology:

is a mythology that's based on the insight of duality. And so our religion tends to be ethical in its accent, sin and atonement, right and wrong. It started with a sin, you see. . . . And then they eat the apple, the knowledge of the pairs of opposites, and man and woman then cover their shame, that they're different; God and man, they're different; man and nature, as against man.[10]

Myths from other belief traditions don't contradict this foundational dualism; in fact, many re-affirm it. Asked about an archaeological site in a cave in the harbor of Bombay (Mumbai), Campbell described a large central mask as representing eternity, God. And about two side figures:

Whenever one moves out of the transcendent, one comes into a field of opposites. These two pairs of opposites come forth as male and female from the two sides. What has eaten of the tree of the knowledge, not only of good and evil, but of male and female, of right and wrong, of this and that, and light and dark. Everything in the field of time is dual, past and future, dead and alive. All this, being and nonbeing, is, isn't. . . . The mask represents the middle, and the two represent the two opposites, and they always come in pairs.[11]

10 Interview with Bill Moyers, Episode 2: *Joseph Campbell and the Power of Myth*, "The Message of the Myth," at billmoyers.com.

11 Ibid.

In explaining our origins, whether metaphorically or literally, the Bible opens: "In the beginning, God created the heavens and the earth."[12] Already, fundamental oppositions are explained as created by God, the Author of the logos: God and not-God, heaven and earth. The first chapters of the first book, Genesis, go on to create the most fundamental oppositions, in rapid succession. The earth is formless, then formed. There is light and darkness; day and night; land and water; sky and earth. There are plants and animals made in their kinds. And of course God made male and female, but both in his image, so the male/ female binary dualism is conceived in the mind of God.

---

12 Genesis 1:1.

CHAPTER TWO

Mathematical Realism

W E CAN THINK OF THESE oppositional dualisms in one of two ways. Either they are objective "out there" features of reality, or they are real only in the sense that we form them in the mind and project them onto reality. (This either/or is itself an oppositional dualism.) Dualisms are a type of mathematical concept. Oppositional dualisms are information, in the same way other mathematical relationships are information. The tension between oppositions yields meaning, just as other mathematical relationships yield meaning. Does that meaning inhere in some way in the physical reality around us, or is it only in our minds? Are oppositional dualisms and other mathematical relationships extant in the universe in some way, or are they only mental projections originating with us?

Mathematical relationships inhabit the realm of the ideal. We don't dig in the dirt or look in the sky for a message that reads: "2 + 2 = 4." On the other hand, clearly the relationship of 2 + 2, and the number 4, are manifested in the physical universe in countless ways. So mathematical relationships inhabit the realm of the ideal, but are manifested in the real. We can count instances of physical things, and add them to two, and double that two, and grasp the sum, four. Does that mean those instances, and those pairs, and the resulting sum of four, are real in the universe? Or do they remain ghostly ideas in the mind, only? Does the realm of the ideal in which we find mathematics (and virtues and other ideals, as we will see) "exist" only in the sense of being manufactured by mind? Are they physical only in the sense that the physical brain in some way physically supports these products of mind? Or are these mathematical relationships real in the sense that physical reality is not merely measurable and expressible through them, but in the sense that they actually inhere in that external physical reality before we undertake to discover them there?

Before proceeding, we should address potential confusion in definitions. In philosophy, "idealism" is sometimes used to mean that which exists only as an idea, and "realism" to mean that which exists only independent of mind. This has become problematic. If something exists only as an idea, then it does not correspond in any way to anything we apprehend in nature. If something is real but not an idea, then how would we know it? Most philosophy proceeds on some mix of these concepts, so grasping the intent behind the words "real" and "ideal" depends on context.

"Idealism" is also used to correspond to that which is real but immaterial or extra-material, like virtue or beauty. This meaning for "idealism" is behind Plato's forms, and Aristotle's final cause, and corresponds to that which is superlative or aspirational. We consider it a good thing to be "idealistic" because it means aspiring to some good which is not necessarily reducible to tangible matter, as with the desire to improve the condition of others. It is the usual meaning applied outside specific avenues of finely-graded philosophy, and is the meaning applied here. The ultimate ideal is God, who we might say is the ideal of the ideals. As we will see, the attempt to overthrow idealism (on this definition) necessitates the overthrow of God, and ultimately, the overthrow of God means the overthrow of idealism.

"Realism" is used here simply to refer to that which is within the scope of reality, and we apply it when its real nature is not otherwise obvious, as with something we can talk about and conceive as part of reality, but not point to physically. "Mathematical realism," for example, is the idea that mathematical principles do not only exist in the mind, but in the physical universe, as well. Therefore, when mathematicians do math, they are thought to be discovering something that is there, rather than inventing something and mentally projecting that invention onto the physical world.

Mathematical realism is sometimes referred to as "Platonism," referring to Plato in his conception of ideals in the abstract. The contrary point of view is mathematical formalism, which holds that mathematics is a logical system complete unto itself, perhaps helpful in understanding physical things, but not inherent in them. Lest you think this distinction is a lonely irrelevance in a cul-de-sac of egghead philosophy, you might look to a recent popular revival of this question generated from, of all places, a social media post by a high school student, Gracie Cunningham. She was evidently studying math concepts going back to Pythagoras, and asked rhetorically whether they were "real." Exactly the question addressed here. Her question generated some learned responses, one of which can be found in an article by Dan Falk in *Smithsonian Magazine*, citing the stances various mathematicians and scientists take on the subject.[1] Science relies on the realism of mathematics, but science is at its core an empirical discipline; that is, a study of that which is physical. Scientists devoted to a materialist worldview see mathematical realism as a threat, because if mathematics is real, ideals in general are real. And if ideals are real, there is a reality beyond nature: i.e., super-nature. A dualistic reality, physical and spiritual, logically follows, in place of the monism of empirically-observed materialism. Expressing the concern strict empiricists have to admitting the realism of mathematics, Falk rhetorically asks: "If proof of the Pythagorean theorem exists outside of space and time, why not the 'golden rule,' or even the divinity of Jesus Christ?"[2]

Mathematical realism means that when mathematicians explore mathematical relationships, they are delving into something that is real. When physicists, chemists, engineers, and any other person employing mathematics to understand the physical universe uses mathematical measurement and relationships, the mathematics is real, not merely descriptive, and not merely a mental projection onto physical things. If mathematical facts are true at all—and almost no one seriously contends that they are not true—then something must make them true. They are so completely an abstraction that they are in no sense "true" unless they are made true by being real in the physical universe. Consider this. Science is universally done using math. If a scientist tests a hypothesis by using mathematics, but mathematics is a meaningless self-enclosed set of symbols and relationships, how could it operate to test the hypothesis about physical things? If mathematics isn't real, why is it used in science?

The realist conception of mathematics, including dualisms, applies to all ideals, and ultimately to the ideal of the ideals, God. So the concept of mathematical realism is extremely important. It informs not merely mathematics, but ideals more generally, and therefore, necessarily, the ultimate ideal: God. Numbers and mathematical relationships exist in a

---

1 Falk, Dan, "What is Math?" *Smithsonian Magazine*, September 23, 2020, available at: https://www.smithsonianmag.com/science-nature/what-math-180975882/.
2 Ibid.

non-physical realm, in the same way other ideals do. They may describe what is physical (or what is physical may be described by them), but they are not physical themselves. Mathematics is perceived and perceivable in the physical brain, and emerges as a property from external physical things, onto which the brain projects its thoughts. It is like beauty, in that respect. This requires mathematical realism: the conclusion that mathematics is real in the physical universe.

This suggests a relationship between what we call "truth" and realism, including but not limited to mathematical realism. If mathematics is real, then other abstractions like beauty and truth and goodness are real. Not just in the limited sense that we apply those concepts to real physical things, but in the deeper sense that physical things embody them. Beauty is not merely in the eye of the beholder, but is a real feature of certain physical things. It is there, it is not merely our projection. Imagine yourself looking across a mountain lake at the Grand Teton National Park. Sure, the mountains are there; they're real enough. But they're beautiful (beauty-full), too, and their beauty is also real. Similarly, actions are good or evil unto themselves, they are not merely described that way by us. And truth is not merely a description we apply to propositions or facts. They are true or false unto themselves. In this way, we conclude that beauty and goodness and truth exist objectively.

Now about the opposing point of view, mathematical formalism. The idea here is that mathematics is not real, but is a self-contained process unto itself, a manipulation of signs according to prescribed rules: a self-contained logic system, like the game of chess. As in a game with no direct correspondence to the outside world, so in mathematics there is no direct correspondence to real physical features of the universe, on the formalist view. In essence, formalism means mathematical principles are tools for helping us understand the universe, but the universe does not divulge those tools to us. We mentally impose mathematics on the universe, to aid in our understanding, but the universe does not provide them.

Formalism holds that mathematics does not emerge from the physical cosmos, nor does it exist in the part of the physical cosmos that is our brains, and yet we are mentally able to construct it. Formalism supposes that mathematics is just a set of syntactical rules we follow to push numbers around in interesting ways, as if it were all a game with no consequence outside the game. This would be like your computer doing calculations, but of course with no self-awareness, and with the calculations having nothing to do with anything outside the computer itself. Or like the calculus student who gains proficiency at manipulating numbers according to the computation rules of calculus, but without grasping its underlying principles, and therefore having no clue as to what real-world applications calculus might have.[3] Formalism holds that mathematics is in this way untethered from anything physical.

The same concept applies to other ideals, though "formalism" is not typically the word used to describe it. Beauty, truth, and goodness are not transcendent ideals, on this formalist view. Beauty (and ugliness) would indeed be only in the eye of the beholder. Nothing would be true (or false) unto itself, but only in our calling it so. Likewise good (and evil) would not inhere in acts or propositions or concepts, but would only be conceived as such in our individual minds, and projected outward.

The formalist view of mathematics leaves us with an insoluble conundrum as to how mathematics so well corresponds to the physical universe, allowing us to understand it in ways we could not otherwise. Mathematical formalism took a serious philosophical blow with the incompleteness theorems of Kurt Gödel in 1931, in which he proved that logical systems, including mathematics, cannot prove themselves true. Any system, whether of logic, as in mathematics, or of anything else, cannot be provable within itself. It will always require unprovable assumptions not contained in the system. The implications are large, to include the necessary existence of God. Gödel himself generated an ontological proof for the existence of God, near the end of his life.

Gödel's idealism no doubt caused him to intuit a problem with the claim that a logical system could be complete unto itself. His proof demonstrates that certain unacknowledged assumptions are unwittingly built in, in the same way unacknowledged ideals are behind so much of human activity. Gödel didn't just do math, he addressed meta-mathematics, because his proof not only resolved a mathematics question, but also the meta-mathematics question of whether mathematics describes an objective truth existing in the external world and not just in our mental processes. He was a mathematical realist.

Eminent mathematician G.H. Hardy wrote on the subject of mathematical realism in *A Mathematician's Apology* (1940):

A mathematician, like a painter or a poet, is a maker of patterns. If his

---

3 This provides a clue as to how mathematics might be made more palatable to students who do not intuitively grasp the "real" nature of mathematics. It should be a voyage of discovery, not a pointless exercise in symbol manipulation.

patterns are more permanent than theirs, it is because they are made with ideas. A painter makes patterns with shapes and colours, a poet with words. . . . A mathematician . . . has no material to work with but ideas, and so his patterns are likely to last longer, since ideas wear less with time than words.[4]

This certainly suggests his view in favor of mathematical realism, but he left no doubt by speaking to the realism/formalism debate specifically:

> I believe that mathematical reality lies outside us, that our function is to discover or observe it, and that the theorems which we prove, and which we describe grandiloquently as our 'creations,' are simply our notes of our observations. This view has been held, in one form or another, by many philosophers of high reputation from Plato onwards, . . .[5]

This is strong support for the idea that numbers and mathematical relationships exist as objective truths in physical reality. The number 2 is not merely a mental construct we impose on the physical world. If we observe two apples, we do so because a collection of two actual apples bears that property. It is the same with the relationship $2 + 2 = 4$. This is a proposition which resides in physical reality, not just in our heads. Indeed, a mathematical realist who thinks like Hardy might conclude that mathematical principles, like the dualisms which produce meaning in the universe and internally in our rational processes, are in a sense more real than physical things. Hardy:

> [T]his realistic view is much more plausible of mathematical than of physical reality, because mathematical objects are so much more what they seem. A chair or a star is not in the least like what it seems to be; the more we think of it, the fuzzier its outlines become in the haze of sensation which surrounds it; but "2" or "317" has nothing to do with sensation, and its properties stand out the more clearly the more closely we scrutinize it. . . . Pure mathematics . . . seems to me a rock on which all idealism founders: 317 is a prime, not because we think so, or because our minds are shaped one way or another, but because it is so, because mathematical reality is built that way.[6]

---

4 Hardy, GH, *A Mathematician's Apology*, Cambridge University Press, Canto edition 1992, p. 84-85 (first published 1940).

5 Ibid., p. 123-24.

6 Ibid., p. 130.

Theoretical physicist George Stanciu similarly writes of the beginning of his conversion to Christianity, when he discovered mathematical truth in high school:

> [I]n the tenth grade, I was changed forever by Euclid's proof that the prime numbers are infinite, an exquisite proof that surprisingly showed in six lines of text an eternal truth. Until that point in my life, I thought truth did not exist; everything about me changed, the seasons, my body, and people. My experience of the human world was that everything was in flux, sometimes bordering on the absurd.

This eventually led him to God:

> In my first encounter with the truth and beauty of mathematics, my fourteen year-old mind saw dimly that I was being called to the transcendent, in Christian terms to God. . . . When in my thirties and still dim-witted, Socrates pointed out to me that since I could grasp the eternal truths of mathematics, there had to be something in me that was eternal, something deathless.[7]

We invoke oppositions in order to do mathematics. We see two apples and not one because we distinguish apples from other non-apple blotches of color around us, and perceiving them as such also quantifies them as two and not one. We think in dualist oppositions because they are fundamentally mathematical. We find dualism in Leibnizian binary number systems, as we've seen, but in addition one can readily find dualisms in simple set theory. The set of letters in the alphabet, for example, is comprised of the subsets A and not-A, B and not-B, and so on. We distinguish between two things because each is not the other. We make ever greater and more nuanced conclusions about physical reality around us by making this-not-that divisions in ever finer gradations. We invoke oppositions in order to think.

We can easily take for granted the oppositions of light and dark, but the Bible uses this opposition by way of analogy countless times, for example, using it as a visual to describe the oppositions of good and evil; life and death; oneness with or separation from the Father; heaven and hell; truth and falsity. Our default state is the Nothing of utter darkness, and we spend our whole lives seeking out light wherever we can find it. We often look in the wrong place for some sliver of corrupted light, but

---

7 Stanciu, George, "Physics, Beauty, & the Divine Mind," *The Imaginative Conservative* (on-line journal), September 28, 2016.

God shines a light into the darkness,[8] and Jesus is the light of the world,[9] the bright morning star to wash out all darkness.[10]

In the nineteenth century, the physicist James Clerk Maxwell proved the existence of electromagnetic waves, which would later be shown to include light. He developed a short series of mathematical equations which together comprise the classical theory of electromagnetic radiation. He discovered them, he didn't create them. These mathematical relationships constitute real elements of the physical universe, as with information more generally, and truth, and transcendent ideals. If you were creating the universe, and you wanted to create a universe with light, you would have to create it using the equations Maxwell discovered. That is what God did. He spoke this information into his physical universe: "Let there be light."

8 E.g., Isaiah 9:2.
9 John 8:12.
10 Isaiah 60:19-20; Revelation 22:5.

CHAPTER THREE

Ideal of the Ideals

MATHEMATICAL REALISM is just one instance of Platonic idealism. If numbers and mathematical relationships and algorithms and dualisms are in no sense real, then we're just sitting around working puzzles all day for amusement.

As with mathematics, so with truth in the abstract. If truth is only what "works," as the philosophy of pragmatism suggests, then it's not an "out there" transcendent truth. And so with beauty, and with virtues like honesty, courage, and loyalty. If these ideals are not in any sense real, then neither are the objects of metaphor and analogy and myth. If the Resurrection didn't actually happen, it's only a story to illustrate a concept, but the concept itself is not real because ideals are considered in no sense real. What's in play here, besides all the details you already know about Christianity, is the idea of transcendent idealism in the abstract. If the Resurrection is only an analog or metaphor, and not a real event, then its power leaches out because then we're only telling stories that suggest virtues to which we're told we should aspire. But why should we?

This is why C.S. Lewis, an expert on ancient myths, was so struck with Tolkien's formulation of Christianity as the myth that is factually true. If the Gospel (and Abraham, the Exodus, crossing the Jordan, etc.) is just metaphor, then it's only part of a metanarrative we create for ourselves because it's useful. If it's not literally true then what goes down the drain is not just a helpful lesson, but idealism itself. So truthy-seeming metaphors fail to establish actual truth, ultimately. This is not to say all metaphors are invalid, nor all myths invalid. Quite the opposite. They point us to something. But if there is no something, ultimately, to which they point, then they're just literally pointless stories. If the Resurrection is just one more myth pointing us to something else, rather than the ultimate thing to which all myths point, then your faith is in vain.[1] The Resurrection is the capital-T truth which upholds all the other ideals.

The dualisms we have discussed are mathematical expressions. Mathematics is real, and not merely a mental game. Dualisms are clearly a real feature of the universe we experience, and not merely a construct we place on it. Meaning is generated by the oppositional nature of dualisms. That meaning is not merely part of a mental game. It is information, just as fundamental to existence as physical substance. It is real. Ideals, like the transcendent ideals of beauty, truth, goodness, and justice (and their binary opposites), and like virtues such as honesty, charity, and compassion (and their binary opposites) are also real, and not merely a mental game. These realities of the universe around us take us directly to a hierarchy of value, at the top of which is God.

Consider good and evil. Both belong to the set of matters with some property of morality. If A belongs in the "good" camp, and B in the "evil" camp, then A is a subset, defined as the subset of matters that are not B. And vice versa. The same analysis applies to beauty (ugliness) and truth (falsity). We invoke mathematics to perceive oppositions that produce meaning, and we find meaning not only in physical things, but in abstract ideals other than mathematics itself. In this way, mathematics underlies, or supervenes upon, all of reality. Therefore, mathematics is not an ethereal ideal only, but is real and fixed into reality. It is an "out there" phenomenon, existing not just in the cranium but in the world around us. Just as mathematics is real, so are goodness, beauty, and truth, and virtues like honesty and charity and compassion and justice. They exist in the mind but they exist also in external reality, just as does the physical world.

On the widest and most abstract level, one could view the whole universe as the logical system that cannot be provable within itself; that is, it must have its origins outside itself, it can in no way be self-generating. This is a variant of the no-something-from-nothing argument for the existence of God, but Gödel's theorem further supports a necessary realm of ideal that is also a real feature of the physical universe. Gödel was a Platonist,[2] which meant he was an idealist. Plato conceived of things in the physical world as instantiations of an ideal for that type of thing. There is a higher truth, an abstraction, for which physical things

---

1   1 Cor 15:13.

2   Goldstein, Rebecca, *Incompleteness: The Proof and Paradox of Kurt Gödel*, 2005.

are examples, which is a way of saying that ideals are in a sense more real than the physical, because they are unchanging and eternal. Reality is dualistic in this fundamental way: it consists in real, physical things, which are manifestations for an ideal of those things. As for physical things, so with non-physical concepts. Specific instances of, say, courage or cowardice, exemplify the ideal.

The implication is that reality is comprised of a realm of ideal, not just physical stuff. Moreover, the ideal is on a higher level of abstraction, though real. That which is physical instantiates the abstract ideal. The ideal in that way runs in and through the physical in addition to existing apart from it. This is dangerous thinking, for those who are resolute materialists, because where does this hierarchy of idealism take us? If we experience beauty, as with a mountain landscape we would describe as beautiful—full of beauty—then we are invoking the ideal of beauty. But beauty is just one kind of ideal. In invoking that ideal, aren't we thereby invoking the concept of idealism more generally? Idealism in the abstract instantiates types of ideals, which in turn instantiate physically. A hierarchy of idealism emerges whereby physical things are subordinate to an ideal for that thing, and then the ideal for that thing is in turn subordinate to idealism generally. The pinnacle of this hierarchy is the ideal of ideals, which is also real. The properties at that pinnacle coincide with our conception of God. God embodies the ideal of the ideals. We can present this graphically in Figure 1:

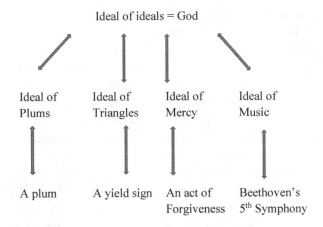

Figure 1

It may be self-evident that the dualisms we form without having to think about it are not all equally important. The dualism of night and day might not be immediately pressing in the same way the dualism of friend and foe can be, for example. There is also a distinction between importance and immediacy. I might be particularly conscious of hot and cold in the weather as I walk out the door, but less immediate and more abstract dualisms are ultimately more important, like presence and absence, or being and non-being. God's existence or non-existence is a fundamental dualism of extreme importance, yet I can put it to one side as I engage quotidian concerns.

That some dualisms are more important than others suggests a hierarchy of dualisms. Being and nothingness is a dualism quite fundamental in all our thinking, and it is therefore hierarchically more significant, even if we don't actively contemplate the abstract nature of existence while deciding whether ketchup should exist on our french fries. Presence and absence are similarly fundamental and abstract and hierarchically significant: in the active contemplation of any idea there are excluded others. We give greater hierarchical value to the one present idea than to those absent. The dualisms we engage all day every day include creators of hierarchy: significant/insignificant; important/unimportant; momentous/trivial.

God creates hierarchies. God is distinct from his creation; from contingent caused things; from imperfection; from presence (in his omnipresence); and from weakness (in his omnipotence). There is a great divide between God and all that is not-God. This might be described as the ultimate dualism. He created the universe in which there is pervasive, semantic logos, and this includes information imparted by oppositional dualisms.

Though there are certainly hierarchies resulting from this logocentric construction of the world, this does not mean that in every opposition one part is greater and the other lesser, as with God and the not-God creation. To say it differently, though there are hierarchies, they do not inhere in the fact of binary opposition in the abstract. They may exist based on the substantive nature of the opposition, but they don't exist just because two ideas can be placed in binary opposition. In an example that is politically contentious, consider the dualism of man and woman. They are in binary opposition, but the opposition by itself does not mean male is to be regarded as predominant. Hierarchy is implicit in some logocentric dualisms, like God and creation, but not in others, such as inside and outside. It is a mistake to find hierarchy a given just by virtue of the binary opposition. A hierarchy imagined in such cases may be created by misunderstanding, or because of one's personal biases, or intentionally for polemical purposes. But of course in other cases it may inhere in the nature of the opposition.

Consider the opposition of truth and falsity. It's fairly obvious that we ascribe this binary division in order to get to the truth (or falsity) of a principle or proposition. But there is another kind of dualism in play, too, and that is between the truth of the proposition itself, and the concept of truth in the abstract. While we're engaged in evaluating the truth of a proposition, there is another truth question lurking in the background: why is truth an ideal in the first place? Why do we bother isolating truth by distinguishing what is less true or misleading or outright false? Without much real thought about the mental process we invoke, we create hierarchies beginning with placing truth above falsity.

We can think of this process as having vertical and horizontal axes. On the horizontal axis we distinguish like from unlike, then distinguish specific instances among those which are like, further distinguishing, among those, like from unlike. On the vertical axis we distinguish specific instantiations of the ideal for the thing we've identified, and then ideals in the abstract.

Truth/falsity determinations cause us to assemble facts; the assemblage of facts causes us to distinguish principles; and the distinction among principles generates values. The hierarchy derives from oppositional dualisms as in Figure 2 below.

Note that in formulating this hierarchy of ideals, we group like with like before ascending a level to identify the ideal which informs the like-with-like grouping. If we were to abandon the project of grouping like with like, we would abandon also our ability to discern anything, whether physical and present, or mental and conceptual. To say there is a class of fruit called plums is to say plums are distinct from other classes of fruit, and fruits are distinct from other kinds of plant edibles, which are distinct from other plants more generally, and so on. These classes of like with like constitute universals. That is, we mentally classify things together because they share certain features. All things that share those features belong in the class. We don't have to have certified all the plums in the world as belonging in the class. We can confidently speak of plums without having examined every one of them.

If we deny the existence of universals, or ascribe to universals no hierarchical significance, we adopt a *nominalist* view of reality. We should understand universals as a kind of ideal, or at least as pointing to the necessary existence of ideals, and grasp the barrenness of nominalism.

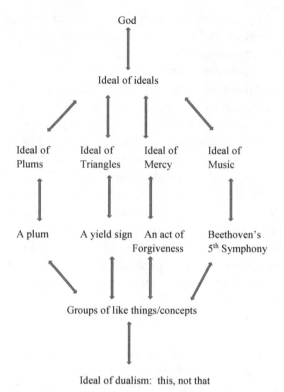

Figure 2

We get to this by extrapolating further from our understanding of mathematical realism. If mathematics is a real thing, as opposed to a formal system of logic which is not extant in some way in the universe, then we can think of mathematics as an entity distinct from its countless instantiations all around us. It exists in a realm of ideals, in other words. We know of this conceptually from Plato. We know from Aristotle a competing view: the criteria by which we group this from that is not some idealized entity but rather merely a common taxonomical feature of the thing under consideration. Still, we don't think of Aristotle as purely a nominalist, because he employed an idealistic element to his own explanation of causation, finding a "final cause" of purposefulness in material things. Platonism primarily informed early Christian thought, for example, with Augustine of Hippo (354-430). Aristotelian thought eventually re-entered Christian philosophy and was further developed by Thomas Aquinas (1225-1274). The tension between Platonic and Aristotelian perceptions of reality greatly informed late-medieval speculation on the true nature of things.[3] The medieval project of working out a rational proof of the existence of God was greatly enhanced by this tension.

Aristotelian thought also contributed to a breakdown in perception of a necessary hierarchy of ideals, however. William of Ockham (1287-1347) rejected both the Platonic and Aristotelian systems of thought, finding both unnecessary mental superstructures by which to evaluate things and ideas. A nominalist, he essentially held that things just are what they are, there are no universals to be inferred from them, and therefore no ideals, and therefore no hierarchy of ideals with God at its apex. Ockham therefore rejected both Thomistic proofs of the existence of God, and the Platonism of Augustine. This did not turn him to materialism, however. Instead it turned him to fideism, which amounts to belief in belief: he regarded God alone as the only entirely necessary entity, all else being contingent. Reasoning our way to God, he held, is a futile exercise. Ockham acknowledged that we have common conceptions (and words) we apply to differentiate things but deemed them not to describe metaphysical universals. Instead, he regarded them as universal only in the sense that multiple singular things bear the same word description or applicable concept.

William of Ockham was a churchman, no doubt pious, and certainly did not reject Platonism in order to collapse the reasoned hierarchy of values inhering in religious thought. But his philosophy has that effect, if we don't go all the way and embrace his fideism, too. It has the effect of climbing the ladder of faith without the benefit of reason, and then kicking away the ladder upon reaching God. The problem with nominalism is that once the reasoned basis for God is rejected, the basis for objective truth must be rejected, also. Many are willing to climb a ladder of reason, because God gave us brains. Few are willing to climb a ladder of pure faith, because why step on that first rung, especially if the society you live in does not encourage it in the way Ockham's society of fourteenth-century Europe did?

We can think of our systems of thought, or fundamental assumptions, or ideology, as a set of meta-principles by which we mentally bind cohering beliefs. Nominalism amounts to an abandonment of organizing principles, though it's actually an ordering principle itself: there is no set of universals to which we can subscribe in making sense of reality. Instead, everything just is what it is. That leaves us with materialism,

---

3 As depicted visually in Michelangelo's *School of Athens,* a Sistine Chapel fresco painted 1508-11.

because we're down to examining stuff as it is, with no principle to unify it with other like stuff and formulate a hierarchy of meaning from our world.

There's a bit of a paradox with modern materialists who purport to subscribe to Ockham's nominalism. Science, that church of materialist empiricism, actually relies on universal ordering principles. So if, as ardent nominalists, we deny any ordering principle other than the reality of things as they are, on examination of those things we nonetheless invoke unifying, universal principles in order to systematize our understanding. We separate mammals from amphibians, for example, because we adopt certain organizing principles of taxonomy, grouping like with like so as to delineate phylla and species, enabling us to make further universal generalizations helpful to understanding biology.

So if we are materialists and perforce nominalists, denying ideals except as useful taxonomical principles, we harbor intellectual dissonance. On the one hand, we engage universals in order to do science on a materialist presumption. On the other hand, we deny universals as existing outside the limits of materialism. In this way, methodological materialism elides to philosophical materialism. We can be nominalists philosophically, yet universalists in our science.

This takes us, however, from materialism into irrational vulnerability to philosophical exploitation. If we're not thinking in universals, we're not thinking in terms of ideals, and everything just is what it is. But then along come purveyors of pragmatism and existentialism, new truth-generating vehicles with their own necessary superstructures of thought to replace those of Plato and Aristotle. With nominalism we set aside universals which would support systems of thought apart from lifeless materialism, but then we're to re-impose on ourselves a new system of thought with new universals. Ockham's famous "razor" really ought to be brought out again, this time to pare away superstructures within postmodernism, rather than Plato's hierarchy of ideals, or Aristotle's causes. Nominalism disarms us from the ability to employ idealistic thought, but then postmodernism re-arms us with a set of universals alien to ideals altogether. We're vulnerable to adopting them because, though our universals have been purged from us, our urge to find universals has not.

A nominalist collapse of hierarchical ideals takes us away from religiously-informed ideals, but our indelible orientation to universals remains. Instead of ridding ourselves of unnecessary ontologies in explaining a God-infused reality, as Ockham advocated, we form new

thought structures built on God-absent materialism: man-made ideologies, including dangerously pernicious ones like Nazism, Maoism,
and Stalinism. We all have a mental superstructure in place, when we
confront any proposition. This may be a very basic set of ideas or ideals
about how one should live peaceably with one's neighbors, or it may be a
highly-developed systematic philosophical system. We are rational creatures, and faith must be based on reason. This is true for faith in God,
and it is true for faith in competing ideologies. If we do not conceive of
God at the pinnacle of a hierarchy of values he decrees, we may place
our faith in the State, or in a deterministic universe, or in racial hierarchy, or in collectivist utopia.

CHAPTER FOUR

Realism of Information

WHETHER NUMBERS and number relationships merely describe the universe, or are found in the universe, they certainly comprise a logical system of symbols manipulated by syntactical rules. We readily see that numbers and mathematical relationships convey information. In this way they are like language. Our language is a logical system of symbols (visual, if written, or aural, if spoken) manipulated by syntactical rules. It conveys information. We can ask about information the same question we ask about mathematics: is it real already in the universe, or is it only made real in the sense of being generated in the human brain, and then used to describe a cold universe-as-such to ourselves?

The idea behind mathematical realism must be applied to other logical systems, like language. Language—conveying meaning rather than gibberish—is either entirely a product of brain, or it is a product of mind. The brain is the physical organ in the cranium, operating on electricity and organic tissue. The mind is the subjective consciousness we experience, the locus of thought. Even if mind and brain are identical; that is, if rationality is merely a description of brain functioning, then the language it produces is necessarily a real and extant feature of the universe because the brain is a physical part of the universe. Even if there is some mysterious other component to mind, like the soul, the physical brain is involved in the thinking process, so language, and the information it conveys, is an extant feature of the physical universe, the brain being part of that physical universe. Language, and the meaning associated with language, is an extant feature of the universe because it is a product, at least in part, of the brain—a physical thing.

Materialists would perforce say language is a product of the brain only, so a materialist cannot fairly deny the "realness" of information and its expression in language. Theists generally suppose an extra-physical component of human consciousness, perhaps conceived as the soul, but they do not generally deny the physical brain is a component, too. So for theists also there is a "realness" to information conveying meaning, manifested in language or in that which is reducible to language by us.

Language requires rational processes of mind. Mental processes are rational because they are logical. They are logical because they are linked to the ordering criteria of truth. Truth is necessarily, therefore, a real and objective "out-there" phenomenon. It is ontological, meaning that it precedes existence. Existence itself is meaningless without the concept of truth already in place. It is true or not true that physical things even exist. It is nonsensical to speak of a thing's existence without having already conceived the truth of the thing's existence. All of our mental processes are oriented toward this truth, as they would have to be, if we were to ever understand anything anyone else says. When we speak, we appeal to the truth orientation in the other. We all have this truth orientation. Logic is the system of successive inferences we draw in the direction of external, objective truth.

Language, in the form of words and consistent syntactic rules conveying information, implicates realism much like mathematics in that there is semantic content and grammatical order, just like arithmetic, computer programming, the structuring of oppositional dualisms, and this sentence. To put a label to it, this is logocentrism: the centrality of the word, semantic meaning, to physical reality. This is the word, the logos, information everywhere, more fundamental even than physical substance, generated by dualisms and by mathematical relationships in the cosmos, by consciousness, and by DNA—all messages implying a Messenger and a purpose for the message being imparted to us who are able to decode and receive it. It is ultimate reality, a reality infused by God who speaks truth into the world.

It is often observed that many mathematical constants in the universe have to be "just so" in order for there to be a universe at all, or for it to be one that can have an earth which can sustain life. This Goldilocks phenomenon is sometimes referred to as the "fine-tuning" of the universe, and of the Earth. The phrase implies One who does the tuning. The necessary precision of mathematical relationships in the universe suggests they are not accidental. They certainly constitute information, which again implies One who informs. We can think of information as being a brute fact of physical existence, but it would seem information exists to be imparted. A message, in other words, spoken into physical reality (not just emerging from it with no inherent purpose), to be received by us or anyone else.

This brings us back to mathematical realism. The real-ness of mathematical principles, like dualisms, also relates to information. As we've seen, the tension between dualisms creates meaning, which in our minds creates understanding. We make sense of the morality of an act because we distinguish the concepts of good and evil. We weigh the truthfulness of a proposition or assertion because we distinguish concepts of truth and falsity. We evaluate the beauty of a thing or person or theorem or poem because we distinguish conceptually on the basis of beauty and ugliness. The tension in these oppositions generates meaning.

The meaning thus produced is reducible to semantic content; that is, it can be put into words. There is a flood of semantic content in the world. We are deluged with it, but in the same way fish are deluged with water. It is our natural habitat, and so we don't see it as such without making a special effort to do so.

Information does not exist as an isolated feature of reality unattached to any other. It's not like a rock we might envision hurtling through space, with its origin and destination unknown. Information is imparted from informer to recipient, or from informer through a medium with the potential to be received and understood. Unlike (perhaps) that rock, it carries a message. Information begins as a product of mind, and it is understandable by mind. Information imparted in language is a relational phenomenon, connecting origin and destination in mind. You can write down a secret and shoot it up into space with no serious expectation that it will ever be read. But it's still information. Writing it down is an act of communicating, even if you think it is only symbolic communication to the universe.

Science amounts to decoding the messages in physical reality. The explosion of scientific understanding in modern times (say, since the 1600s) did not result from inventing physical principles and projecting them onto physical reality. It came from discovering what was already there. The information is real and extant in the universe, in the same way ideals must be. Information can be thought of in the same terms as mathematical realism, that is, as an "out-there" phenomenon of the universe. Its existence could be something we consider an invention of our minds, as opposed to something there to be discovered. But if it is a mental invention only, then how does it originate so as to be understood by us? If it only exists as a self-contained puzzle in the same way formalism construes mathematics, then how can it point back to anything true in the universe?

Even a mathematical formalist would be hard-pressed to explain how the formalist conception of mathematics—as unconnected to the physical world and merely useful in describing it—could also apply to information. Information—such as the mathematical constants of the universe, and DNA, and meaning generated from dualistic oppositions—cannot be generated internally and then imposed externally on the physical universe. It is not purely human intellectual product overlaid onto the universe. It is integral to the functioning of physical things. Prescriptive, not merely descriptive. One might imagine mathematics as merely descriptive, but communicated information is necessarily prescriptive. DNA, for example, prescribes how the body functions. It is not merely a way of describing the body's functioning, as a formalist might argue mathematics to be.

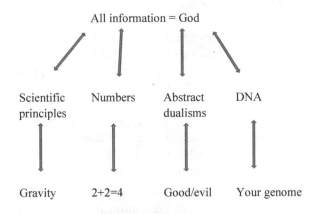

Figure 3

Information exists for us much like ideals, in that it is not physical, but runs in and through that which is physical. Information in the abstract governs physical stuff. It therefore holds a hierarchical relationship between informer and informed, much like the hierarchical relationship between ideal and physical. Where does this hierarchy take us? If we unravel the mystery of DNA, the essence of what we find is not the physical structure—as with the double helix and the various amino acids—but rather the information it contains. A car is not in essence wheels, engine, and body, but rather the knowledge of its designers in making those elements function together as a vehicle of transportation. Likewise, the essence of the universe is not the dust and ice balls and mosquitoes that populate it, but the pattern of their movements in synchrony, dictated by physical forces reducible to information. Information is instantiated in physical systems which in turn instantiate in material and forces acting on it. The resulting hierarchy looks much like the hierarchy of idealism we observed. At the pinnacle of this hierarchy is an ultimate communicator, which just like the information itself, is real. The properties of that pinnacle coincide with our conception of God as omniscient, as we see in Figure 3.

Thus, information is a real and extant feature of the physical universe; it is not merely a projection of human mind onto the physical universe. The mathematical realism we considered applies conceptually to information, too. Both are subsets of multi-tiered, dualistic reality. Language is symbolic of meaning, and so we can observe that symbolism, too, is an extant and real feature of our physical reality. As Richard Weaver wrote in *Ideas Have Consequences*:

> Symbolism is a reaction against the deification of the material world, because the symbol is always a sign of things that are not compresent in time and space. The symbol by its nature transcends and thus points to the world beyond the world.[1]

A symbol acquires meaning only as a representation. It is a higher-order concept, and therefore points to taxonomical value hierarchy, in the same way thought relates to its subject-matter, and mathematical realism relates to its instantiations in the universe. The word "symbol" derives from Greek words meaning the gathering of like things with like, in a meaningful way. The representation of those things, the symbol, stands in for that group of like things, and against unlike things. The opposite of symbolic is "diabolic," meaning that which casts and separates. We thus perceive symbolism to be integration, an orderly binary opposite of entropic degeneration into disintegration and chaos. As such it is another instance of hierarchical value formation in the mind and as communicated to other minds, and again presents a compelling analog to continuing hierarchy culminating in the mind of God.

Information and language are not interchangeable concepts, and yet each alone is incomplete without the other. Language exists to im-

---

1 Weaver, Richard M., *Ideas Have Consequences*. Chicago: University of Chicago Press 2013, p. 75 (first published 1948).

part information. Information is not information until it is in some way communicated. Both exist as a dynamism suggesting the presence of a Communicator into the world. Language is a logic system, by which information is conveyed, but both information and language are structured on the basis of continual refinement in distinctions, oppositions which yield meaning which in turn can be communicated meaningfully. Both the information and the conveying of the information follow an orderly structure. We can draw inferences about the reality of the order that underlies both. When two people talk, they do so for the purpose of conveying information. True information or deliberately false information, both aligned according to a criterion of truth. Truth is the arbiter to which we all appeal, in every communication. We may disagree on what is true, but we don't disagree that truth is what we seek. We share a truth orientation. This truth orientation points to the objective nature of truth, and to the transcendent source of that nature.

The truth orientation is so much a part of the operating system of our lives that it's possible to overlook it as evidence. It's fundamental evidence of the objective nature of truth even though we may miss it as such, when we engage in discussion on the objective nature of truth. If this truth orientation did not exist, there would be no rational ordering principle for the direction of our thoughts. Thoughts would proceed randomly. Nor would there be a rational ordering principle for the communication of those thoughts. We might ask why are there objective features of our surroundings that lend themselves to being understood in binary terms like true and false, but then we should also ask why the question itself presents in a way that can be comprehended, and accurately communicated. Truth, we can say, is therefore bound up in the very fact of objective physical existence. At the first moment there is something rather than nothing, truth is spoken into the world.

Truth can be said to inhere in existing physical things that don't have subjective experience, like rocks and air. Numerous mathematical constants are necessary to the existence or continued existence of those non-biological things, and as we have seen, those constants are both real and truly real. Even physical objects like rocks are thus imbued with informational content, including mathematical truths, which require no proximate human to appreciate, but do require an active universal Mind to author.

We will see that in postmodernism, the idea of objective, "out there" truth is compromised. "Truth" might attach from a process, which is in turn imagined for negotiating power. A power orientation can therefore take the place of a truth orientation—in theory only, of course, not in fact. With a truth orientation, the normal process is to reason to a conclusion. With a power orientation, this may be reversed, so that one may have a conclusion and then develop argument to support it, and yet invoke "truth." The word for this is irrationality.

Rationality means thinking in accord with reason and logic. If we take away the ordering principle of the logos, then reason is the connectivity of inferences on some criterion other than truth. Objective truth is necessary to rational thought. Again, we can disagree about what is true, but irrationality results from rejecting truth as the ordering principle for thoughts, the reason thought A leads to B, and not X, Y, or Z. Even in using this analogy, the appeal is to our shared and logical use of an orderly arrangement of sounds and symbols in language. Rationality is the logical progression of ideas, from observation to inference to conclusion. Rationality is related to the truth orientation because rationality involves a connectedness of linked thoughts, and that connectedness is the process of one thought causing another according to a truth orientation. That directedness toward truth is logic, and it is the logos. This is the source of both semantic content and syntactical structure in our thoughts and communication, a pre-existing ordering criteria linking thought to thought. Random thoughts are meaningless, unless linked to other thoughts on some ordering criteria apart from the thoughts themselves. That ordering criteria is the orientation to truth. We know truth to be objective and external to us both, which is why thinking is not pointless and communicating thoughts is not pointless. We can communicate. And what we communicate is information we discover out there in the universe, not random chaotic utterances unlinked by any ordering criterion of truth or falsity. There is a kind of substrate of truth spoken into the world by universal Mind, imparting rationality to lesser human minds in the uncountable rational inferences made in every waking moment.

What is noblest about mankind finds its source in something higher. Platonic ideals, mathematical systems, universals, symbolism, and language all point inexorably away from meaningless materialism, and toward a meaningful hierarchy of values founded on objective and even transcendent truth. This describes a logocentric view of reality, wherein the word, the logos, is central to how we perceive reality. Logocentrism is a necessary element of religious tradition. God's revelation to mankind is in words, imparted to us as sacred scripture through human prophets. Jesus the Christ is himself described as the Word, being the physical manifestation and fulfillment of this revelation. This is why the apostle John opens his gospel: "In the beginning was the Word, and the Word was with God, and the Word was God."[2]

---

2 John 1:1.

CHAPTER FIVE

Transcending Opposition

I T MIGHT SEEM HARSH to embrace the fact of fundamental oppo- sitions in our existence. The idea of it, even in the abstract, might suggest antagonism and conflict. It is not surprising that one might con- sider the tension between oppositions as a root of conflict more gener- ally.

These oppositions are inescapable, however, and moreover neces- sary in our effort to make sense of anything, not to mention, find ulti- mate purpose and meaning for our lives. If this grasp of oppositions is to be construed as conflict, then so be it—it is conflict, then, which gives rise to meaning. We should approach the tensions generated by these oppositions as opportunities to better understand reality, rather than try to wish them away. Binary oppositions in reality cannot be simply collapsed, so as to pretend they're not operative at all. The oppositions remain, and the tensions they create, as well. Naturally, we want to re- solve tension. We can choose between oppositions, or accept them as is and transcend them. What we can't do is simply collapse them.

We would extinguish the opposition between us and God, for ex- ample, by denying God's very existence, thus attempting to crash the opposition. That amounts to an attempted erasure of God. We might alternatively attempt to erase the self, the other end of the opposition, and the most common way to do this is to step outside the individualist self-perception and into the collective. We can mentally step away from the sense of self that bears personal responsibility, and into the sense of self that is merely part of a collective, diluting that feeling of subjective weightiness. God is not so terrifying if he holds society responsible in- stead of me. Difficult choices are not so difficult if they are made by the collective. My failures sting less if they are said to be the result of my identity or place in the society around me.

The myriad attempts we make at collapsing fundamental oppositions in our life will fail. We don't do away with evil, for example, by pretending it doesn't exist, or by refusing to call it what it is, or by making it indistinguishable from good. We can't collapse this dualism by declining to discern between good and evil. We can't deny this dualism by pretending that one opposition or the other isn't real. Our way to address this opposition should be to accept the reality of it, and then attempt to transcend it. We do so by choosing good and avoiding evil. We will still do evil, however, sometimes. This is a difficult truth. The way to deal with that reality is not to deny our guilt, or call that which is evil good. The way to deal with it is to figure out where good comes from, and where evil comes from, and align ourselves with the source of good. This takes us to God. We find that God is just: he holds us responsible for moral failure. But God then transcends the dualism of justice and mercy on our behalf, by his forgiveness of our evil through the means he provides. We can't entirely eradicate evil on our own, even within our individual selves, but we can strive toward the One who is wholly good, in gratitude that he redeems us from the consequences of the evil we do.

We may feel that resisting binary oppositions will result in having their fretful extremes levelled out, so we can all just get along. Perhaps it would be more pleasant to live hidden from the all-seeing eye of a just God. But this urge, if it could be realized, would also have the effect of eliminating the highs and lows of human experience. If we imagine God out of existence, we bring about this levelling whether he's real or not. If we persist in subjectively imagining away the boogeyman of difference and divide, we end up diminishing ourselves and the society in which we live.

It's natural, unfortunately, for us to want to reject God because we'd like to be gods ourselves. We are not like the God who is, but we continually overstep, thinking we are. Some deep humility is called for, to remember who we are in relation to him. But that's not as instinctive as we might think, because we also have this instinct of our own significance. And it's valid. Our yearning is valid. Our capacity for imagination and mystery and love are meaningful. They constitute evidence of this all-important question of God's existence. Who are we in relation to God? Why do we always see ourselves as gods? Why aren't we gods? We are significant, and we are not destined to oblivion. Why this raging "I am!" at the clouds?

We're complicated. The questioning shouldn't end like a cartoon character with one of those thought balloons that looks like a bunch of tangled wire followed by an exclamation mark. Is there a God? If there is, it is certainly true that we cannot in this life properly apprehend him. But on the other hand—well there is no other hand,[1] if we are to preserve what it means to be made in the image of God, even metaphorically. What becomes of us otherwise? Are we just smart animals? Clothed apes? Instinctual but perfumed creatures, only?

If we're only animals, it's high time we stopped putting some of our fellow human-animals in prison. Or bothering with an upwards call to the sublime in art, literature, philosophy, political principle, or moral reasoning. On this view, all of that is just flotsam left over from the outmoded God hypothesis and crammed down our throats by humanist philosophers holding on to their livelihoods. In reality there is only all against all, and power rules[2] because that's what power does in this bleak and pointless landscape. Sex, wealth, prestige, and power are the objects of all striving. And if you think otherwise, so goes the message, you are a pitiful naif, captive to the wishful thinking of your fellow losers who look to the sky for return of an invisible mitigator of these treacheries, One who is expected to re-reveal himself, when he gets around to it, as the ultimate victor on our behalf, despite his previous appearance as ultimate victim and scapegoat, no better than a slave, a non-person, acquainted by perverted choice with sorrow and despair, visible in history only because he was heralded loud and long by witnesses among a band

---

1 As Kierkegaard put it, "either God – or, well, then the rest is a matter of indifference; whatever else a human chooses, he misses either/or." (Kierkegaard, Søren, *The Lily of the Field and the Bird of the Air*) translated and with an introduction by Bruce H. Kirmmse, Princeton University Press 2016, p. 40). By "either/or" he meant the aesthetic (or sensible or sentimental or carnal or earthy) choice rather than the austere ethical choice that God presents. If we dismiss God, then we don't even get to Kierkegaard's "either/or." Instead we live in animal stasis, not worthy of God's calling, to be sure, but also not worthy of considering our humanity as anything other than another kind of animal.

2 You'd be right to recall Nietzsche's "will to power" in this context. E.g., Nietzsche, Friedrich, *On the Genealogy of Morals*, translated by Walter Kaufmann and R.J. Hollingdale, 1989, p. 87, second essay, section 18 (first published 1887). Nietzsche and a host of philosophers subsequent to him point out that power struggle is the inevitable result of the overthrow of any god-like extra-human authority. As Yuval Noah Harari puts it, modernity offers us a deal: "Give up meaning in exchange for power." (See Scruton, Roger, *The Turing Machine Speaks*, about Silicon Valley guru Yuval Noah Harari's chilling post-humanism, as reported in *City Journal*, Summer 2019.) Scruton quoted Harari: "There is no purpose in the world, only the unending chain of cause and effect. . . . modern life consists of a constant pursuit of power within a universe devoid of meaning."

of Jews preaching not just to other Jews but to the rest of the world.

God communicates a hierarchical physical reality. Not in the sense of worldly powers like princes and popes and the dictatorship of the proletariat, but by something more fundamental. He created a cosmos discernible by means of binary oppositions, and us with the ability to know and be known through them. Some of those oppositions are more significant than others, in that they involve abstract principles which underlie everything else: existence and non-existence; something and nothing; rational and irrational. There are unquestionably higher and lower orders of principle involved, which also stand in opposition: higher and lower orders of good and evil; truth and falsity; beauty and ugliness.

Ask not for a levelling of these. If we could re-orient the world according to our own security- and fear-driven desires, we might try to eliminate what is evil and false and repulsive, but we don't have the option to truncate those from our experience and leave their oppositional higher orders in place. Evil is understood only in relation to good. Falsity in relation to truth. Ugliness in relation to beauty. We can pursue the higher order principle, certainly, but the lower is not thereby eliminated. It serves, in fact, to point the way. If you would be morally better, you make good choices, and each choice is between the morally higher over the morally lower. There is a hierarchy of moral choices, made such by oppositions. If you seek truth rather than falsehood, you discern truth from the many shades of falsehood that present themselves. Beauty is not merely in the eye of the beholder. It resides in the object or language or principle or theorem or person, and we identify it because we can also identify its opposite.

God is in opposition to we who are not-God. We understand what we do of him on the basis of the disclosed characteristics he has that we do not share. He is eternal, omnipotent, omniscient, omnipresent. He has no limits, therefore, which is another way of saying that he alone is beyond any opposition which serves to define him, other than not-God—all that is finite in time and space, and weak and ignorant and foolish and sinful, and most of all, *unfinished*. In Aristotelean terms, God is the Prime Mover, the purely actualized Being upon which all other things, including living things, are contingent.[3] In Platonic terms, all that exists is an imperfect instance of a perfect ideal of those things,

---

3 Expanded upon by the author in Norton, Albert, *Intuition of Significance/Evidence Against Materialism and for God*, 2020, pp. 14-16. See also, Feser, Edward, *Five Proofs for the Existence of God,* 2017.

and those ideals are specifics of the ideal of perfection, and the ideal of the ideals is God.[4]

Imagine a flat sheet of paper. Now cut a spiral into this imagined paper. Then grasp the mid-point of the spiral. You can pull the spiral up and a little ziggurat appears. If you hold the sheet flat and release, the spiral will sag down in a negative of the upward-formed ziggurat. This provides a visual of the oppositions in play, with regard to virtues we regard as being of a higher order than their negative oppositions. Courage is up; fear down. Compassion up; indifference down. Sexual rectitude up; promiscuity down. We can easily choose the downward end of the same oppositions. It happens if we barely even try. God creates the higher, aspirational oppositions. God pulls the spiral up; we don't push it up. If we try, we get a man-made ziggurat, like the Tower of Babel, and it will be abandoned and unfinished and pitiful, eroding in the sun and wind and occasional rain of the timeless Valley of Shinar.

Would you give up the glorious sunset to stay indoors where it's not too hot or cold? Would you forego love because your heart might be broken? Do you not climb the mountain because you might fall and get hurt? Do you not play the game because you might lose? Do you isolate yourself because friends might disappoint? We act on fear instead of courage far too often, and we do it because the swing in these oppositions frightens us. How many times does God admonish us not to fear? To be strong and courageous? Why does he do it? Yes, he has plans for us, and wants us to actualize them, but also his project is to pull us upward. He doesn't want us to descend to self-destructive negatives, but he is also not satisfied that we stay safely in an intermediate zone of quiescence. We'll find no rest there. When we stop there, we find desperation instead of shalom.

"The mass of men lead lives of quiet desperation," Thoreau wrote.[5] We recognize in this the resignation in living a conventional, middle-brow existence, something we all experience in some degree or another, and so this quote resonates. The sentiment exists in any society, including Thoreau's early-1800s New England that was conventionally and nominally Christian. Around the same time, writing in a similarly nominally Christian Copenhagen, Søren Kierkegaard acknowledged the same despair as "the sickness unto death."[6] Thoreau wasn't seeking

---

4 Norton, Albert, *Intuition of Significance/Evidence Against Materialism and for God*, Resource Publications, 2020, pp. 28-31.

5 Thoreau, Henry David, *Walden*, 1854.

6 Kierkegaard, Søren, *The Sickness Unto Death*, 1849.

an explicitly Christian answer, but Kierkegaard certainly was. Why were the good, polite, middle-class burghers of conventionally religious Copenhagen in "despair?" Because it is a common condition. One kind of despair, consciousness of our sin, makes us regular church-goers and otherwise followers of the herd in our religious "duties," but there is another kind of despair that ought to drive us further, to see that the dance with God isn't about following a set of social rules that keep us out of danger. The despair exists because we're actually fighting God, when we stay in control by ordering our priorities to a safe inoffensive middle zone, not overly vigorous in either direction, with a hat-tip "yay God" once in a while, just in case the lion gets loose. There's despair instead of the freedom God promises because we don't trust him, and we think we've done enough by merely acknowledging the virtues rather than soaring with them. This is an internal thing, it's not about adding one more social responsibility to a list already too long. The internal thing is to recognize the outrageousness of God's call on our lives. The despair that Thoreau and Kierkegaard recognized, and that we all know, is a symptom of having collapsed to a muddy middle instead of facing the oppositions as they are and seeking to transcend them.

Kierkegaard was right in decrying an "established Christendom" in place of Christ. For just one example of his thought, he lamented the growing enthusiasm for Christmas celebration, as part of the watering-down of genuine Christian faith. Imagine him in contrast to his contemporary Charles Dickens, who wrote *A Christmas Carol,* celebrating the soft sentiment of Christmas celebration. Dickens was nominally Christian, with a strong aversion to what he considered its extreme expression among evangelicals. Kierkegaard had a different view. He remarked about Christmas that "the Savior of the world was now a child," thus mitigating the demands of moral and spiritual challenge that faith in a suffering, selfless Christ entails.[7] In this way, the dangerous God is thought to be pacified and folded into the manageable fabric of society. Kierkegaard desired earnestness in seeking Christ, silence in awe of Creation which in turn leads to a fear of the Lord. As we read in the Old Testament: "The fear of the Lord is the beginning of wisdom."[8]

Kierkegaard desired earnestness in seeking God, because its lack among Christians was quite apparent to him when he wrote in the first

---

7 Kirmmse, Bruce H., introduction to Kierkegaard's *The Lily of the Field and the Bird of the Air,* reprinted by Princeton University Press 2016, p. xiii. Kirmmse's comments were based on Kierkegaard's journals and notebooks.

8 Proverbs 9:10.

half of the nineteenth century. A process of taming Christ was far along, at that time, though not so far as today. It is important that we have some sense of God's movements in history. Christians tend to think that time ended at the Ascension, that we've been holding our collective breath since that day, waiting for Christ's imminent return. Of course we don't know when that return will be, but it's a mistake to be ignorant of all that has transpired since the last day he was among us as a man. All of history is in the providence of God, and it all has meaning.

We may say we want God, but what we really want is a paper cut-out of God. We want the lion, but we want him caged. We want to collapse the dualism of God and self, to close the gap between us and him. We want to be elevated, so we imagine him reduced. We want God less dangerous, so we diminish the gulf between ourselves and him. We don't want the helplessness that goes with our estate in contrast to God's, so we mentally collapse the contrast. By denying this ultimate dualism we think we can manage him as one of our projects, so we can put him back on the shelf while we're occupied with other things. We want a God who will recede into the background when we're not directly engaging him. This has a flattening effect because God constructs the world, we don't. The best we can do—we unfortunately think—is try to pull ourselves up to the flat level of a society uninformed by God, by complying with the norms society dictates for us. But in this way of thinking, we won't build higher in any sustained way. The landscape of our lives will be dotted with pathetic unfinished towers of Babel.

That's one way we attempt to cage the lion. Another is to simply imagine him out of existence. This does not entirely relieve the tension, however. For one thing, there likely remains a nagging doubt. Suppose there actually is a God? Because if there is, he might expect something of us. We might entertain flashes of insight that if God does not pull us up, our trajectory is down.

But for another thing, where would that leave us? One would have to keep the mental shield up, so to speak, to go with the daily flow and not think about the implications. What would be the point of living, in a God-less reality? Why do good, instead of evil? On what basis do we ascribe authoritativeness to what we call "good?" How would we sustain a workable polity, if the only tools at hand for social cohesion were cultural opprobrium and ever more engulfing legal regulation? On what basis would there be any consensus of values? Are we to dispense with any attempt to explain the sense of our own significance? Do we try to live without meaning? Do we resign ourselves to the resulting all-against-all struggle for power?

It might seem that these questions are overblown. We're not living in a real-life dystopian anarchy, after all, nor under the thumb of oppressive fascist dictatorship. At the moment. So what's the problem? The problem is that we can't assume a static environment in which current ideals carry forward. They haven't in history, and they won't in the future. We're living now (in the West) on the fumes of liberal bourgeois nominal Christianity; what was normative in the time of Thoreau and Kierkegaard. Those values seem stable enough that they will remain if we tweak them in "progressive" ways to something better. They seem permanent enough that we can take them for granted.

But we can't. Ideals like charity, compassion, trustworthiness, and self-reliance are indeed written on the heart by God, but they can certainly be corrupted if we disregard their source and imagine them to be only emergent artifacts of biology which continue to evolve. The problem is that individually, we have no reason to strive, morally, beyond the boundaries we imagine society sets for us. I might consider my behavior adequate if the society around me says it is, and what I do or say or think in private is out of society's reach anyway. I am what I think you think I am. If you don't know about my secret vices, they don't count as vices. So now imagine everyone as the me just described. There is no meaning to my existence, in a God-less vision of reality, and no reason for us to sustain, individually or collectively, the values that inhere in the meaning-full God-filled understanding of reality. Disaffection, disappointment, and despair result. We are ever more conscious of the meaninglessness of our existence, as we are ever more successful in unimagining God. As the reality of God recedes from us, that meaninglessness looms larger. And with it, despair.

Nor is this avoidable by going down our own road, setting up our own little moral kingdom within the one we actually live. Just as the moral and ethical structures of an advanced civilization are not self-sustaining, our individual, internal systems of value are not self-sustaining, either. If they are not upheld by our recognition that God authors them, then we look to society around us to sustain them. This necessarily means that our values are society's values; there is no real distinction. This is why many people actually believe—whether they are able to acknowledge or articulate it or not—that an action or attitude is good or bad only as society determines it to be. Moral values do not originate with the individual, and certainly not with a putative God, on this view. A collective approach to everything results. This only accelerates the despair, upon the imagined removal of God.

CHAPTER SIX

Individualism and Collectivism

INDIVIDUALISM SOMETIMES gets a bad rap. We have a tendency to equate it with selfishness, so something to be avoided. Many social critics point to the ravages of unbridled pursuit of individual personal autonomy as the source of personal and societal self-destruction. There's a valid point there. If individualism is taken to mean only maximal personal freedom to behave any way we want, unguided by moral principle or social constraint, chaos will ensue, and "individualism" on that understanding is an unqualifiedly bad thing. But let's think a bit more deeply about individualism and its opposite, collectivism. How do we think of ourselves, in our relations with others? Is the first instinct to self-identify in terms of one's part in the various groups to which we belong, such as family, workplace, church, citizenship, etc.? Or is the first instinct to self-identify in terms of the inviolable self, one person engaged in navigating external relationships?

Orthodox Christianity is crystal clear that we individually have salvation or don't. Enmity or reconciliation with a just God is an individual matter. We don't remain at odds with God because of our social memberships, nor do social memberships redeem us. It is between the self and God. We are personally and individually responsible to God, in an unmediated relationship. In this way Christianity requires an appropriate individualism. A collectivist outlook would mean that one's self-perception is filtered through social associations. A collectivist might perceive his relationship with God to be mediated, in this way, attenuating individual responsibility.

The tension is emphasized in the distinction we make between brain and mind. This is the age-old mind-body problem of philosophy, and

61

increasingly, of neuroscience. We intuit different meanings for "brain" and "mind." The brain is the organ in the cranium that we understand to operate on chemistry and electricity as we think. But more goes on in brain interaction, including, in particular, our sense of self. We think in the sense of calculating from perceptions, but we're aware that we think, and we're aware that others like us are similarly self-aware. This is something more than just thinking about the fact that we're thinking. It is the subjective "me" that is the focal point for that thinking, the in-eradicable context or position from which anything can be evaluated. Foundational to the first thought is awareness that it is me doing the thinking. My awareness of my awareness is meta-awareness. It therefore corresponds to other meta-realities, such as the ideals for which physical things are instantiations. That meta-awareness is a feature of human consciousness, by which I am aware that all the processing of data from the outside world is taking place in me, the self. And in addition, all the thinking of me in relation to the outside world, with all the history and emotion that entails, takes place in me, the self. This position of subjectivity is so fundamental to our thinking that it takes a strong exercise of imagination to consider any other perspective, such as a collective hive awareness or God-like omniscient awareness.

This subjective self-awareness is consciousness, and it is inexplicable as merely brain-functioning. In the seventeenth century, René Descartes argued that the mind and body are distinct in substance. This is considered the origin of mind-body dualism, in philosophy. Philosophers and scientists have grappled with this dualism at least since Descartes. Clearly there is a connection between the mind and the brain, but most people intuit an essence distinct from mere brain functioning. The brain is the locus of activity supporting consciousness, but the mystery of consciousness is so profound that the material brain is an insufficient explanation by itself. There must be something more than physical brain functioning, to constitute the sense of individual self and self-awareness with all the uniquely subjective features of consciousness.

We don't take in and evaluate ideas or propositions or facts or sense impressions from a position of distant neutrality. We are self-contained and self-motivated and self-controlled. I am in here looking out. The individual self is an irreducible and inviolable point of conscious perspective. Our thoughts are certainly influenced by innumerable interactions and awareness of social expectations, but it is the individual thoughts that are so affected. We would do well to consider the curious phenomenon of selfhood, the "I" which thinks, and processes the various social interactions, and navigates the world. Personal subjectivity involves the internality and privacy of our thoughts and is also the platform on which sense impressions are received and addressed. It is the irreducible "I" that is engaged, even in thinking about the nature of the self's interaction with humanity around me. In addition to independence of thought, we individually have moral agency and free will—or at least we feel that we do—in the integral and separated self. When I engage with the world around me, it is my mind that engages, not a hive mind of which I am but a cell, like a midge in a midge swarm, or a single bird in a murmuration of starlings. A person's subjective experience of the world is a little kingdom unto itself. Enlivened by interaction with others, certainly, but nonetheless an irreducible unit of awareness and intelligence.

On the other hand, it is certainly true that an important part of our individual consciousness is its intersubjectivity with others, so that we are necessarily social creatures, too. We are sufficiently social in our self-perception, in fact, that it is possible to conceive of self only in relation to others. The tendency to do so is collectivism. Extreme collectivism amounts to hiding or subjugating or subsuming the self in the collective. This means collapsing the individual/collective dualist opposition, and in turn the creator/created opposition. It amounts to an erasure of self, and may result from the desire to avoid the harshness of unmediated responsibility to God.

The words "individualism" and "collectivism" are bandied about in all kinds of situations, with every shade of possible meaning. It is important that we try to understand something of this oppositional dualism, however, because doing so will help explain the undeniable tension in our lives. Does God relate to "us," as a people? Or does God relate only to "me," an individual person? Both, perhaps, but if so, how are these ways of relating different? Is one primary? Both I and the society around me are the not-God opposition to God. The distinction between society and me constitutes another opposition. Perhaps more of the frictions among people turn on this dualism than we realize. And, this oppositional dualism informs our understanding of God and his relationship to us more than we may realize. So it's important to get some understanding of it, and it's important to consider what happens if we manage to partially confuse the divide between individual and collective.

Each of us have a conception of how we fit in with others, and this conception is inseparable from how we conceive of God. Our relationship to God and our relationship to others are not two entirely distinct topics, however much we might wish them to be. We each have corporeal integrity and subjective conscious integrity. There is no overlap bodily or mentally, with others. Our respective bodies and minds are distinct. And yet, our relationships with others and with mankind in the abstract affects our understanding of God. Likewise, our understanding of our relationship with God informs our understanding of how we are to relate to others. "Individual" and "collective" are not categorically distinct, therefore, but are oppositions in which each defines the other, and meaning is provided by the opposition, in the context in which it is applied.

It would not be easy to say one person is more an individualist, and the other more a collectivist. It's an internal thing, not something we can easily recognize from the outside. Moreover, no one is purely an individualist, and no one is purely a collectivist. While most people prize their individuality, almost no one characterizes themselves as a collectivist. We think of collectivism as conformity to social norms, and while that is a necessity to some degree for all of us, we prefer to think of ourselves as going our own way, complying with social norms only incidentally and only by our own consent. And yet, the most individualistic among us is also a collectivist, in some form or degree. We tend to separate our personal feeling of sociability from our ideas about how society should be organized.

We might think of individualism in terms of simple physical separation, such as describing a person who lives alone and is not undone by it. Imagine Robinson Crusoe. He's a fictional character, but he'll do, for this purpose. Daniel Defoe invented this character as a castaway, a person shipwrecked alone, in large part to isolate for examination questions about man's perceptions of reality in the puzzling modern age.[1] For our purposes, what is noteworthy about the Crusoe character is that he seemed to thrive in his isolation. He was ever looking for means of self-improvement and for improvement of his condition; daily in communion with God; and never given to despair. Importantly for how we think of individualism, he was entirely self-sufficient, though in his case of necessity. For all that, however, we find the most impactful moment in the entire novel to be that when he sees evidence of another human being: Friday's footprint in the sand. He was incomplete with no society at all, notwithstanding his thriving otherwise.

Self-sufficiency is a recurring theme of rugged individualism, es-

---

1 Kirsten A. Hall, "Crusoe at the Crossroads/On Robinson Crusoe, Lost, and why we keep returning to mysterious islands where science blurs with the supernatural," *The New Atlantis*, Summer 2019.

pecially in the United States, with our stories of Daniel Boone and hardy westering pioneers, and our cultural approval of spirited individual initiative. The American cowboy is an archetype not just because he is more or less uniquely American, but because he seems to embody a principle of self-sufficient individualism. This individualism does not mean isolation and it doesn't mean an absence or even diminution of social interaction. It is most marked by independence, that is, a habit of mind in which the first instinct is to solve one's problems without the aid of others and to chart one's course in life without deference to what society around us is imagined to prescribe. In short, individualism in the American imagination is twined with personal freedom.

The Bible is clearly a message to individuals, about how they are to be reconciled with God. Even in its teaching on how we're to live with others, it is directed to the individual, addressing the individual's interaction with others as a central element of one's moral development occurring through unity with Christ. God's chosen people were the Hebrews, and much of his interaction with his people was collective in nature, so much so that the looked-for Messiah was expected to be a political savior for the nation of Israel. At the same time, clearly God was in the process of developing individual conscience, as when the law was brought to the Israelites through the prophet Moses. The Ten Commandments are primarily injunctions directed to the individual.

It's quite true that the Old Testament, in particular, is addressed to the "people" of God, to the nation of Israel and to the Hebrews as a tribe to be separated from the tribes around them in consecration to God through his covenant with them. God certainly addresses that nation, as a nation, through his prophets, and so in that limited sense it is collectivist. The Old Testament is nonetheless an individualist project, primarily, as we see in instances when individuals defy God's commandments. The whole people may suffer for it, but the wrongdoing is that of an individual. The Old Testament is collectivist in that the chosen people-group, the Hebrews, is to consider itself separated (and separating) from the pagan perspectives of the people-groups around them. It remains a teaching to individuals, not just to the tribe collectively. The moral standards of God apply individually.

In the New Testament, there is again the notion of the people of God, and instances in which the word of truth seems to be taken or rejected as a group, rather than individually, as with the household of the Philippian jailer,[2] or when the fellowship of believers was said to hold possessions in common.[3] These must be seen as vignettes specific to circumstances of the persons involved, however, or to early attempts at living out the Christian life as it was then understood. Jesus did not preach collectivism or individualism as a way of thinking about social organization, specifically. He did teach in such a way as to create self-examination within each individual. That necessarily means an outworking of one's faith in relationships with other people, but it is an essentially individual undertaking.

Most importantly, it is clear from Christ's teaching that we are individually to choose or reject him: that in the final day, he will separate out those who have aligned themselves with him from those who have not. The imagery is of oppositional separation: sheep (his followers) on one hand, and goats (those who continue in God's wrath) on the other.[4] We are not his on account of belonging to a group, nor are we rejected on that basis. It is for each of us individually to choose, just as it was hundreds of years earlier, as related in the Old Testament story of Joshua leading the people of God across the Jordan, admonishing them to individually choose definitively whether they will or will not serve God.[5]

There are many practical teachings in the Bible for how we are to conduct ourselves, of course. Most have to do with how we are to relate to other people. People in that day, as in this, had some sense of empathy and mutual help with those closest to them, who they would regard as neighbors. Jesus taught us to expand that natural feeling to others, including strangers, including those to whom we might initially react with wariness or even hostility. This is often taken by collectivists to mean a universalist concept of humankind, such that our project is to break people-group barriers wherever we find them. Individualists would turn the focus around to the subject of Jesus's teaching: the individual who is instructed to open his heart to people in need regardless of tribe.

Similarly, Jesus taught often about feeding the hungry, clothing the naked, and caring for the widow and orphan. A collectivist approach might be to find the most practical way to accomplish these things, even if it means invoking the coercive power of the State to force universal participation. In this way the State, rather than individuals, exercises

---

2 Philippians 16:31.

3 Acts 2:44.

4 Matthew 25:31-33.

5 Joshua 24:15.

charity by proxy. Individualists are more likely to see these teachings as being about the heart of the giver, rather than the physical needs of those to be helped. For them, a coercive (and statist) collectivist approach is not called for nor necessary, and is likely counterproductive both for material aid to recipients and moral improvement of givers.

The Bible seems to speak to both individualists and collectivists. To this day, Christians on the left read it through collectivist lens, and Christians on the right read it through individualist lens. There is significant division among Christians, for this reason, but the collectivist and individualist divide is not limited to those who internally call upon Jesus. Given the Christian influence on Western culture to this day, the individualist and collectivist divide exists across society and tends to be a significant point of division: indeed, more so than one's belief in a personal God, or disbelief.

A Christian may actually be a collectivist first, and a Christian only second, superimposing the dictates of the former onto the latter. It is a dangerous thing, however, to have anything ahead of personal faith. Jesus did not call for socialism. He called for loving one's neighbor. He stood for justice, not divisive and counterproductive "social justice." He stood for individual love of God, first, not love of mankind in the abstract, and certainly not a coerced form of "love." He sought to open our eyes and our minds to the coming kingdom of God, including the kingdom presently growing inside us and in the midst of us, not to direct us toward a utopian sameness that will inevitably usher in tyranny and greater material neediness.

In the New Testament, the individualist nature of the Bible's teaching is more explicit. Jesus was the culmination of the Old Testament revelation. The Old Testament canon, formed before Jesus' Advent, directly follows the genealogy of Jesus, to the point of including writings relevant to his human forbears and excluding writings that are not. Jesus' teaching was explicitly directed to individuals in one-to-one correspondence with the God of the universe. To be at peace with God means individual spiritual unity with Christ. It is not dependent on tribe or kinship, but on the exercise of individual agency.

The moral element of the Bible's teaching is strongly directed to how an individual is to interact with others. The Golden Rule, for example, invites us to empathize with others and thereby to consider their interests just as our own. This is not an injunction to a purely collectivist perspective, however, wherein we are to value ourselves only insofar as we meld our personalities with the people around us. It is essentially individual, by the very fact that we are called out of ourselves, in a manner of speaking, to develop love of others. The teaching is necessary because of our perspective of subjective personal self-interest. The object of the teaching is not to eliminate that individual perspective, but to get us to imagine the same perspective in others, and to then act on that understanding in love. This teaching, a summary of the latter six of the Ten Commandments,[6] is necessary precisely because of our individualist perspective. It reinforces that perspective, rather than eliminating it. The individual/collective opposition is not collapsed by the Golden Rule, but is transcended.

There is a collectivist trend in philosophy, expressed in culture, and it contributes to the attempted breakdown in oppositions of thought, pulling us from God and each other. This collectivism coincides with the breakdown in belief in objective truth, and with the transcendence of ideals. We will see the development of these truth-alternatives in pragmatism, coherentism, and existentialism. The elision of self into society facilitates these truth-alternatives, and is in turn facilitated by them.

---

6 The Ten Commandments, see Exodus Chapter 20. The first four are properly understood to involve our "vertical" relationship to God. The latter six involve our "horizontal" relationship with others.

CHAPTER SEVEN

Intersubjectivity

ALTHOUGH THE OTHER-NESS dualism between person and person is insurmountable and irreducible, that does not mean we're all atoms occasionally bouncing off each other but otherwise independent. We're not the billiard balls knocking against each other that philosophers of causation use for analogies. A collectivist element to human nature is built in, so to speak. This makes the individualist and collectivist divide a bit murkier, but does not eliminate it. We should understand how this works because we are capable of shifting, in our self-conception, to a more purely collectivist way of thinking, as a means of erasing self and the self's distance from God.

Our self-image is ineluctably informed by our relationships with others. It is an ineradicable element of human consciousness that we see ourselves as others see us. In fact, it can be truly said that I am not what I think I am, I am not what you think I am: I am what I think you think I am. In my mind I hold a picture of myself that is formed by what I think is in your mind. In my mind I see myself on the screen of your mind. In the same way, I see myself on the screen of what I imagine to be a collective mind—how I think I appear to society generally around me. Without really having to think about it, we all do this all the time. It affects our dress, our mannerisms, the customs we follow, the language we speak, and even, to some degree, the thoughts we think. This is a self-aware and social element of human consciousness.

We say we're "self-conscious" in those moments when we think about how others who perceive us have the same kind of intentionality of consciousness that we ourselves possess. We're "self-aware" when we are thinking about something but simultaneously thinking about the fact of thinking it, as if there were another part of the brain out there looking in on what goes on in the mind subjectively. It is a third-person point of view that we can adopt at will. We are self-aware creatures, meaning that we are aware of being aware.

I am aware of objects in my environment, and I am aware of you, but you're not an object, you're a subject, another like me.[1] That means you have awareness of me. I'm conscious of that. I'm aware that you're aware of my awareness. I know that I exist in your mind, that you see yourself on the screen in my mind just as I see myself on the screen in yours. Because of the subjective nature of your awareness, I know you know much about me just on sight, and significantly more if we are in greater proximity over time.

So we're not only self-aware, we're also other-aware. Not merely of another person's presence, but of another person's also having the kind of self-awareness we do. We perceive other people not as objects in our environment, but as subjects, another like me who also has other-awareness, and so sees me as subject, also. A kind of double-feedback then occurs from this subject-to-subject mutual awareness: intersubjectivity, by which each is aware of the awareness of the other. It creates a shared set of assumptions that needn't be uttered in each verbal exchange. Indeed, it exists without words. This is culture, or the mutual other-awareness that exists in a society as small as two people, or as large as the population of the whole world.[2]

This seems to be an essential element of human consciousness, in fact—so much so that in utter isolation we wither in ways only beginning to be understood. Prolonged segregation in prison, for example, has only recently come to be seen as little short of torture. We can say this is evidence that we're social animals, and that's certainly true, but how is that manifested in us individually? It would seem to be manifested in this double-awareness that is so much a feature of human consciousness.

And yet, despite the phenomenon of intersubjectivity, and the resulting shared culture, there's going to be a little that an individual can

---

1 This is the title and theme of a novel by the author: Norton, Albert, *Another Like Me*, 2016.

2 It is this shared mutual awareness that at times builds into a societal tension requiring release in scapegoating individuals or minority groups. This is among the frailties of socially organized mankind that Jesus exposed by being scapegoated himself, yet rising literally above it all. René Girard, in his *I Saw Satan Fall Like Lightning* (2001) insightfully explains this phenomenon. Scapegoating is described as one among several means of resolution of tension from binary opposition, suggested by Wood and Petriglieri infra.

hold back. There's an interiority that I can withhold even though I know you not only hear my words but also see my actions and the context for them, and the shared participation in a society with shared assumptions. You can infer much, but you can't see inside that dark interiority I keep all to myself.

Because I see myself through the eyes of other people, my relationship to them is going to be a function of how thoroughly I am known by them. The intensity or coolness of my love for another will be a function of many things, but a significant contributor will be how well they know me. So we run around trying to ingratiate ourselves with others and spend all day on Facebook, and so on, because we want to be known. Except we don't really want to be fully known. We want to be selectively known. We want to curate the image of ourselves that other people will feed back to us. We want to filter. We hold part of ourselves back, because we fear rejection and betrayal. The reason we fear is because of something we know about ourselves. Deep in the interior of my consciousness there is that little room that stays locked, and I don't let anyone in there, because if I did, they would not love me, I feel. It is a secret place, full of regret, for good reason. And even more significantly, a place in which my real motivations and my real self are readily apparent. My selfishness, my cruelties, my indifference, my callousness, my self-indulgence. I fear that it makes me unlovable.

Everyone is this way. Everyone has a locked, dark room, and this acts as a governor, a limitation, on our relationships with other people. It partially constrains our ability to love, because it limits the degree to which we allow ourselves to be known. This is the reality of good and evil in each of us. How are we to transcend it? Deny evil? Call evil good? This opposition exists in the heart; we can't run from it. We might try to collapse the internal opposition of good and evil, by simply denying evil. But it never works. We might try to collapse the opposition by killing the host, so to speak: by obscuring the self in which this evil resides, such as by losing the self in the collective, or in some even unhealthier way, like altering the consciousness with substance abuse. Good and evil are propositions of truth. Perhaps truth and falsity can be merged or re-created, to the effect of eliminating the self's awareness of internal good and evil.

If we don't try to crash this opposition in one of these unhealthy ways, we're left with this uncomfortable reality about ourselves. There is something rotten inside, and it makes us sick if it's left to molder and breed more evil. We want it cut out, or cured, to make the sick tissue whole. Evil is real and it is real inside each of us. It is an ineluctable part of what we are in this lifetime. If we were like the animals, not discerning good from evil in the same way, and not morally responsible, we wouldn't carry this sickness that clings to us like a sneering sentient shadow, like a smell of corruption that won't dissipate. What are we to do?

We find partial and temporary relief in confession, apology, and repentance. The weight of our offenses can be partially lifted in this way. But it is incomplete. There is an ineradicable corruption, and the fact of it, if not the specifics, is still known to others, because our intersubjectivity means we all know that we all carry this festering cancer. The only way to address it is to acknowledge the oppositions of truth (and falsity), evil (and good) and their presence in human nature, including mine. The answer is to seek the means available to transcend the oppositions of good and evil in the human heart.

What if there was someone who could see into that interior room? Someone who had the key, so to speak, and could come and go at will, but instead of being repelled by the stench, loved me anyway? By loving me anyway, knowing me even in this fetid depth, how could my love in response not be deeper and more profound than any love I am otherwise able to experience in this life? What if that interiority of my consciousness were accessible to such an all-seeing One? I might not like it that God can breach that interior space at will. I like having my secrets. I might object to being known so thoroughly. I might even react by imagining him out of existence, so I can continue to store away whatever rotting odds and ends I'd rather not have out in the open. If he's real, however, the fuse of this desire sputters out. If he's real and knows me, he knows me, regardless how I may feel about it.

I might instead adopt the opposite strategy. Instead of resisting God's knowing, I might desire greater knowing of him in return. I might find that he actually knows me better than I know myself, and loves me more, too. That knowing is a necessary feature of an all-knowing and all-caring and all-powerful being. That is, God: omniscient, omnibenevolent, omnipotent. Why would I not surrender to this flooding love?

If mankind had invented God, instead of the other way around, expiation of guilt would be the reason, not tribal cohesion or some such attempt at a naturalist explanation. But if we buy into God as merely symbolically a scapegoat for expiation of sin, as wishful thinking about how to band-aid the problem, we're still left with the difficulty of explaining the presence of that evil in the first place. Explaining evil requires explaining good as well, because good and evil exist together in binary opposition. Neither makes sense without the other. So it would be not just evil that must be explained naturally, but good, as well. Good is inexplicable without a Source. A naturalistic version of evolution would be an attempted explanation of some elements of goodness, such as co-operative interaction with others, but it wouldn't explain good thought and conduct in general, nor by what authority we call such interaction morally "good."

The moral compass, the conscience, applies to private thoughts and actions just as it does to those expressed or visible to other people. We respond to pangs of conscience even though the relevant thoughts and actions are private because we acquire a perspective that goes even beyond person-to-person intersubjectivity. We adopt the perspective of a sentient entity so powerful that even private thoughts and actions are open to it, our own and everyone else's, because we are self-aware that everyone else, too, has a conscience. The question is whether the explanation ends there, or whether this social feature of consciousness exists because a creator, God, is the Author of it.

We feel instinctively that we are known. We endlessly store guilt if we think it stays locked up privately forever. Something more than simply being discovered in our fault is going on. Confession, repentance, apology are soul-healing activities for a reason. We have an instinct against burying our wrongs. A sense that, left buried, they will fester and make us ill. This derives from the instinct that we are known even within that interiority not open to other people. We are known by God, and we are aware of his knowing, on a deep level, even if we attempt to deny it. This is what makes us uncomfortable in our guilt. It's what makes guilt, guilt. It's what makes evil, evil: the opposition to goodness, which is of the essence of God who knows us.

Being known, then, correlates to our feeling of love. We may articulate reasons why we feel affection for particular others, and usually it has to do with qualities we ascribe to those others. But in large part, my feeling of love has more to do with how those persons know me. Your love for a long-time friend may have more to do with the passage of time than his remarkable qualities, because it means he knows you well.

Individualism considered as an extreme of isolation would leave no room for love. Perhaps an extreme of collectivism would, too, because the love requires heightened attachment to one or to a small number. Loving everyone is the same as loving no one. If the attachment you feel to your spouse or sibling was the same as the attachment you feel to someone you've never met, the description "love" for that relationship no longer fits. Love arises out of the dynamic of oppositions between self and others. And it arises especially from the dualism of known and unknown.

Most people have experienced loneliness, in some form or degree. Loneliness can be most profound when one is surrounded by other people, as in a big busy city. Loneliness is not alleviated by proximity of other bodies. It is alleviated by relationships in which one is known. Love of all kinds—brotherly love, familial love, friendship, romantic love—arises out of being known. Being known in turn requires openness, overcoming the guardedness we all maintain to some degree. This is a difficult thing for extreme introverts or people withdrawn by virtue of personality or perhaps painful past associations. Loneliness results from indifference, and indifference is the dispassionate opposition to love.

Love requires the intersubjectivity that arises out of subject-to-subject connection. In the presence of another person, we know that other person knows us. I am aware of your awareness of my awareness. We know each other. Perhaps the strength of that knowing is weak, as when we're among slight acquaintances, but it may be stronger, as when we're in the company of a close friend or spouse or sibling.

Imagine being a celebrity. Being a celebrity means being known. Could this be the draw so many have to achieving fame? Or imagine young lovers, each infatuated with the other. It's not just worship from afar, like the admiration one might have for the celebrity. Instead, an essential element of that swooning head-over-heels feeling we have in the throes of new romantic love is a deep sense of being known. The relationship infatuates because of the newness of being known more deeply than in other kinds of relationships, more deeply especially because of the mutual expectation of exclusivity which drives the depths of that knowing.

We described consciousness itself as being defined in part by the phenomenon of intersubjectivity. Our self-awareness incorporates our perception of what others think of us as self-aware beings. The social component of our being is ineluctable because it is not just sort of the way people are. It is a feature of our very consciousness as human beings. The awareness play-back causes—and is caused by—our deep desire to be known, so we can say that being known, also, is integral to our very consciousness.

If we hold in mind the full playback intersubjectivity of human mutual awareness, resulting in special relationships of love we have with some people who know us well, we can readily extrapolate to yet greater depth of being known, by One who knows us thoroughly even in that secret interior space. If we grasp this about God and know also that he doesn't reject us, despite knowing us as he does, then we can begin to grasp the height and width and depth of his love. We might then be impelled to reciprocate, seeking to know him more deeply. The nature of this love would exceed what we know humanly, of love. The long story of God building up a people-group, culminating in the self-sacrifice in Christ, is the story of that love.

If God is as understood by the Jews and then Christians, he knows us entirely. We respond either by yielding and embracing that love for ourselves, or with resistance, perhaps even resentfulness, that we are known so thoroughly. Our resistance may take the form of denying the very existence of the Knower, as if pretending he is not there prevents his penetration of our illusory god-like sovereignty. We may so desire the impregnability of our self-made castle that we imagine out of existence the Besieger.

If this thesis is correct—that our consciousness incorporates the desire to be known and thereby the ability to receive and give love—then with respect to God, there would seem to be no middle ground. We choose between extremes of love and rejection. Denying the very existence of God is rejection, but so are other ways of attempting to collapse the uncomfortable opposition between ourselves and omnibenevolent God, such as imagining him to be indifferent, or imagining ourselves within a collective rather than in a position of individual choosing. We may mentally extend the moment of indecision, perhaps by engaging the mind with busyness at trivial things. Or we may unwittingly adopt the philosophy of hesitation that inheres in existentialist thinking, which in turn has its place in postmodernist thinking.[3]

---

3 Derrida, Jacques, *Violence and Metaphysics and Writing and Difference,* as cited by Jack Reynolds of La Trobe University, Australia, in his contribution on Derrida to the *Internet Encyclopedia of Philosophy,* iep.utm.edu/derrida (section 5).

CHAPTER EIGHT

Modern Philosophy

POSTMODERNISM IS abandonment of objective truth and objective right and wrong. Our culture today is polarized between those who hold to the idea of objective truth, and postmodernists, who hold truth to be a human construct.

On the one hand, truth can be conceived as an extant reality in the cosmos, there to be discovered by us, real and not invented. On this understanding, objective truth explains an inexorable orientation in our thinking to differentiate truth and falsity. Things are true if they correspond to the way the world is. Christianity, correctly understood, and theism more generally, is necessarily based on this view of truth.

Postmodernists, by contrast, conceive truth as a mental construct imposed by us on the external world to mitigate or effectuate power relationships. Postmodern conceptions of truth have their roots in coherentism, existentialism, and pragmatism—philosophical movements concerning the origin of truth that are atheistic, and necessarily so. These can be understood in how they attempt to avoid the effects of dualistic oppositions. To understand this, it would be helpful to take a high-level view of philosophical developments leading to postmodernism, especially the jump from medieval to modern philosophy, and then modern to postmodern.

But first, let's ask: How is philosophy relevant to begin with? Sometimes philosophy seems remote to human experience. How many angels can dance on the head of a pin? If a tree falls in the forest and no one hears, does it make a sound? Who cares? These questions, and their answers, if there be answers, have no practical value whatsoever. If this is what philosophy produces, we might think, then philosophy is twaddle,

76

safely ignored. But actually these kinds of questions help us to understand how we perceive reality, even if they're intentionally silly hypo-
theticals. Are there angels, and if so, of what are they constituted? If
you're a late-medieval or early-modern scholar trying to come to grips
with the natural/supernatural divide, this is a legitimate way to isolate
the question, though it is self-evidently and intentionally a silly question, from a practical standpoint. Likewise, the tree-falling question iso-
lates philosophical starting points for both ontology and epistemology.
For that purpose, it is actually helpful that the question is so impractical.
It is not about trees or hearing; it is about the basis for all knowledge,
and what it means to exist.

Philosophical questions matter. That philosophers produce words
and concepts and thoughts, rather than food or medicine or clothing,
does not render the exercise of philosophy pointless. Large movements
in philosophical thought trickle down to everyday thought patterns.
What Plato said 2400 years ago may seem irrelevant to our lives, but
it assuredly is not. Likewise with Aristotle and the whole pantheon of
ancient thinkers, continuing down to those whose thinking acquires
resonance in the present day. One could debate whether art or theology
or philosophy or even music are initially the more influential in changing thought patterns.[1] But it is beyond dispute that major philosophical
movements over time are hugely influential on your thinking and mine
in the present day.[2]

Before jumping to philosophical developments, however, it would
be wise to consider how they came to be philosophical developments.
As philosophy began to emerge as a discipline distinct from theology,
and specialists began to make names for themselves, what they wrote or
said became notable by virtue of being departures from more orthodox
thinking of the time. Famous philosophers like Immanuel Kant or Friedrich Nietzsche or Jean Paul Sartre did not become famous by clearly ar-
ticulating then-current thought, but rather through radical departures

---

1 Among Christian thinkers, Francis Schaeffer (1912-1984) was an example of one who
attempted a synthesis of cultural trends in the modern age in order to demonstrate the
philosophical underpinnings of current Christian thought. See *The Complete Works of
Francis A. Schaeffer*, (2nd ed.) 1985.

2 Czeslaw Milosz opens his brilliant book *The Captive Mind*, about the destruction
wrought by communist philosophy, this way: "It was only toward the middle of the
twentieth century that the inhabitants of many European countries came, in general
unpleasantly, to the realization that their fate could be influenced directly by intricate
and abstruse books of philosophy." Opening lines, *The Captive Mind*, New York: Vintage
International, 1990 (first published 1951).

from it. New philosophical developments have an outsized impact by virtue of being new. This is not bad in itself, necessarily, but we should take note that this is a criterion for influence distinct from correspondence to ultimate truth.

Likewise, we should consider a flip side to this radicalist tendency. Philosophy, more than most disciplines, develops its own canon. A philosopher who engineers a new system of thought doesn't crystallize it from the ether. He first digests existing strains of thought and "does philosophy" by finding new ways to think about a system or sub-system of philosophical problems. Philosophical work that is well recognized becomes a benchmark for later philosophy, or as a particularly important node in a network of philosophical thought.

Finally, we should consider that philosophers don't become famous and widely read by sitting around in an ivory tower, getting up from time to time to toss a brilliant manuscript out the window to an eagerly waiting throng. Philosophers are made famous by others: publishers who publish their work and not others; cultural influencers who recommend their works and not others; and cultural currents more generally, which may applaud a philosopher this year who would have been laughed at last year. And of course, some philosophers are more assiduous at self-promotion. The point is that philosophy builds on itself but not in quite the same way as science, say, or engineering. A philosophical school of thought can take a wrong turn, yet be highly influential. What counts as a "wrong turn," after all? The project is to question everything, including what makes something wrong or right. If objective truth is among the assumptions tossed out by developing philosophy, for example, how does one say that it's right or wrong, true or untrue?

This problem becomes acute with postmodernism. Falsity is not converted to truth because it is combined with a body of other falsehoods. When a modern philosopher like Immanuel Kant or even the skeptic David Hume undertook fine distinctions of thought, it was done in the direction of given absolutes, typically. They didn't question the very existence of absolute truth, or beauty, or goodness. They only questioned what comprised those absolutes. In postmodern thought, by contrast, philosophers reject absolutes, even as they incoherently invoke them by using the format of argumentation that can be understood by others. Postmodern thought might more or less cohere, but that coherent ball of intersecting propositions floats entirely free of a concept of truth as an "out there" phenomenon for us to pursue. It can be regarded as "true," therefore, only on the basis of rational consistency with other beliefs one already holds. Coherency as a truth criterion by itself encourages thinking on the margins: logical thinking from one proposition to another, but without tracing the chain of inferences back sufficiently to erect a self-contained way of thinking. Coherency as a basis for formulation of truth nonetheless has superficial appeal. We try to make an integrated whole of what we believe to be true because there is an inescapable underlying truth orientation in all of us. But we have to do that for the whole of our understanding of reality. Propositions are not made true just because they cohere with other beliefs we hold. It could be that many of our existing beliefs are wrong, too.

Thus, if God exists but a philosophical school of thought assumes him away, then it will attract other cohering beliefs: that is, beliefs that require or are at least consistent with the atheist proposition. Jacques Derrida's post-structuralist deconstruction, for example, provides a unique perspective, including a validation of the role of dualisms that form a central thesis of this book. But his entire philosophy assumes these dualisms subtly advance power interests in a social dynamic for defining, rather than discovering, truth. Ultimately it is a philosophy of negation and polemics, rather than a system of thought with independent explanatory power.

To begin to grasp the truth-denying elements of postmodernism that are so influential in the culture today, we must back up a bit to see how this philosophical thought developed. To do so, let's first distinguish between modern and postmodern philosophy. In the history of the West, the modern age is sometimes said to have commenced around 1600, roughly a marker for an explosion in scientific progress. Other dates are often used, for a variety of valid reasons. In his magisterial *Modern Times*, for example, historian Paul Johnson places modern times entirely in the twentieth century,[3] though in a separate volume he puts the birth of the modern in the early nineteenth.[4] Often the descriptor "modern" simply means recent, perhaps in the context of developing technologies. Certainly "modern" is post-medieval. It could be placed after the Renaissance of the fifteenth and sixteenth centuries. It might coincide with or be placed after the Enlightenment period, which is itself difficult to pin to a specific range of years without more context.

In philosophy there may be a bit more uniformity in the dates one would assign to "modern." In his *Modern Philosophy*, Roger Scruton tells

---

3 Johnson, Paul. *Modern Times*. HarperCollins, 1983.

4 Johnson, Paul. *The Birth of the Modern/World Society 1815-1830*. HarperCollins, 1991.

us "The modern era is held to be contemporaneous with the rise of natural science, and the decline of the centralising tendency in Christendom. Hence Descartes is described as a modern philosopher, while Aquinas is not."[5] Descartes wrote in the first half of the seventeenth century and had such a profound impact on philosophy that he is reasonably cited as a pivotal thinker well into the modern age. So around 1600 would be a reasonable date to use as a transition marker to the era of modern philosophy.

But then we have "postmodern" philosophy, which many see as a legitimate distinction from the modern. That necessitates finding dates and criteria for delineating between modern and post-modern. It is common to situate the rise of postmodernism in the 1960s, following publication of works by Jacques Derrida, Michel Foucault, and Jean-Francois Lyotard. An earlier date is proposed here, however: approximately 1900. Why? The most significant reason to distinguish modern and post-modern philosophy is abandonment of belief in God, followed by abandonment of belief in objective, transcendent truth in the abstract. In philosophy which was almost exclusively secular commencing at the turn of the twentieth century, that abandonment occurs within philosophies of pragmatism, coherentism, and existentialism. Postmodernism is nothing if not hyper-skepticism, not only about God, but about claims to transcendent truth reflecting the idealism in metanarratives more generally. Postmodern philosophy concerning knowledge of truth presents alternatives to the proposition that truth is an objective, "out-there" phenomenon which is discoverable but can't be created. It is a turn from the correspondence theory of truth as consisting in relation to reality.

The single most important turn in philosophy was the overt abandonment of theism. Over the course of the nineteenth century, philosophy proceeded as if there were no God, or if there were, he was an incidental add-on to the materialist conception of reality. Søren Kierkegaard was a notable exception, and certain later thinkers like William James discussed the concept of God from a decidedly heterodox point of view. But explicit atheism became central to the thinking of many in the nineteenth century, as with Karl Marx, Sigmund Freud, and of course Friedrich Nietzsche, who, in the latter half of the nineteenth century, famously declared God "dead." Rejection of God and rejection of objective truth coincided, which is natural because God is the embodiment of objective truth.

---

5 Scruton, Roger, *Modern Philosophy/An Introduction and Survey*, New York: Penguin Books, 1994, p. 1.

In Western culture outside the United States, Christianity was in sharp decline even by the time of the First World War of 1914-18.[6] Explicitly atheist ideologies drove the bridle-high bloodshed of the Second World War (1939-45). The 1960's postmodernists wrote largely in reaction to these events, and their work excluded God because they wrote in reaction to metanarratives that drove ideology. Importantly, not left-wing metanarratives, but only those of National Socialism in Germany, the imperialism of Japan, and the fascism of Italy and Spain. When postmodernists speak of "metanarratives," they mean Christianity and racialist right-wing metanarratives, not the leftist metanarratives of Marxism as manifested in Russia, Soviet satellites, China, Cuba, Venezuela, Cambodia, and many other places. The shock of right-wing ideology in Europe led these thinkers to reject idealism generally, substituting Marxist theories of reality. Atheism is taken for granted in Marxism, and therefore in all postmodernist philosophy. In most philosophy it was taken for granted well before post-Second World War philosophy. There was a tipping point at which presumptive atheism took hold. It would be reasonable to place it roughly around the turn of the twentieth century. So, we'll call modern philosophy that which developed from around 1600 into the early twentieth century, and postmodern philosophy that which has its roots at the end of nineteenth.

Following the Advent, Christian philosophy dominated in the West throughout the medieval period and into the Renaissance of approximately the fifteenth/sixteenth centuries, giving way to the modern period commencing in about the seventeenth. These are conventional names and date ranges. Obviously history flows continuously. It is not really marked off into neat segments, but we do so conventionally, in order to gain a foothold in our understanding of the sequences of ideas prevalent in a society over time. This is how we gain a foothold in understanding of anything, after all: setting off two concepts in opposition so we gain understanding by how they're different. Even in something as second-nature and task-specific as separating history into modern and postmodern periods, we engage in oppositional thinking. It is the tension between the oppositions from which we derive meaning. The differences in thinking from one period to the next allows us to understand the evolution of ideas.

Philosophy in the medieval period consisted largely in developing reasoned, objective support for a systematic Christian theology, distin-

---

6   An excellent summary of this evolution is found in Alan D. Gilbert's *The Making of Post-Christian Britain/A History of the Secularization of Modern Society*, 1980.

guishing it from pagan notions of fate. This was tied to the authority of the church, rather than being a subjective and individual undertaking. It was collectivist in that general sense because truth was thought objective and there to be discovered, with the church the collective institution for that effort. Underpinning all the philosophical ruminations of the time was the assumption that there was one truth to be discovered, and as such, it applied to everyone.

The modern period is usually pegged to the scientific revolution, which is in turn pegged to the seventeenth century, with such luminaries as Francis Bacon and Isaac Newton. The cosmos came to be seen as understandable, through natural laws that applied to all physical things. Just as truth in the abstract was objectively there to be discovered, so truth about the nature and movement of physical things was there to be discovered, as well. The scientific revolution meant increasing reliance on observation, and reason applied to that observation. Observation occurs subjectively in human beings over time, however, so the emphasis on reason in the Enlightenment period of the seventeenth and eighteenth centuries coincided with a turn to the subjective, in philosophy.[7] This meant a turn toward making sense of the world with an understanding that the sense-making process occurs in individuals and is subjective; therefore, one must account for the features of individual consciousness and cognition through which the world is negotiated.

This was primarily a modern development, meaning it commenced in the seventeenth century, more or less. Among philosophers, as with much else in philosophy in the modern age, it is often traced to René Descartes (1596-1650). Implicit in his statement "I think therefore I am" was the supposition that reality relies first on individual and internal thinking, which at a minimum proves the existence of the thinker. The turn to the subjective was also significant in the thinking of Immanuel Kant (1724-1804), especially in his reaction to the more overtly rationalist and empiricist English philosophers of his age. What it meant was that the perspective of this philosophy was centered on the individual. It was an exploration of our reception of the world individually, through the senses.

In the eighteenth century, both English and so-called continental philosophical developments were strongly influenced by Jean-Jacques Rousseau (1712-78). Rousseau is often thought of as a leading figure in the romanticism of the eighteenth and nineteenth centuries. Romanti-

---

7 This way of phrasing it was employed by Charles Taylor in *A Secular Age*, 2007.

cism and the turn to the subjective are necessarily associated with an individualistic, rather than collectivist, way of approaching reality. The monolithic authority of the Church had been shaken by the effects of the Reformation and progress of the industrial age. Church authority was giving way to the authority of self. Monarchy was on the way to being replaced by republicanism, and the aristocracy by the nation-state. This was within the Age of Reason, which meant the reference was to one's own mental faculties, rather than received authority. It was individual, as a result, not collectivist.

With the American Revolution, a more radical departure from tradition and old-world thinking could be accomplished on literal new soil—new at least to European Americans—and the American project was distinctively liberal in that authority of aristocracy, state-sponsored church, and the State itself were rejected in favor of idealistic individual freedom. The foundational principles were these: (1) individual rights were pre-political; that is, from God, not the State; (2) the State's purpose was to preserve those rights; and (3) the State's authority was confined by the consent of the governed.[8] Thus, "pursuit of happiness" was to be an individual, and not collective, undertaking. Politically this individualism vis-à-vis the State was compromised by the outcome of the Civil War in the 1860s, but well into the twentieth century, Americans could conceive of the country and themselves as citizens distinct from the country's limited government.

The American experiment was closely watched in Britain and the European continent. Liberal political ideology worked violent revolution in France beginning in 1789 and fitfully in the years following, resulting in a forever-changed political and cultural environment not only in France, but in a watchful (and often French-dominated) Europe, during the early nineteenth century. These upheavals corresponded to a more individualistic, self-sovereign conception of one's place in the world.

Rousseau's romanticism did not make a straight line to individualism. In fact at the same time Rousseau lacquered romanticism over individualistic reason, he also advanced an idea that happiness was only to be found in a society yielded to a new kind of collectivism. Rousseau reacted negatively to the kind of expression of self-interest that found its answer in social prestige, thinking it distinguishable from mere economic self-interest asserted in the working economy. He developed a

---

8 Declaration of Independence, Congress of the United States of America, July 4, 1776.

paradoxical notion that freedom would follow from subjugation of one's individual will to the "general will." He famously wrote, in fact, that if one resists this subjugation to the general will, he "will be forced to be free."[9] He likely meant freedom in the sense of moral freedom, much like the Christian conception of freedom in Christ, but for Rousseau, moral freedom meant putting aside prestige as a motivator, embracing equality, and living in a less corrupted and more natural or primitive state. Because this general will was to be secured by the State, the individual would be freed from the private wills of other persons or institutions. Rousseau's idea of freedom was not entirely nonsensical, perhaps, given his premises, but it was certainly thoroughly collectivist.

As a matter of individual, personal autonomy, Rousseau's freedom was illusory. The contemplated compulsory participation in the "general will" would necessarily mean freedom only to give oneself over to the small-d democracy, which was Rousseau's ideal. This meant collectivism. Individualism of the kind which would set a person apart from that political process was not what was contemplated by Rousseau. By associating individualism and freedom with their opposites, collectivism and compulsion, Rousseau presaged collectivist ideologies developing from other directions in the nineteenth and twentieth centuries. The collectivism of Rousseau precedes his desire for freedom and his desire for understanding God, and this is true for his many collectivist intellectual heirs as well.

Rousseau influenced the thinking of Georg Wilhelm Friedrich Hegel (1770-1831), who had a profound and lasting influence on philosophy and in turn on the everyday thinking patterns of people in Western society, from that day to this. Like Rousseau (and many other philosophers of the modern era), Hegel's systematic philosophy was in large part a philosophy of the desire for human freedom. He was particularly concerned with development of ideas in history, thus introducing a sense of direction to history which persists in our operating assumptions about the working of the world to this day: in fact, this idea of historical consciousness now obtains to such an extent that we're scarcely conscious of it.

Hegel introduced the idea of *geist*, meaning a spirit or consciousness that evolves over time, and thereby provides a meaningful progress to history. A word in common usage today, *zeitgeist,* meaning the spirit of the age, borrows from Hegelian terminology. Hegel explored the means

9 Rousseau, Jean-Jacques, *On the Social Contract*, translated by G.D.H. Cole. Mineola, NY: 2003 (first published 1762).

of development of historical consciousness in history. He employed a conceptual dialectic for which he acknowledged Johann Gottlieb Fichte (1762-1814), by which thesis and antithesis result in synthesis—a dissonance and then conflicting strains of thought resolved in a kind of negotiated settlement of the conflict, while setting up new conflicts to similarly be resolved. The rolling-forward effect of this constitutes the changing historical consciousness by which a *telos* to history is expressed society-wide. Superficially, this would seem akin to the meaning-making of oppositional dualisms, but this dialectic works through the *geist*, collectively, and applies to social consensus of meaning rather than the subjective cognition by which individuals make sense of the world. Thus, in Hegelian philosophy, the collective historical consciousness evolves by the collapsing of oppositions into a synthesis (or "subsumption") as a means of resolving the meaningful tension those oppositions create. It presupposes that dialectical process is one of dissolving those dualist oppositions into something else, a process-negotiated position that becomes the new current thought. Moreover, the process is not necessarily one for finding truth, but rather for developing what will be called truth. Hegelian philosophy is fundamentally collectivist, and necessarily so. The idea of *geist*, or historical social consciousness, is akin to Rousseau's general will. It imagines a shared movement of ideas, rather than a means of recognizing disparate and individually-formed ideas. The process resolves collectively, so there is an implicit expectation that the point of this natural resolution is to bind the wills of those who participate in the society, which forms the basis of the collective consciousness.

In a sense, we're all Hegelians now. It's not that Hegel's theories were true or accurately reflected reality. It's that the ideas became prevalent and then became the reality. Though the names of philosophers (like Hegel) may not even be known among influencers in society, there is a top-down deployment of philosophical ideas so that they attain common currency and become part of the fabric of our lives. They are the background shared cultural memory that we don't question. So, for example, we don't stop to think where this dialectical idea of opposition resolved in synthesis even came from; it just seems to be natural and we don't question it anymore. When we speak in politics or culture of "the narrative," for example, we are invoking Hegelian historical consciousness.

Indeed, if we take Hegelian dialectic as merely a description of what naturally happens, there is already some truth to be found in it. We want to get along with others, after all. We routinely compromise our independent intentions and ideas, in order to live peaceably and in harmony with others. We do this in small things and large; it is a necessary element of that shared cultural memory that derives from intersubjectivity. In this way, the content of the shared cultural memory is formed and sustained.

And yet, there is a difference between the all-in embrace of Hegelian collectivism of thought, and the kind of interpersonal buffering that occurs between and among individuals in a heterogeneous society. The total collective way of thinking requires conformity, number one, but number two, finds the substance of the collective *geist* in social consensus, the push and pull of power struggle for ideas. To fast-forward to the present day, how has this collectivism played out? Collectivism is an attempt to collapse the me/you opposition so that self is subsumed into society, thereby subjectively compromising or softening oppositions of God/not-God, good/evil, salvation/damnation.

Within Hegelian thinking, the concept of a "marketplace of ideas" is inapposite. There's not a marketplace in which a person evaluates the ideas on offer and accepts or rejects them on their merits. Instead there is a process which exists to yield a consensus. A power struggle ensues because one's purpose is to dominate the conversation, not to persuade others based on external but commonly-accepted criteria. I'm not trying to persuade you that X pleases God. I'm screaming X because I want X to dominate the resulting "consensus" synthesized by resolution of the conflict of thesis and antithesis. The object is not to find the foundational truths that exist *a priori* and objectively. In the consensus society, the idea of abstract truth is an anachronism. We are no longer about discovering truth, but about creating it. We no longer engage in debate and exchange of ideas in order to get closer to a cosmic truth existing apart from all of us engaged in the discussion. We engage in debate to bring the social consensus closer to what we individually want. This is the all-against-all power struggle we inherit upon the putative death of God. It is an expression of Nietzsche's will-to-power.

Public debate is undertaken as an argument over what is "good" and "right" and "just" and "true," ideals which are invoked as objective and foundational apart from what individuals and society think about them. And yet, behind that invocation is a stance that those are not true ideals at all, but merely labels useful against those who still attach meaning to them; those who subscribe to objective truth. In fact they are shibboleths, vague words of approbation bleated in false deference to an ideal that really no longer exists. Eventually the mask comes off. The public discussion itself over time becomes understood as a process toward consensus, rather than finding objective truth. The power struggle thus becomes the norm. The antagonists no longer fraudulently cloak their purposes as a search for objective, foundational truth. Instead, the public conversation becomes more nakedly the struggle for dominance in the formation of coerced "consensus." In this way we replace the individual with the collective in our dealings with each other and with God. Our dealings with others become attenuated and impersonal.

There was an idea at one time that paganism involved "direct duties"[10] of each person to another. Christianity was thought to interrupt those direct duties, because our duties were instead redirected to God, who thereby mediated our relationships with other people. We behaved a certain way to our fellow man in order to please God, it was thought, so God amounted to a sort of middle-man, setting us off each against the other. But it turns out that neo-pagan secular society accomplishes division more thoroughly than Christianity could. Society itself becomes the middle-man, through which our relations with specific other individuals is to be mediated. Duties aren't direct, as it turns out, when neo-pagan materialism is substituted for theism. We relate with others on the basis of an ever-shifting social consciousness, a political correctness in the air which must be sniffed out so as not to call down upon ourselves the new gods of social opprobrium.

Our dealings with God are unchanged, in reality, but evolve in our imagining. Instead of hiding from the glory and justice of God in the cleft of the rock,[11] i.e., in Jesus, in order to yet see God, we hide from God entirely in the bosom of our society. That comes at the expense of a more developed sense of self that Christianity would provide, and a corrupted understanding of how reconciliation with our Maker is possible.

10 As referenced by John Stuart Mill, for example, in *On Liberty*, 1859.
11 Exodus 33:22.

CHAPTER NINE

Divorce of Theology and Philosophy

I N THE ENLIGHTENMENT period commencing in the late seventeenth century, many influential thinkers felt much freer to express religious skepticism. Skeptics included David Hume, Denis Diderot, Voltaire, Thomas Paine, and many others. By the French Revolution (1789), the rejection of the Catholic Church, as one arm of an *ancien régime* that included the aristocracy, meant for many the rejection of the God that the Church represented.

By the mid-nineteenth century, Karl Marx adopted Hegel's dialectical method and adapted it for materialism. The result was dialectical materialism, which excluded Hegel's spiritual reality. Marx advocated class struggle, to resolve the alienation of workers from the means of production and the wealth generated by it. Significantly, his philosophy required abandonment of any conception of deity, even an unorthodox one, as with Hegel. This overt break from nominal theism is often lightly passed over in histories of philosophy, but it shouldn't be. It is a significant turn in philosophy, because elimination of the idea of God as sustainer of transcendent truth means that transcendence is open to question, which means the very source of truth is open to question. Perception of truth and of morality as objectively real phenomena would eventually suffer. What followed was further evolution of ideas in infinite directions, still following the logical rationality that the truth orientation dictates, but without its foundation.

One has a sense that Marx and his collaborator, Friedrich Engels, started with the absence of God and a conviction that an underclass was exploited, and then went about looking for a theory to support practical ways to rectify it. It is no accident that their ideology excludes God. It is an essential element of overtly socialist and then communist theory that no God enters into the genuine motivations of people. In fact, Marx was among thinkers like Sigmund Freud and Friedrich Nietzsche who viewed religion with suspicion and hostility, imputing nefarious motives to its practice because, they believed, its truth claims were self-evidently false. Given there is no God, they reasoned, what could be the purpose of all this highly developed religious belief? Some purpose other than what is stated, they thought. In essence, they held that because the God of Christians and Jews was a fiction, the whole religious construct existed for reasons other than the truth of what it asserts. Typically, such thinkers held that religious doctrines therefore existed to maintain order and give advantage to ruling classes of people in society.

Marx thought religion was like an opiate of the masses, useful to keep the proletariat docile. His theory of emancipation through political collectivism rests fundamentally on atheism. People don't actually believe this nonsense, thought Marx and Engels (and later, Freud and Nietzsche). They just think they believe it. This is a mental dissonance: a disconnect between actual belief and what one thinks one believes. Truth and belief are not necessarily connected, by this way of thinking. This suggests an interesting comparison to Kierkegaard, incidentally, because Kierkegaard in a way was saying the same thing: merely being part of a Christian society and mouthing the words of belief does not make one a Christian. Genuine belief must be internally felt and not merely a cerebral construct. So Kierkegaard implicitly acknowledged the dissonance between actual belief and what one thinks he believes. That's why he believed a leap of faith was necessary.

Marxism is nothing if not automatism. That is, the diamat (dialectical materialism) presupposes a hyper-rational, materialist universe, in which the past is linked to the present and future deterministically. Marxism, especially in its Leninist-Stalinist form, embraced and harnessed this automatism in its culture and governance. When we see an expectation of automatism in our nominally capitalist society, we are seeing this symptom of burgeoning Marxist philosophy in Western belief systems. One starts with reductionist materialism, which is thought self-evidently true, and admixes a bastardized version of Hegelian historical consciousness, and the result is what Stalinists called the New Man, or Soviet Man: a person with beliefs devoid of any sense of transcendence, and the self subsumed into the State, just as with fascism.

Marxism's emphasis on historical consciousness means there is no "trans-historical" truth; that is, "truth" is derived only from the power structure and the interests that inform it. Thus, "truth" has no independent authority but is contextual to time and culture. Clearly, this view excludes eternality of truth—nothing is true at all times and all places. There is no foundational principle for something being regarded as "true." For this reason among others, it is essential to Marx's thought that Christianity and the existence of God must be rejected.

The move toward collectivism and materialism in philosophy was aided by a sentiment among some writers that Christianity, being individualistic, was also essentially selfish. One could go so far as to see the Golden Rule as a limitation, rather than an expansive view of how one should behave. This perspective would be implicit in the philosophy of Emmanuel Levinas,[1] for example, in the latter half of the twentieth century. This perspective has deeper antecedents, however, contributing to widespread rejection of orthodox Christianity among radical elites. At mid-nineteenth century, the novelist Mary Ann Evans (who wrote as George Eliot) generally treated cultural expressions of Christianity with some indulgence,[2] but an internal impact of Christian belief is curiously absent in her characters beyond their embrace of conventional, Christianity-influenced morals. Evans rejected first the doctrine of free will, and then the whole of Christianity. She maintained it was a religion "based on pure selfishness"[3] because of its doctrine of personal and selective salvation.

Around the same time, in *On Liberty*, John Stuart Mill found Christian morality essentially selfish because it replaced what he considered a classical (and pagan) moral inducement of direct duty to others, with Christianity's self-interested motivation of eternal reward.[4] This is an objection to the mediating effect of God in person-to-person relations. All duties flow to God, not others, according to Christianity: "Against you only have I sinned, O Lord," David prayed after sinning with Bathsheba.[5] Mill's distinction between direct duties and duties mediated by

---

1 E.g., Levinas, Emmanuel, *Totality and Infinity*, 1969; *Alterity and Transcendence*, 1999.

2 As with *Scenes From A Clerical Life* (1857): long on genial cultural Christianity, short on doctrinal significance.

3 Rée, Jonathan, *Witcraft/The Invention of Philosophy in English*, London: Allen Lane, 2019, p. 323, citing 1842 letters of Eliot's friend Mary Sibree, recounted in Cross, John Walter, *George Eliot's Life*, Vol. 1, p. 162.

4 This idea of "direct duties" being an element of paganism was shared by Kierkegaard, and was among the reasons he thought a leap of faith was necessary.

5 Psalm 51:4.

God is not wrong. We might think of two people in discourse as two points on a triangle, with God (or at least, objective truth) as the third point. Both people speak of truth while referring to that third point. That is, you and I might disagree about what is true, but we both refer to the third point, objective truth, in doing so. We only disagree about what the objective truth is; we're not disagreeing over the very existence of objective truth. Without that common reference, we have only the push and pull for dominance as to our respective truth claims. The pagan "direct duties" of Mill's imagination also mean direct conflict unresolvable through common reference to objective truth.

Mill's ideas had an air of self-justification in keeping with radical elite trends of the day, however, because we don't start out indifferent to other people before remembering God. But in any event, this objection also signals a retreat into collectivism. Christianity's individualism means individuals stand alone before God, and some are saved and some are not. A way to try to avoid this harsh-seeming reality is to collapse the I/you opposition in order to hide in the collective, rather than transcending the God/not-God opposition by identification with Christ. This idea of Christianity as essentially selfish opened the door to its replacement in collectivist and materialist presumptions. In philosophy and theology there is a correlation between the trends from individualism to collectivism, and from theism to materialism. In fact, the inclination to collectivism precedes the desire for personal freedom, and the desire for communion with God. The objections of many, including but certainly not limited to Eliot and Mill, were based on Christianity's proposition that not all are saved. Individuals respond to God's offer of reconciliation, or they don't, and that determines whether they have eternal life with God. The logic of the objection had to be this: some, not all, are saved according to Christian doctrine; therefore, people subscribe to Christianity on selfish motives; therefore, Christianity itself is selfish; therefore, it is false; therefore, there is no God. The first step in this progression puts the collective at the center, rather than the individual. The objection is not that a person doesn't have an avenue to salvation. The objection is that some won't take it, in this system of theology. The objection is made on behalf of the collective.

This offense taken at the theological principle causes some to turn to collectivism, because losing oneself in the collective is a way of avoiding the harsh reality of the either/or of God's existence and justice. If the self stands alone and trembling before almighty God, perhaps it's more comforting to lose that solitary self in the crowd. The scary saved/

damned dualism is then just ignored, and a more comforting princi-ple of universal salvation is substituted. This squares with a collectivist's idea (rather than God's) of what's right.

The doctrine of hell should be re-examined in this light. We wrongly conceive it unfair that anyone would go there. Even if we don't reject God entirely, or Christianity in its particulars, we may nonetheless dis-regard the doctrine of hell in favor of annihilationism: the theory that unsaved people just cease to exist and only saved people live on after life in the body. This is another effort to collapse an inconvenient and frightening dualism. It is ultimately untenable, theologically, because it means eternal life for some and not others. Why would that be so? We're tempted to embrace it in order to avoid the seeming unfairness of se-lective salvation. Another way to attempt to resolve this tension created by the collectivist perspective is to collapse the dualism in "universal-ism:" we're all saved. But that renders meaningless Christianity's clear call to action and belief. Yet another attempted collapse is to reject the idea of an afterlife altogether. The attempt to collapse necessary oppo-sitions whereby Christ is deemed an offense,[6] thereby becomes a chain of inconvenient and untenable beliefs, each hooked in turn and dragged along like a string of fish, until the whole of Christian doctrine is gut-ted of its essentials, leaving only the sentimental association with vague Niceness. The frightening heaven and hell binary opposition is in this way eliminated, we think, and another, collectivism and individualism, takes its place so that we can hide ourselves in the crowd.

Henry James (1811-1882), the father of philosopher William James and novelist Henry James, exemplifies this notion that Christianity is essentially selfish, and could be improved upon through a collectivism he deemed less selfish. He and his contemporaries were all too aware of the despair to which modern scientific materialism would lead them, if there is no God. In that way, they anticipated the current climate. But he too was troubled by what he saw as Christianity's selfishness. He thought "sense of self;" i.e., individualism, was the curse of mankind, rather than sin as conventionally understood in Christianity. His views illustrate the pivot from a Christian understanding of reality to modern secular-ism. He wanted to accommodate Christianity's religious impulse into a modern secular faith that also would steer clear of disenchantment borne of scientific materialism. In this way he anticipated the pragma-tists, especially John Dewey. Henry James sought to dispense with the

---

6   1 Peter 2:7-8; Matthew 11:6

"faith in selfhood" inherent in traditional morality. He understood that traditional morality from the Bible was highly individualistic, not just in that it was addressed to individuals rather than societies, but also in the structure of twice-born metaphysics.

James also reacted negatively to the expectation of strict conformity with cultural Christian norms, especially the concept of God as One who kept strict debtor-and-creditor moral accounts with people based on behavior, rather than genuine piety based on love. In this he had a point. Western culture has been lost to Christianity in large part because of this kind of joylessness. One can escape this with a militant atheism, and we have seen much of that in recent years. But the more usual course is to try to neuter the harsh impact of individual moral scrutiny and responsibility by turning to collectivism, without first directly repudiating God.

James was wrong, however, to attribute selfishness to Christianity in the first place. As were Eliot and Mill and others before them. There's no doubt they saw Christianity as selfish because of selective salvation, but is it really? If there is a God at all, and he is just, then his wrath should remain on us who are infected with sin. It would be just to leave us all to condemnation. That would certainly end any discussion of fairness. But God gives us an opportunity of salvation. That actually is unfair, but unfair in our favor. It is not unfair that God declines to interfere with our exercise of free will in accepting or declining his offer. So the charge that Christianity is "selfish" is not well thought-out, and rests on a flawed understanding of basic Christian doctrine. If we pretend there is no condemnation even apart from Christ, we also must pretend there is no agency on the part of human beings to make moral decisions, and must live like animals for whom transcendent truth is irrelevant. We imagine we can give up the negative part of our God-imaged selfhood, but retain the positive. It doesn't work that way, however. The lows must go with the highs, and vice versa. And in any event, we don't choose one reality over the other. There is but one, and we accept it or live in delusion.

The glide out from under the awful weight of meaning commences by first throwing off the yoke of individualism. One repudiates self rather than God because that seems easier, initially. Then there is apparent rest in the storm-haven of collectivism, for a time, before its meaninglessness ushers one gently into outright atheism. One may be dimly aware, however, as was Henry James and his radical contemporaries, that this leads to the despair of materialism. Collectivism seems a way to navigate between Scylla and Charybdis, between what seems soul-crushing obedience to wrong-headed Christian moralism, and the despair of meaningless materialism. This is why there is a desire for insignificance as well as significance. We would like to hide in the cleft of the rock[7] from omnipresent meaning—from God—but not if that cleft is Christ because that is taken to mean religiosity, the culturally-enforced deference to rites and practice and institution and mutually-reinforced hypocrisy, man-made substitutes for genuine love for God. We intuit (and are told in Scripture) that Christ means freedom, but we create churches that confine the soul. It's no wonder that some associate God with constraint rather than freedom, and drift into the seeming anonymity of the collective instead of looking up through clenched trembling hands at the God who *is*.

By the late nineteenth century, there was quite a broad field of overtly atheist philosophical and popular writing and speaking. In the culture, the "freethinker" movement was at a zenith against a largely Christian, if sentimentally Christian, backdrop.[8] In this milieu William James wrote, adopting a metaphysical view that borrowed only loosely from Christian theism. His goal wasn't to advocate overtly against religion, but rather to develop his philosophy of pragmatism, a new theory of truth, which later in the century would become, along with existentialism, a foundation of postmodernism. James's writings suggest he followed the selfishness motif of his father (and others) in that he felt the "sense of self" was the curse of mankind, rather than Christianity's concept of sin. What was happening here was a continuation of the shift away from both Christianity and individualism to the collectivism and alternate truth theories that erode theist belief.

Yet another way to avoid the harsh choice of Christianity is to undermine the need for salvation. In this way the selective nature of salvation is irrelevant. Along with the other erosions of doctrine, secular philosophers found (or assumed) essential good in people rather than the religious perspective of original sin deemed to infect humanity. This seems to follow, if "sense of self" is the curse of mankind rather than sin. The selfishness identified (or perhaps more accurately, felt) in these trends was to be ameliorated by crossing the person-to-person divide, collapsing the me/you opposition. Generally, in philosophy, this involves various means of subverting alterity, but it is never quite successful. *Pace'* Levinas, other-ness remains ontological. It is an opposition that can be

---

7 Exodus 33:22.

8 Susan Jacoby elucidates this point in her history/advocacy *Freethinkers* (2004), especially chapter 6.

transcended through Judeo-Christian principles, but not eliminated in paganism or postmodern neo-paganism.

Near the end of the nineteenth century, an entirely different set of reasons for dispensing with Christianity was presented, by Friedrich Nietzsche. He objected to Christianity not because it was selfish, but for an opposing reason: it induced a slave morality in its followers. His rabid denunciation of Christianity further enabled unapologetic rejection in a society which was still, despite tendrils of "freethinker" movements, nominally Christian. Nietzsche's writing emboldened later philosophers to leave dualist metaphysics at the door, so to speak, like a wet umbrella. Spiritual truth could be ignored, which was the same as rejecting it *a priori* in philosophy. Philosophy thereafter, for the most part, proceeded as if there were no God, and never had been.

And yet, in 1889 Nietzsche lamented: "I fear we are not getting rid of God because we still believe in grammar."[9] Meaning is expressed in language, and is intelligible because of its structure. Structure inheres in grammar. The rules for structuring the logos exist to divide this thought from that. It is a system of oppositions in the mind of both the speaker and the hearer. In his characteristic way, Nietzsche threw off this line on the way to another thought, but it suggests a lingering doubt that the logos can be summarily deconstructed. Postmodernists would nonetheless try, however, as with Jean-Francois Lyotard: "oppositional thinking . . . is out of step with the most vital modes of postmodern knowledge."[10]

Kierkegaard aside, philosophy in the nineteenth century largely proceeded as the product of divorce from theology. It's not as though all the philosophers in the West got together and said "let's henceforth exclude all theories involving God." Instead, the supernatural element of Christian religion was broadly questioned, then rejected among many; Christianity came to be regarded more and more as an ethical system founded on a series of myths, and then thinkers were more and more open to a reality explainable without God and limited to physical things. There was a general understanding among educated people that the influence of Christianity still permeated Western societies, of course, and genuine Christian belief was still strong among some segments of society. But among intellectuals, including most prominent philosophers, it was

---

9 Nietzsche, Friedrich, *Twilight of the Idols III.5,* translated by Duncan Large, Oxford: Oxford University Press, 1998, p. 19.

10 Lyotard, Jean-Francois, *The Postmodern Condition/A Report on Knowledge*, 1979, section 5. Discussed in article by Alan D. Schrift, "Nietzsche and the Critique of Oppositional Thinking," *History of European Ideas*, Volume 11, 1989, pp. 783-790.

mostly thought merely a useful cultural artifact to be transposed into a new form of social cohesion (as with Emile Durkheim, John Dewey, and later, Ronald Dworkin), or else rejected in its entirety, to be purposely replaced (as with Karl Marx and Friedrich Nietzsche).

CHAPTER TEN

What is Truth?

THE EXTRACTION OF theological inquiry from mainstream philosophy had a profound effect on thought concerning the nature of truth. Philosophers developed new ways of defining truth. This was not the result of concluding overtly that because there is no God, all bets are off on how one determines truth. It is doubtful that individual thinkers purposely undertook a re-thinking of truth because the absence of a putative God seemed to open the door to it. But this was the practical effect.

With very few aberrations or intellectual detours through the ages before the twentieth century, thinking about truth took for granted some species of what we would now call correspondence theory. The correspondence theory of truth exists in a few varieties among carefully parsing philosophers, but in essence it is the idea that what is true corresponds to the way the world is. It is objective, and it is a real feature of reality. This was thought to be self-evident for many generations of thinkers. How could such a basic ideal unravel? Or to ask the same thing conversely, why did that basic idea remain in place for as long as it did?

The monotheisms assume the existence of an absolute truth: God. Truth is therefore transcendent, transcending the realm of the ideal to the realm of the physical. God authors truth, and truth is of the essence of what God is, along with other essential attributes like goodness, love, justice, and mercy. God is therefore the external and unchanging referent for any appeal to truth or morality. Truth and goodness in the abstract are understood, therefore, to be external to human beings. As with mathematical realism and idealism in general, truth and goodness are among the ideals we discover, rather than invent. They are objectively real. Just as we might say mathematics is in some way extant in the natural world rather than merely a self-contained game, so the concepts of truth and goodness and beauty are built into the external universe.

For truth to exist, something must be actually true. For beauty to exist, something must be actually beautiful. For goodness to exist, something must be actually good. For the ideal of truth to exist, there must be an instance of a true thing apart from our subjective evaluation. If we subjectively believe something to be true, it is because an ideal of truth exists apart from our subjective belief. If we subjectively believe something to be true, but it is not true, it is because the reality of the thing departs from the ideal of truth. If the reality of a thing's truthfulness can depart from an ideal of truth, then truth or falsity exists in the reality and not solely in the ideal. Truth or falsity exists in the reality and not solely in the ideal, if the reality includes any concept which can be true or false.

Truth or falsity attaches to every statement that can ever be made about any physical thing or force. Is not a feature of any existing thing that it truly exists? Because if it does not truly exist, then any statement about it is false. If gravity exists, then the concept of gravity is true. If gravity does not exist, then no statement about gravity can be true. Still, the argument might go, it is the statement about gravity that is being evaluated as true or false, not gravity itself. So the argument would go that any truth statement remains in the realm of ideals. But if we remove from our understanding of physical things or forces any statement about those forces including their very existence, what is left? Physical things and forces as brute facts of physical existence? No, because we have to exclude even the concept of existence. If we exclude the concept of existence, we necessarily exclude the truth claim that they exist. Truth is ontological because it is a concept inseparable from anything that might be conceived. In this way, truth precedes existence. It is nonsensical to speak of a thing's existence without having already conceived the truth of the thing's existence.

Imagine two people talking. There are assumptions they both make about the nature of reality, of course, but they also assume that many, or most, of those assumptions are shared. That is, the two people don't have to spend countless hours of spadework defining the terms they use in their mutually-understood speech, nor do they have to explain the whole of their respective grasps of reality in order to converse. They take a lot for granted. What they take for granted we would call the culture, at least as it pertains to these two imagined people. Among the most fundamental things they take for granted is the dualism of truth and falsity, and the ways in which it is or is not transcended. Truth is preferred over falsity, in the same way good is preferred over evil, and beauty over ugliness. These two speakers don't have to prove these propositions to each other in order to be understood. They're obvious.

So it must be that they have a mutual understanding of what makes something true. If the shared understanding between these two speakers is that God is real, then they will understand truth to be unitary, objective, and external to them both. When they speak of what is true, and make statements intended to be taken as true, and find truth in some of what they hear, they are intuitively making reference to that external and objective measure of what is true. The two people may disagree about whether a particular proposition is true or false, but they will not disagree that there is a real and external absolute truth in their shared existence, to which they both appeal. To renew this visual, we might think of the relations as a triangle, in which each speaker is at a corner, and external truth is at the third. The speakers relate each to the other, but also separately to the external truth which governs their shared understanding.

This understanding of the origin of truth has a long history. In the fourth century Socrates lived and taught, and we know of him through Plato. You may know that Socrates stood trial and was sentenced to death. His crimes? Corrupting the city's youth and failing to honor the city's gods. He contended that he honored "the god" or "the gods," depending on translation, by remaining truthful, more so than by following prescribed rites and practices. In other words, by critical thinking rather than slavish devotion to received conventional wisdom; by reason rather than sentiment or collectivist conformity. Plato gave us (in his *Apologia*) the closing argument of Socrates, delivered after the prosecution's closing argument. It was delivered to the jury, which in that day meant all the elders of Athens. Its opening lines go like this:

> I do not know, men of Athens, how my accusers affected you; as for me, I was almost carried away in spite of myself, so persuasively did they speak. And yet, hardly anything of what they said is true. Of the many lies they told, one in particular surprised me, namely that you should be careful not to be deceived by an accomplished speaker like me. That they were not ashamed to be immediately proved wrong by the facts, when I show myself not to be an accomplished speaker at all, that I thought was most shameless on their part—unless indeed they call an accomplished speaker the man who speaks the truth. If they

mean that, I would agree that I am an orator, but not after their manner, for indeed, as I say, practically nothing they said was true.[1]

The question we ought to ask is what makes something "true?" That it corresponds to facts; the way world actually is? Or is it what society gets together and agrees upon? Shouldn't we care what is objectively and absolutely true? And be prepared to disavow the false "truth" foisted on us by the mob? That's what Socrates thought, and it's what he tried to convince the men of Athens. But they killed him. The story of Socrates' trial is canonical in Western civilization because (among other things) it illustrates the virtue of correctly perceiving the nature of truth, and of facing down mob rule. Socrates was right and the mob was wrong. Socrates would not live by lies. He died for the principle of objective truth. He could have avoided the trial and the sentence at any step along the way.

Sound familiar? Four centuries after Socrates, and twenty centuries before today, a certain Galilean also had something to say about the source of truth. The Jewish accusers of Jesus could not bring him to the justice they thought he deserved for blasphemy, so they took him before the Roman governor, Pontius Pilate. The accusers violently disagreed with Jesus's truth claim that he and the Father were one. But in doing so both they and Jesus invoked an external, unitary, objective and absolute understanding of truth, in the person of God the Father. True or false: Jesus was one with the Father, or he was not. There was no in-between in which to hide. Jesus brought this about. Jesus told Pilate that his purpose in coming into the world was "to bear witness to the truth."[2] Further: "Everyone who is of the truth listens to my voice."[3] This should be taken as both a claim that something is true, and a claim about absolute truth, by which we should measure truth and falsity. Pilate responded: "What is truth?"

What is happening in this exchange is not just a disagreement about whether or not a particular proposition—that Jesus is the Christ—is true. The very concept of truth itself was in play. The Jews, including both the accusers and Jesus, subscribed to one unchanging, eternal, absolute of truth in God the Father. Against this standard all questions of

---

1 Plato, Apology 17a, b. From Plato, *Five Dialogues/Euthyphro, Apology, Crito, Meno, Phaedo*, translated by G.M.A. Grube, revised by John M. Cooper (2nd edition), p. 22, Indianapolis, IN: Hackett Publishing Company, 2002.

2 John 18:37, and the story is told in all four gospels.

3 John 18:38.

truth or falsity are to be measured, and when any two speak of truth or untruth, it is to this unitary standard external to them both to which they appeal. In asking "what is truth?" Pilate took himself outside that paradigm, calling into question the universal applicability of objective truth to which both Jesus and his accusers subscribed.

This idea of objective truth has been at the heart of our thinking from ancient Athens down through the centuries until the twentieth century *anno domini*. Over the course of that bloody century, there was a shift, unprecedented in the history of the world. A shift from objectivity to subjectivity, in our determination of truth. We now look within to find it. We rely on how we feel emotionally. Our emotions induce compromise of an ethical principle to find comfort in the collective. We see truth as universal, but not because it's objective and therefore applicable to everyone. We see it as universal because it is formulated collectively. But then it is internalized individually. Some will hold out, but they'll be coerced to embrace the collective "truth." They'll be coerced so as to force universality from the subjectivity of me-as-god thinking.

Postmodern philosophy stands in Pilate's shoes. It tosses into the trash bin the very concept of universally-applicable external, objective, and absolute truth. It does so because the way is made for this, upon rejecting the embodiment of absolute truth in the person of God. A postmodernist considers truth to be whatever coheres with other beliefs he already holds (coherency theory), or whatever works for political goals he favors (pragmatism), or something self-generated to give meaning to life (existentialism). As a result of the new malleability in "truth," we tend to talk right past each other. And it's getting worse. The divide grows wider every day.

The postmodern perspective requires rejection of the God who embodies truth. The gradual shedding of belief in God is not incidental to the direction of public discourse. The gap in understanding is ever widening, and it is not the result of a passive drift away from religion. There is a militant aspect to this separation.[4] The postmodern perspective grounds truth in the collective, which means truth is basically what society says it is. The difficulty is that society as a whole doesn't get together and vote on a common creed, such as the existence or non-existence of God. It never could. Genuine theists would never agree that God's existence depends on what people think about it, for just one example of why this is so. For another, people never actually defer to collective

---

4 Dewey's statement at the conclusion of *A Common Faith* Yale University Press, 1934.

truth, even as they theorize truth is generated collectively. What they want is their own idea of truth made collective. Diversity of thought is an enemy of postmodernist ideas about the origin of truth. The reverse is true as well: postmodern "truth" is an enemy of independent thinking. Remember the question here is not whether a particular proposition is true, but how truth originates. If truth itself is a product of the culture, then deviations from the "truths" the culture pronounces are false. If your idea of truth is something other than what society says it is, to a postmodernist you're just a liar, and you deserve to be shouted down.

Truth, even on this collectivist definition, is attenuated in the postmodern perspective. Social interaction generates consensus which becomes truth, but who gets to say what the consensus is? Or more realistically, why would we suppose the ostensible consensus is genuine common agreement? The social locus of "consensus" truth means the externality of the source of truth shifts from absolute ideals to social consensus. Instead of both parties to a debate referring vertically to the absolute, they instead refer horizontally to social consensus, as if we're all in a massive episode of the game show *Family Feud*. Social "consensus" becomes the arbiter of truth, rather than idealistic truth. When people disagree about what's true, they disagree based on that social consensus measure. The argument shifts to disagreement over truth by that measure. Disagreement is not thereby eliminated; in fact, it is heightened. Because social consensus is not merely a reference point for truth, but defines truth, the battle ratchets up from propositions of truth to truth itself. The disagreement is not just over the truth or falsity of things. The disagreement is over what truth and falsity even mean.

Moreover, as a source of truth, consensus must be truly consensus, which means dissent from the consensus is falsehood rightly denounced. This is rather obviously a recipe for unending division and escalating disputation, even among those on board with the postmodernist truth paradigm. Instead of simply disagreeing with someone about whether something is objectively true, you disagree about what the social "consensus" holds to be true, which means you fight to form and then interpret the social consensus. Truth is something we create, not just appeal to, and that process of creation is never-ending all-against-all social ideological battle. The reason we've experienced a sea change as of 2020 from which we likely won't recover as a nation and as a people is that political and cultural developments go forward on the basis of differing formulations of truth, rather than differing opinions of what is true. It doesn't make any sense to speak of mere "bias" because that means unaware deviation from objective truth. If truth no longer refers to the objective and absolute, but is instead fidelity to personal sentiment writ large in social "justice" consensus—that is, in the bully-approved "narrative"—then fidelity to objective truth is irrelevant. The accusation of bias or of intentional bending of truth falls flat because the debate is between differing conceptions of truth. We no longer argue to a common point of reference. It's as if we're arguing in different languages, each not understanding the other's, and we raise our voices and become violent because somehow that's supposed to make us understood.

In the medieval period, heretics were called such if they were deemed to have departed from objective truth. In the postmodern period, heretics are those who defy the social consensus. In the medieval era, the appeal for truth was to authority. In the modern era it was to objective and external reality, if not necessarily a reality to include God. In the postmodern era it is to social "consensus," internalized through existentialist subjectivism, so we mistake it as coming from within. Beginning c. 1900, the appeal for truth is no longer reason, but rather what works. So it is irrational, and open-ended. The object (the thing truth is to "work" toward) is a perpetual battleground.

This is the complaint against political correctness. People who quaintly subscribe to a notion of truth as an objective and real phenomenon are often puzzled over it. Your thought might be: so what if there's a consensus view of things? That doesn't make it true. It is not above re-examination. But to a postmodernist, that *does* make it true, and it *is* above re-examination. And into the bargain, you're a lying dolt for questioning it. There is no room in this paradigm for dissent. This formula for generating truth requires total participation.

That means coercion. Because of the postmodern conception of truth, public discourse consists in attempting to move the "Overton window"[5] in one's desired direction. The Overton window amounts to a shifting of acceptable public opinion to encompass one's point of view and exclude others'. It functions much like the brackets John Rawls would have us draw around acceptable public discourse in order to exclude "comprehensive doctrines"[6] like religion, but not dogmatic secularist irreligion, because that anti-metaphysical view seems to be

---

5   The "Overton window" is named for Joseph P. Overton, who used the idea of a window framing politically acceptable opinions in public discourse. Giridharadas, Anand, "How Elites Lost Their Grip in 2019," *Time Magazine*, Nov. 21, 2019.

6   Rawls, John, *The Law of Peoples* with "The Idea of Public Reason Revisited," Harvard University Press, 1999.

invisible to those who hold it. The battle is identified by Jean-Francois Lyotard as rejection of "metanarratives," again, like the metanarratives of religion, or capitalist pluralistic freedom, or structural hierarchies of ideals, but never the metanarrative of Marxism. The battleground does not take place in quiet think tanks, but in the public space of hyperreality: the internet and ubiquitous and constant media in a dizzying variety of forms.[7] The postmodernist construction of truth is Nietzsche's will-to-power in applied form.

How did postmodernism come to stand in Pilate's shoes? Remember that some version of correspondence theory prevailed for most of history, and truth on this way of thinking refers to actual facts in the universe. Alternative theories of truth sprang up from time to time, but did not get widespread traction until around the turn of the twentieth century, what we are calling here the postmodern era. In philosophy there are many variations on these alternative theories, but we can usefully summarize them into three: coherence theory, pragmatism, and subjective existentialism. Postmodernists employ all three, in various ways at various times, holding with Samuel Johnson and Ralph Waldo Emerson that "a foolish consistency is the hobgoblin of little minds."

Coherence theory (or "coherentism") is the idea that you hold certain beliefs in mind already, and when you encounter a new proposition, you accept it if it adequately coheres with beliefs you already hold. At a superficial level, this seems valid. We do this all the time, really. We evaluate propositions on the basis of what we already believe to be true. A problem arises only if the propositions we hold to be true are not themselves rooted in objective reality. To be rooted in objective reality means to be rooted in a hierarchy of ideals that reaches up to the absolute of transcendent truth. If you hold to a constellation of beliefs that cohere well, but are not objectively true, then you simply hold cohering, but false, beliefs. Coherentism can lead us further and further astray from objective truth. We can gobble up new planets to add to our constellation of beliefs and form a whole mental universe that is entirely illusory.

---

7 The postmodernist philosopher Jean Baudrillard is often credited with the idea of hyperrealism, by which he meant that society had "replaced all reality and meaning with symbols and signs, and that human experience is a simulation of reality." There is value in Baudrillard's perspective. What is meant here, however, is that heterodox views on ultimate questions are more difficult to sustain because the very pervasiveness of public space reinforces the collectivist engine for defining truth. We draw ever closer to Baudrillard's conception of reality as being only that which becomes part of the public space, as when a person feels their vacation is not "real" until they post photos of it on Facebook.

The problem is not with the cohering nature of a proposition. It is that the coherence is understood to make the proposition true.

If you believe, for example, that there is no God and that all of reality is composed of matter in motion, then you will evaluate a new proposition on the basis of whether it coheres with that existing belief. Suppose the new proposition is the Resurrection of that certain Galilean in Judea 2000 years ago. Resurrection from the dead cannot be explained by natural processes, but your existing beliefs only allow for natural processes. The Resurrection does not cohere, therefore it is false. This chain of reasoning sounds all right, on one level. If your existing materialist beliefs are true, the Resurrection is in fact false. But we're not talking here merely about evaluating truthfulness of a proposition. We're talking about creation of truth. If you have, subtly or otherwise, bought into a coherentist theory of truth, you may reject the Resurrection simply because it does not cohere, rather than evaluating it independently as a truth claim. If you were to do so, and this led you to believe the Resurrection occurred, then it is the existing belief (against the supernatural) that would be upset and have to be revisited. This may have been what Samuel Johnson (and Emerson) were really getting at, denouncing unthinking insistence on consistency. Sometimes our conclusions need re-evaluating, in light of evidence and reason.

After all, if coherence and non-coherence create truth and falsity, then we should ask: "cohere or not cohere with what?" The example in the preceding paragraph uses one's own subjective existing beliefs. But suppose the object of coherence is some other source, like the collectively-derived "truths" postmodernism yields. If the expectation is that we're all to embrace as true a societal (fought-for) consensus, then we will accept any proposition on the basis of how it coheres with that coerced consensus, not the subjectively-held internal beliefs that I hold inside my inviolable self. In this way, my very selfhood becomes compromised, and false beliefs rapidly accrete to other false beliefs because they're not just beliefs. They're "truth," and are therefore no longer subject to scrutiny. This is how totalitarian ideologies are propagated.

CHAPTER ELEVEN

Pragmatism

MANY THINKERS in the nineteenth and early twentieth century, like Auguste Comte, Emile Durkheim, and John Dewey, were inclined to think of religion as naturally evolving in societies, but no more true for that. Theirs was a project of enlisting religious impulse for positive aims like social cohesion.[1] The social cohesion element of religion was to be grafted onto a collectivist, centralized approach to social organization, which necessarily involves some form of compulsion in law or disingenuous moral persuasion.

Dewey's perspective is especially instructive. He was eager for social change during the height of his influence in the first half of the twentieth century. He was a militant secularist who sought to co-opt religious practices for social participation in a new secular "faith." He was instrumental in advancing the pragmatism of William James and C.S. Peirce and others, and that involved developing an entire new source of truth as being that which proves practically successful. The arbiters of success are of course to be people like John Dewey himself, bent on reform of society to what he regarded as self-evidently superior leftist, collectivist, progressivism. His impact especially on education was intentionally formative of collectivist thinking habits, rather than just imparting facts of history, math, literature, and so on. Dewey was suspicious of any kind of dualism, having rejected any form of Platonism which distinguished between being and experience. It is no accident that atheism and "progressive" collectivism coincided in his thinking.

The roots of postmodernism were in Dewey's collectivist pragma-

---

1 E.g., Dewey, John, *A Common Faith*, Yale University Press, 1934.

tism. He employed the logic William James articulated. In the context of religious belief, one's openness to the God proposition is understood to be a necessary condition to accepting it as true. Conversely, doubt is a necessary condition to rejecting it as false. Perhaps a will to believe is necessary to accept any proposition of truth; or a will to disbelieve, to reject. This sets up a participation between the erstwhile believer, and the proposition. Truth, James concluded, was therefore not entirely external to the person who believes or disbelieves.[2] This does not by itself create a breach in the truth/falsity dualism, but creates a fuzzy area in between, one might say, that remains undefined. The proof then can be found in the pudding.

Early pragmatists (C.S. Peirce, William James, John Dewey) extrapolated this idea to an entire new source for truth. In James' words, "truth in our ideas means their power to work."[3] On the surface this sounds silly, because one would have to take a proposition as true and then see how it weathers before confirming its truth. That could never be a test for the proposition of God's existence, for example. Moreover, it multiplies contingencies. We would have to ask about a proposition: "work" to what end? Truth in this way is subjugated to some other goal; it is not the end unto itself. The actual goal is a vague and shifting idea of social cohesion, because social cohesion is the understood but unstated object. What moves us closer to it might be regarded as truthful, but in actuality, there is no look-back to discover truth from process because who cares? We've moved past it, and truth was not the goal anyway; it's just an artifact to match with outmoded ways of speaking and thinking still in use by some. Those resisters are to be appeased in their own language of objective ethical principle, because after all, the project—social cohesion—requires at least that much deference to their outmoded thought. It is not social cohesion if dissenters straggle around out there in the cold. They must be made to come in. They must, in Rousseau's words, be "forced to be free." Today's "progressives" are philosophical heirs of Dewey's pragmatism. Social cohesion in the abstract must be free to shift over time. It is nonetheless thought self-evident, to collectivists who oppose those for whom the end-game is objective truth above all; whose god is God, the Author of personal ethical principle.

Richard Rorty is a postmodernist intellectual heir of Dewey. In his view, as in Dewey's, truth is found in what gets things done, and the

---

2 See James, William, *Will to Believe and Other Essays in Popular Philosophy*, 1897.

3 James, William, "Pragmatism," an essay first published in 1907.

things to get done are invariably leftist political projects. He advances a process of "redescribing" situations in a way favorable to a leftist outlook, rather than engaging in direct argument concerning propositions. This methodology is ubiquitous now. A postmodernist technique is to avoid direct engagement on propositions, and instead re-direct and re-define, constantly invoking words and phrases with innocuous meaning, vesting them with subtle new shifts in meaning so that the new meaning is accepted uncritically. This brings about an unobjected-to shift from the old meaning to the new, and unwitting acceptance. The process is one of "redescribing" situations to bring about meaning more congenial to leftist goals of transgressive deconstruction. A narrative dialectic using ever-shifting definitions is substituted for debate over propositions, much to the frustration of those who subscribe to objective truth. Rorty describes this as an "ironist" view:

> Ironists specialize in redescribing ranges of objects or events in particularly neologistic jargon . . . An ironist hopes that by the time she has finished using old words in a new sense, not to mention introducing brand-new words, people will no longer ask questions phrased in the old words.[4]

This is why seemingly straightforward words like "racism," "discrimination," "tolerance," "socialism," "spirituality," and many others are so elastic as to diminish their helpfulness in public discourse. This ambiguity is strategic. The point of opaque or slippery language is to insulate ideas from thorough analysis and consequent criticism. The ideals of postmodernists like Richard Rorty would dismantle objective standards of truth and morality which inhere in the structured value hierarchy of Christianity, while assuming selectively the validity of certain of those values, like the dignity of the "other:" the alien, the ethnic minority, the oppressed, the disadvantaged.[5]

For pragmatists, meaning emerges from action, in that the outcome of action serves as the verifying principle for a proposition. The action-based test for truth also requires a Godless or God-irrelevant context, because action is by its nature a time- and space-bound undertaking. Objective truth, however, is a timeless and space-irrelevant

---

4   Richard Rorty, *Contingency, Irony, and Solidarity*, New York: Cambridge University Press 1989, p. 78, as cited in Groothius, Douglas, *Truth Decay*, Leicester, UK: InterVarsity Press 2000, p. 104.

5   Groothius, *Truth Decay*, chapter 8.

proposition: an unchanging and eternal ideal, a religious concept with eternal unchanging God as ontological Source.

Pragmatism is collectivist, and necessarily so. Individuals don't come up with a true-for-them proposition and then take action based upon it, and then look back to decide whether the proposition was true. To ask "what works" is to ask what works for society as a whole. For pragmatists, human consciousness is socially located, and therefore the truth determination is a social product. That feature of truth theory carries forward into postmodernism. The entire pragmatist paradigm pertains to social rather than individual pursuit of truth. It excludes God because God stands for eternal and absolute truth, and the replacement god of social collectivism requires contingency. Collectivists may have a nagging sense of God's presence, or an attraction to the solemnity and smells and bells of the church. But there is a linear divide in which each side inches inexorably further apart: those called to the eternal and Absolute, in opposition to those called to the temporal and exigent. There is no overlap in these callings, and there is correspondence only in that their adherents co-exist in time and spatial proximity, and can communicate, though without real understanding. Individuals have agency, of course, and can therefore jump from one paradigm to the other, as from one slow-moving train to another. But the two trains move in opposite directions.

Let's consider pragmatism as against a Hegelian and collectivist background. If there is a historical consciousness thought to govern general attitudes and beliefs over time, then we can imagine it accounting for a natural collective negotiation of beliefs, with some beliefs, like Christianity, being jettisoned in their season. Synthesis of competing ideas to create the new normal is a society-wide and necessarily collectivist undertaking, and the resulting negotiated settlement is represented in the *geist*. The very idea presupposes that truth lies elsewhere than in an absolute. It lies in social consciousness, in the setting and re-setting of norms through the dialectic, without reference to absolutes. In this way what we regard as normal is unmoored from external principle, and is hostile to God because he is absolute, and the originator of principles.

If *geist* is the result of a collective process for the setting of norms, then why not nudge it here and there, to get to the outcome one favors? If you want society to be more Christian and I want it more pagan, then we can go into the arena and push and pull for our respective sides. The historical consciousness is not so much a passively-formed society-wide consciousness, as the football we fight over. We can't just go our separate ways, on the question, because we operate collectively. The fact of *geist* seems to require this way of thinking, in much the same way as economic socialism. Just as the thesis and antithesis are purposely advanced for resolution in the public consciousness, so is the resulting synthesis. Formation of the historical consciousness is not to be a passive result of the dialectic. It is the conclusion of a battle fought by warring sides, with eddies of new conflict stirred up in its wake.

Initially this battle takes place between disputants who think they each have the correct understanding of truth based on reference to an absolute. In an age of almost universal belief in God, there was still plenty of dispute, after all. Heresies were identified and stamped out on the basis of reference to ultimate truth. The parties to disputes disagreed about what was in fact the capital-T truth; however, not whether there was a capital-T truth to begin with. It was the same in the Reformation, when the disagreements were over the relationships among God, church and individuals; not over whether an absolute standard of truth even existed.

Hegelian historical consciousness was not the result of such limited ranges of belief, however. Increasingly, even in Hegel's day (around the turn of the nineteenth century), there were heterogenous views about the nature of God, and, more importantly to our thesis, there was an increasing willingness to repudiate God altogether. It would be some time before there was general awareness of all the implications, however. That is to say, it wasn't immediately apparent to everyone invested in the formation of that consciousness that repudiation of God meant repudiation of any objective, external criterion of truth. If truth is what "works," ask: "works for what?" There is a push and pull in society for competing ideas of the "what." If the "what" is to help the underdog, that will appeal to people who cling to ideals as representing real truth. If you believe truth to be objective and transcendent, your belief is just another weapon to use against you in formation of the consensus "truth."

The struggle for power initially takes place in the hyperreal media of internet and print news, opinion journals, blogs, and social media.[6] It is not person-to-person communication, but is advanced by collective media. Media are means of attenuating interpersonal communication, to make it general. Communication is made general in that it is collected and available for everyone. In this way, a newspaper differs from a telephone. Today, even newspapers are largely outmoded; instead we

---

6 A speculation of Jean Baudrillard becoming real.

rely on the internet and ubiquitous electronic programming of various kinds, not to mention social media platforms for content that was provided by anyone, before the recent advent of ideological battles over social media access. These avenues of general communication are not just vehicles for dissemination of information. They transmit culture; collective myth. There's a reason we can all sing the *Flintstones'* song.

The all-society "truth" is, increasingly, the hyperrealism of media which creates and sustains a narrative to which we defer. Interpersonal communication is attenuated to the collective media, which then takes on a life of its own. I don't form an idea of reality based on my interactions with other individuals, but rather my interaction with the collective, expressed in media. Person-to-person intersubjectivity is replaced with person-to-collective media interaction. It feels like we interact with society, but we're actually interacting with this hyperreal collective narrative found in media. This is why "narratives" are fought over. Our individual perceptions of the collective, expressed in media, become our reality. It is hyperreal because it exists in our minds as a reality unto itself, distinct from the physical reality and personal intersubjectivity that was, once upon a time, the only social reality people knew.

Hyperreality is a way to attenuate intersubjectivity. Hyperreality is essentially collectivist. Therefore, hyperreality is collectivism as an attenuated form of intersubjectivity. Being collectivist, hyperrealism induces sameness. Hyperrealism is the new arena for operation of Hegel's *geist*, and in an enhanced and more powerful form. It is the arena for formulating what society will tell us constitutes the good, the true, and the beautiful. This social truth takes the place of transcendent truth as the maker and enforcer of social norms. Or to say it perhaps better, hyperrealism is "transcendent" much like spiritual reality was once thought transcendent, but this hyperrealism is socially, not spiritually, located.

The power struggle initially takes place in the hyperreal media because we are still somewhat civilized. We are somewhat civilized because we live on the fumes of the idealism of religion. We will degenerate so that the power struggle takes place in direct violence or threat of violence. You will feel this first as an uncomfortable pressure to self-censor. Some will recognize it as the early onset of totalitarianism.[7] This is the result of idealism being extinguished to the level that even the moral manipulation no longer works. Self-interest alone motivates. Imagine

---

7   As does Rod Dreher, *Live Not by Lies/A Manual for Christian Dissidents*, 2020. The process is masterfully recounted by Czeslaw Milosz in *The Captive Mind*. New York: Vintage International, 1990 (first published 1951).

the Brits telling Gandhi to go ahead and starve, because they refuse to be manipulated by their own values. Or Americans unwilling to be shamed into abolishing slavery, because idealism itself is dead.

CHAPTER TWELVE

Christian Existentialism

S OREN KIERKEGAARD is often cited as being among the first existentialist philosophers, though he was a Christian and his existentialism, if that's what it was, had to do with how one individually and subjectively reckons with a real God. Kierkegaard held that reason takes us only so far in seeking God. Beyond that point reason fails and faith must take over. This is regarded as essentially existentialist primarily because of its subjective nature. It is regarded as irrational because it is thought to move past reason in arriving at God.

Departing from Hegel, Kierkegaard looked not for development of a collective historical consciousness, but instead for a personal, subjective felt experience of God. This meant coming to a dead-end in the exercise of mere reason, and going the last distance by leap of faith.[1] It is by personal commitment, in other words, that one approaches God. It is the individual, subjective, commitment to a cause or belief system—in Kierkegaard's case, Christianity—that is the primary element of existentialism. One's own choice forms one's purpose, and gives meaning to one's life.

Incidentally, the effort here is to recount a bit of Kierkegaard's thinking, on the way to what will eventually be called existentialism, but not to adopt that thinking wholesale. Kierkegaard's vision of this "leap" is not actually irrational, if irrational is understood to mean a departure from reason. On this question of accepting God, reason takes us to a

---

1 Though this is a reasonable summary of Kierkegaard on this point, one does not actually arrive at a dead end. One arrives at the binary opposition of God/not-God. An analogy better than "leap of faith" would be a crossroads at which one must turn left or right. In either analogy, time impels us forward, so frozen indecision is decision.

binary opposition wherein we turn left or right and there is no other choice, though later atheist existentialism and postmodernism attempt a third choice as a "philosophy of hesitation," experienced as indecisive agnosticism. Contrary to Kierkegaard's formulation, the turn we make, left or right, is going to be based on reason. Even if there were a "leap of faith," there would be a reason one takes the leap. One doesn't flip a coin to decide whether to "leap" or not. The evidence will point to turning one way or the other, even if we take the evidence to be merely preponderant. That is to say, if your doubt is 40% and your certainty is 60%, you still turn to God. You don't turn 60% toward God, because that's not an option. There is only the binary opposition of two choices, right or left. The putative option of hesitation is illusory, because it is time-bound, therefore excludes *ab initio* a turn to timeless reality, therefore equates to turning away from God. This choice of left or right, even with less than entire certainty, is rational, not irrational, decision-making, given the opposition of only two choices. The turn away from God would be irrational only if it resulted from emotion or mood or indifference rather than evidence and reason.

Here might be a better approach than Kierkegaard's, offered later in the nineteenth century by Leo Tolstoy:

> If a naked, hungry beggar has been taken from the crossroads, brought into a building belonging to a beautiful establishment, fed, supplied with drink, and obliged to move a handle up and down, evidently, before discussing why he was taken, why he should move the handle, and whether the whole establishment is reasonably arranged—the beggar should first of all move the handle. If he moves the handle he will understand that it works a pump, that the pump draws water and that the water irrigates the garden beds; then he will be taken from the pumping station to another place where he will gather fruits and will enter into the joy of his master, and, passing from lower to higher work, will understand more and more of the arrangements of the establishment, and taking part in it will never think of asking why he is there, and will certainly not reproach the master.

> So those who do his will, the simple unlearned working folk, whom we regard as cattle, do not reproach the master; but we, the wise, eat the master's food but do not do what the master wishes, and instead of doing it sit in a circle and discuss: 'Why should that handle be moved? Isn't it stupid?' So we have decided. We have decided that the master is stupid, or does not exist, and that we are wise, only we feel that we

are quite useless and that we must somehow do away with ourselves.[2]

Yes, one can "move the handle" on faith without real understanding, but reason follows, it is not dispensed with altogether. Humility about the scope of one's evidence and understanding supports moving the handle while we learn.

When writing on existentialism, historians of philosophy often draw a straight line from Kierkegaard to Nietzsche to Heidegger to Sartre to Camus, all prominent existentialist thinkers in the nineteenth and twentieth centuries. It's true that there is a continuity. They are all in fact reasonably called existentialists. But there is a large jump from Kierkegaard to all the rest. Kierkegaard was a Christian, and his existentialist angst centered on how one is to relate to God. The others did not believe in God, and their existentialist angst centered on how one is to live without God. The project of atheist existentialists would be to find self-made meaning in a reality rendered meaningless precisely because the rumored God turned out not to exist, by their lights. It is therefore fair to say that existentialism is—for both Christian existentialists and atheist existentialists—really about God.

Kierkegaard recognized the tension we all have in life. He didn't use the phrase "binary opposition" to describe it, but he understood there were oppositional ways of thinking that created ongoing unresolved tension. There is "either/or" tension between aesthetics and ethics.[3] By "aesthetics," Kierkegaard meant earthy or carnal or carefree—we might use instead the current meaning of "pagan," or "neo-pagan." By ethics, he meant the responsible moral choices we make, driven by our internal conscience. This drives people to church and makes them behave, but that isn't enough to eliminate the tension, it only replaces one kind of tension with another. Because once one lives responsibly and attends church and does the right things, there is a tension between good behavior and knowledge that unity with Christ as called for in the Christian message is missing. Going to church doesn't make one a Christian, nor does living in a Christian society and calling oneself by that name. We're aware of this problem, as we sit dutifully in church week after week, so there is another kind of tension in play, this time between ethical thinking and "religion," to continue using Kierkegaard's terminology. Most of Kierkegaard's philosophy has to do with how one makes a leap to

---

2 Tolstoy, Leo, *A Confession*, 1882.
3 Kierkegaard, Søren, *Either/Or*, 1859.

religion, because clear-minded reasoning alone won't get us there, to his way of thinking. Kierkegaard didn't say "leap of faith,"[4] but people describing this resolution of tension in his philosophy often do.

This is perhaps best seen in Kierkegaard's treatment of the story of Abraham offering up Isaac for sacrifice.[5] The short version of the story is this. God singled out Abraham to be the founder of his adopted people, and tested Abraham by directing Abraham to offer Isaac as a sacrifice. Isaac was Abraham's long-awaited son through whom God was to honor his covenant to bless and multiply Abraham's descendants. Now Abraham was being told to kill Isaac. Abraham acted in obedience, but at the last moment God substituted a ram for Isaac, sparing Isaac's life and sparing Abraham from having to complete the deed.

Bible teachers stumble over this story because it seems heartless and cruel. How do we continue to think of God as loving his human creation in light of this command? The stock answer is that Abraham's faith was so strong that he believed God could raise Isaac from the dead, so as to make his promise good. In fact, that is an answer given in the New Testament[6] in which Abraham is cited as a hero of the faith.

A traditional Jewish understanding of this story is that it amounted to the overthrow of the pagan practice of child sacrifice, and by extension, of paganism itself. It is hard for us moderns to picture how the practice of child sacrifice could have been so pervasive as to warrant this paradigm-setting story to undo it. Or if not pervasive, how it came to be seen as an egregious extreme of paganism so that Abraham's act and God's deterrence would be seen as a foundational re-direct from paganism. Our lack of understanding stems partly from the fact that this was a specific type of sacrifice, and we don't even understand the sacrifice system as a whole. Children were sacrificed, in pagan times,[7] but so also were animals and grain and drink. All those animals sacrificed and all the grain and drink offerings—what was it for? Evidently the intuition that almighty God, like the gods of the pagan pantheon, would be ap-

---

4   He did, however, refer to "Lessing's ditch," the insuperable divide between facts of contingent history and idealism produced by reason. The idea is that reason takes us to a point and no further; after that, our own action takes us to idealistic truth. So one might say a leap of faith is a leap across that "ugly ditch" described by G.E. Lessing (1729-1781). This idea of truth revealed in action will resurface in the thought of William James in the formulation of pragmatism, which places truth itself in that action of crossing.

5   Genesis chapter 22.

6   Hebrews 11:19.

7   Among many other Biblical references to child sacrifice, see Leviticus 18:21.

peased only by sacrifice for the covering over of sins that call for justice. The Jews sacrificed (not children, of course) in the temple in Jerusalem until it was torn down in 70 A.D., so the system of sacrifices and all it stood for was not incidental to Judaism. Jesus himself was the ultimate sacrifice, and according to Christianity, the sacrifice to end all sacrifices. Sacrifice, therefore, is absolutely at the heart of Christianity, too.

So why doesn't this understanding of the Abraham and Isaac story jump out at us today? It could be because we live in a society informed by millennia of Judaism and Christianity, which successfully overthrew the pagan paradigm, and now pervades our thinking. Our grasp of the significance of the sacrifice system in Judaism and among the pagans has atrophied. It seems foreign to us now. We have to study and think about it to grasp how it's necessary to understanding God's grace, and necessary to understand the path God had the Israelites on for many generations. In our day, this compulsion to sacrifice is not well understood precisely because it has been so thoroughly transmuted (or sublimated) into charity, by pervasive Christian influence. We give of ourselves not to appease the gods or to atone for sin, but to share love. We don't sacrifice animals and grain and drink. Instead we sacrifice time and talent and money as expressions of love. In this way (among others) the love of God is demonstrated. Charity replaces sacrifice as a manifestation of how the God/mankind opposition is transcended, rather than erased by imagining God out of existence.

Because we are at such a distance from the reality of Abraham's world, it takes some strenuous exercise of imagination to place oneself in his shoes, still more to understand a good God who would test in this way. Søren Kierkegaard grappled with it in his *Fear and Trembling*.[8] He didn't dismiss the story as plainly rational or morally sound. Quite the contrary. The story has to be dealt with on its own merits, not wished away. Kierkegaard used it to support his thesis that there is an ongoing unresolved tension in the heart of mankind, with respect to God. We all exist in mid-leap, you might say. On one side is the firm foundation of objective, tangible, earthy reality, and on the other, the idealized reality accessible to our reason but maddeningly just out of reach. We can't quite put our hands on it; it is evanescent. But through revelation—the physical creation, the prophets, the written word, the Messiah—there is a promise that it comes to us though not fully visible in this life. In this life we see as through a glass darkly, but then—when this life is over and

---

8 Kierkegaard, Søren, *Fear and Trembling*, 1843.

all is revealed—we will see as though face to face.[9]

The story of Abraham and Isaac brings into sharp relief how we are to think about this unseen reality. Our conscience would whisper to us that Abraham is no more than a murderer, if he is truly willing to sacrifice Isaac. Who can withstand this teaching? If this is what we're up against, we're doomed, we may feel. There must be something more. This story shows us the distance from us to God, in the same way the dispensation of the law does. This teaching must point us to some way in which the opposition between us and God can be transcended. It's hinted at, in the substitution of the ram, a metaphor for the substitutionary atonement that would come, which we have now seen in the Christ. We don't have it in us to follow the hyper-ethical principle, acting on principle for the sake of principle, when it means bloodying our own hand, and for the loss of something inexpressibly dear to us. We freeze in the face of this dilemma. If you subscribe to Derrida's view, or that of the existentialists, hesitation is the right response. But time impels us onward, it drives us willingly or no, this side of the veil. The story of Abraham and Isaac foretells Christ by metaphor, but also by presenting two features of the nature of God that superficially seem to be in opposition, and so must be reconciled. On the one hand, God is absolute, and his commands are absolutely binding upon us. On the other hand, slaying one's child violates the conscience, which we understand to also be of God. Why would we be expected to take any step toward obedience, as Abraham did? Unthinking obedience would amount to giving up the moral agency which God's word unequivocally tells us we have—it is why we are morally responsible for what we do.

This opposition is only resolved for us if we understand love, expressed by God in mercy. He is willing to pardon but must do so without compromising his justice, and so he takes the burden of our wrongdoing onto himself, redeeming us from the consequences of it. If we embrace the hyper-ethical, ultimately principled action of Abraham in following God, without grasping the significance of the substitutionary atonement in the form of the ram, we might conclude from the story that we're to give up our moral agency, and leave our frustrated conscience unaccounted for. But if there is a redemption event unconstrained as we are by time, as suggested by the substituted ram, then this teaching makes sense. God is perfect and perfectly just. We have moral agency and will exercise it badly, even if only once in the tiniest (by human standards)

9   1 Corinthians 13:12.

failing. Thus there is an unbridgeable divide over this binary opposition, God and mankind, unless God provides the way to transcend it. So a deep reading of this story reveals the coming Christ not just by analogy and story and myth and metaphor, but by ontological necessity owing to the nature of God as Author of love.

We're not to read this story with exasperation, stopping at a seemingly intractable opposition between God and mankind. Instead we're to find the new opposition expressed there, between God's justice and his mercy. Love emerges. This is why Christians should take to heart the absoluteness of God's love, suffusing the world immeasurably for those able to discern. Experiencing this love washing over us like morning sunlight when all is made new, we begin to understand why we're to respond to God in kind and to others of his creation in kind: to judge not, condemn not, but give.[10] Teachings like this can be wrongly understood as conditional, because we're to "give, and it will be given to you . . . For with the measure you use it will be measured back to you."[11] But the imagery of the cup of blessing running over[12] means a kind of participation by us. It's not that we earn a certain-sized cup and God grudgingly fills it. God will give more than the cup holds. But we control the size of the cup by which we receive his love, and we always make it too small. We are to greet the morning light of God's love expansively, trying to do so without seeing it as limited, because it is not.

Abraham's obedience is hyper-ethical, in that he prioritizes ethics over passions or what Kierkegaard might have called "aesthetics;"[13] being given over to internal guidance from a cocktail of reason, emotion, sentiment, and sensation. Ethics we can think of, in this context, as pure, unadulterated principle, resolutely and uncompromisingly applied, as contrasted to a complicated, situation-specific and necessarily somewhat muddled human moral resolution. There are a finite range of options for a choice like this one, or any other moral decision. One acts on the dualism of principle and expedience. We may engage in angsty fine moral shadings in the course of acting on expedience, but the choice of pure principle is already disregarded, in doing so. It is insufficient to speak of "doing what's right," without inquiring into what makes something right. The answer to the latter question in turn rests upon one's concep-

---

10 Luke 6:37, 38.

11 Luke 6:38.

12 Psalm 23:6.

13 In his *Either/Or*, Kierkegaard positions "either" as the aesthetic position, and "or" as the ethical one—another dualism.

tion of ultimate reality. If there is no God, then our moral discernment rests on social "consensus" formed from the push and pull of ongoing negotiation and ideological power struggle. If there is a God, however, he supplies the moral sense, laying it on our hearts whereupon we abide by it, or attempt to explain it away. If the moral sense comes from God, then he is not wrong to illustrate for us the hyper-ethical principle in this story of Abraham and Isaac. In fact, he arms us with understanding as to how to think through the implications of his presence, not just in the face of difficult moral questions, but in understanding more generally the structure of oppositions requiring an either/or choice on our part all through life.

The story of Abraham's willingness to sacrifice Isaac is the paradigm of ultimate constructive, ground-up, building, hierarchical, ethical (vs. aesthetic, in Kierkegaardian terms), and logocentric model of behavior. This is rejected in the postmodern era, of course. The existentialist answer is to re-locate moral decision-making from ultimate principle to individual subjectivity. Misunderstanding the substitutionary atonement taught in the Abraham story seems to justify hesitation before ethical principle. Moral principle is compromised by postmodern thinking. This happens because of failure to accept the binary oppositions in play for what they are, so as to find in God's revelation the means by which he transcends conflict between ultimate principle and subjective conscience. Dualist oppositional thinking is necessary to make the Abraham story intelligible, and rejection of dualist oppositional thinking renders it irrelevant. Jacques Derrida, for example, remarks upon this story with partial understanding. He grasps the hyper-ethical thinking that Kierkegaard alludes to, seeing the story's significance in the top-down construct of metaphysical reality. In fact, a contrast of Kierkegaard and Derrida on this point illuminates the story more than a passive reading of the Bible itself. Derrida's "differance" is the murky background "absence" that, if adequately considered, brings the story into sharp relief. But from there, he would see the story as reason for indecision, for hesitation in addressing complicated moral questions. Derrida supposes the story supports moral inaction, rather than forward action, as with Kierkegaard and, for that matter, the Bible as a whole. Francois Lyotard would second the full turn to situation specificity and away from the universality of principle. Michel Foucault would second the social power adjudication that stands as alternative to pure principle. Hence our becoming ever more mired in moral relativism.

What the story tells us is that in our moral decision-making, we are to be wholly devoted to a top-down, logocentric, ethical, and univer-salist perspective, in which principle weighs 100 percent and 0 percent is weighted to personality, self-interest, social influences, group affilia-tions, and context. Absolute means absolute, and the absolute is God. This flies directly in the face of the postmodernists' and existentialists' focus on inner struggle and hesitation and their dispute with rationality and the centrality of idealistic principle. We live in mid-leap between conceptions of this world and the next. The chasm between has no floor.

CHAPTER THIRTEEN

Atheist Existentialism

WITHOUT THE PURPOSE of seeking God, Kierkegaard's subjectiv-ism can serve to make the individual self-sovereign over an empire in which his created truth reigns. This is the essence of existen-tialism after Kierkegaard. It's not merely a rethinking of how we know truth. What happens first is rejection of God. It's not just that God is the absolute and therefore by definition the repository of all external, to-be-discovered truth. He doesn't merely serve as an avatar for the idea of truth in the abstract. But if he's viewed that way, then it's a short step to disregarding that symbol and finding truth elsewhere. It's a consequence of taking away (in our imagining) God's personal presence, taming him into a trained circus lion that retains the appropriate growls but is caged and monitored so he works for us and not the other way around. It's not as though a generation of philosophers woke up one day and said "You know what? There's no God." It's more the result of a process in which we first imagine God as that avatar symbolizing ultimate ethics, but not personal and not active in the way the Old Testament prophets perceived him. We didn't kill God in our imagining all at once. We made a flat paper facsimile of him so we could ignore the fierce real One with claws and fangs and power. We think of Jesus as the best of us, but like us in relation to God, rather than like God in relation to us.

Neo-pagan atheists like Martin Hägglund[1] agree with Kierkegaard, in one sense. Awareness of death creates tension in life. Those like Häg-glund who see bodily death as the end of existence of the self—"fini-

---

1 Hägglund, Martin, *This Life/Secular Faith and Spiritual Freedom*, New York: Anchor Books, 2019.

tude"—argue it is necessary to prompt us to action in this one life we get, and that its elimination results in an unsustainable, unmotivated eternal boredom. They know not of what they speak, obviously, because they're speaking hypothetically of a reality they say doesn't exist. Time impels us forward and it is the source of anxiety. For atheists, it means do what you're going to do with this life in order to bootstrap meaning before the clock stops. That is existentialism in the tradition of Heidegger and Camus; perhaps Sartre.

For theists like Kierkegaard, death of the body motivates, but it motivates specifically on the God decision: heaven or hell. The clock stops, but in a different sense, because we then enter into timelessness. Timelessness removes the kind of tension we feel now, which is why Christians say we enter into our rest. But that does not imply eternal boredom, except to one whose imagination is terribly stunted. Why would it be thought of as something like present life, but going on forever and tediously? There is no basis for saying that at all. Boredom is a function of time, so timelessness also means boredomlessness. Moreover, if boredom results from life after death of the body, why doesn't it result from living now?

The existentialist problem in atheism arises because if there is no transcendent Source of meaning and life simply ends, it is difficult to find any purpose in it, and despair results. Kierkegaard:

> If a human being did not have an eternal consciousness, if underlying everything there were only a wild, fermenting power that writhing in dark passions produced everything, be it significant or insignificant, if a vast, never appeased emptiness hid beneath everything, what would life be then but despair?[2]

If the personal commitment is not to the Deity who personifies all meaning and all purpose of created mankind, then the goal of that personal commitment is suspect. Existentialism in that case amounts to bootstrapping meaning. In Sartre's existentialism, "existence precedes essence," which means the mere fact of being precedes, logically and sequentially, what one becomes. There is no pre-existing essence, or nature, to human beings. We are what we make ourselves into. Meaning

---

2 Kierkegaard, Søren, *Fear and Trembling*, edited and translated by Edward V. Hong and Edna H. Hong, Princeton, NJ: Princeton University Press, 1983, p. 15. From pseudonymous narrative. The work was first published in the author's native Denmark in 1843, and the first English translation was published in 1919.

to life is self-generated, therefore. Existentialism is sometimes equated to staying out late, listening to jazz, and sleeping around, which would seem to give the lie to self-generated purpose, but does it really? There is no external referent for discerning good vs. bad purpose, on this view, so external restraints of society are a person's only limits in self-definition.

Albert Camus had a more honest take on the implications of existentialism because he seemed to see that if meaning and purpose to a life are self-provided, there remains an absence that cannot be filled by the self-supplied meaning. In his essay, "The Myth of Sisyphus,"[3] he began by asserting "there is but one truly serious philosophical problem, and that is suicide."[4] It is absurd to seek meaning in life when there is none, Camus held, so in the absence of that meaning we are to provide it ourselves, even if, as with Sisyphus, this amounts to eternal self-inflicted toil in commitment to an attitude of defiance. The purpose of the toil isn't what matters; it's the fact of it. One's purpose is defiance against purposelessness. Railing against meaninglessness is itself meaningful.

For both Sartre and Camus, and Friedrich Nietzsche and Martin Heidegger before them, a certain mood takes the place of meaning. For Camus: tragic consciousness. For Sartre: a party scene in a world where all things are possible, at least if one is an acclaimed philosopher. There is no God to supply meaning, in existentialism, and there is no other source outside ourselves for meaning. Existentialism represents the crisis of meaninglessness. If it doesn't lead to utter despair, it necessarily leads to a suspended state short of truth-seeking; a kind of narcotic inaction. This is an attitude of avoidance. If I can impress upon my own inchoate and plastic being a meaning or purpose, then this could consist of an attitude of sustained anti-rational relation to absence. The central question of existence is placed in suspended animation while we tiptoe around it and try not to awaken it. This amounts to throwing over the philosophical project altogether, at least insofar as it veers into theism, insisting that one's atheism is a mere "privative thesis," in A.C. Grayling's formulation;[5] not about anything, really, but certainly not about one thing. This attitudinal stance says nothing about reality at all, other

3   Camus, Albert, *The Myth of Sisyphus*, with translation by Justin O'Brien, New York: Knopf, 1991 (First Vintage Int'l Edition). Camus published this essay in 1942, and it was first translated and published in English in 1955 by Knopf as *The Myth of Sisyphus and Other Essays*.

4   Ibid., opening lines.

5   Grayling, A.C., *The God Argument*, New York: Bloomsbury, 2013.

than whatever it is, it doesn't include a God, because God's nature, if he existed, is to offend and repress. There may not be a point to our lives, perhaps, but it is pleasant to go on pretending otherwise.

There remains that "primordial agitation of mind," however, as David Bentley Hart phrases it,[6] which attends our awareness of being. It is a restlessness not long satisfied by relation to what one isn't, instead of what one is; of what is true, rather than one thing not true. The absence of God cannot form a platform for meaning, and meaning cannot be self-generated. Consequently, existentialism as a totalizing philosophical project unto itself largely came to an end at mid-twentieth century, becoming then subsumed as one element of postmodernism.

Existentialism lives on also as an implicit ingredient in neo-paganism, which runs parallel to and consistent with postmodernism. In "The Myth of Sisyphus," Camus quoted the pagan Pindar, from Pythian III (fifth century BC): "O my soul, do not aspire to immortal life, but exhaust the limits of what is possible." The point is that we're to find it admirable to exist in full light of our temporal finitude. There is no immortal, because there is no soul in the Christian sense. We're animal bodies and then we die. Pindar was writing of immortality in the sense of taking on pagan god-hood, rather than the individual immortality of the soul to which Christians aspire. But the focus on finitude is the main point for Pindar and many pagans, as it would be in the present day with Camus. We are to defiantly and bravely accept that when we die, we die; nothing follows this life in the body. Moreover, our awareness of this finitude is to supply the tension for living a meaningful life, not the promise of life after death as a result of some sort of unity with a purportedly resurrected man-God.

The word "paganism" likely conjures images of the demiurge pantheon of ages past; the Greek and Roman and Norse gods, especially. We haven't reverted to belief in these multiple and limited gods, in neo-paganism, but the "pagan" attitude fits one who locates the tension of life in its very temporariness, and who is further attracted to earthy particulars rather than ethereal ideals. It is no mistake to identify the prevalent modern attitude in the West as neo-paganism, though it involves no deference to purportedly immortal gods who must be appeased in the form of living in compliance with social norms. The conformity to social norms is enforced instead through hectoring into contrived "consensus," rather than immortal but idiosyncratic beings coursing the air.

---

6 Hart, David Bentley, *The Experience of God/Being, Consciousness, Bliss*, New Haven, CT: Yale University Press, 2013.

Atheist materialism takes the place of gods, and seems to free us from the weight of omnipresent meaning. The "faith" in finitude ameliorates the feeling of cloying, meaningful Presence, but takes us to its opposite extreme: an unbearable lightness of being that produces despair.

The tendency to lightness of being and away from the weight of meaningfulness inheres in neo-paganism. We can illustrate neo-paganism with two recent and opposing works. Stephen D. Smith, in *Pagans & Christians in the City/Culture Wars from the Tiber to the Potomac*,[7] described the current culture as neo-pagan not because of widespread belief in pagan gods, but rather because of the openness to finitude—our knowledge of our own mortality—as acceptable because it eliminates the God who is thought to frown down on us from on high, and frees us to live without his onerous constraints. The neo-pagan attitude springs from "[a] persistent and recurring regret for the loss of the 'merry dance of paganism,'"[8] especially as expressed in sexual license.[9] At the same time, the long history of Christianity looms over the individual and the culture, so that overt expressions of Christian belief in any remotely public sphere constitute "a standing affront to dignity, and their [Christians'] presence is an irritant and an insult to the kind of community to which modern progressive pagans aspire."[10]

Martin Hägglund, in *This Life/Secular Faith and Spiritual Freedom*, argues unsuccessfully that we should find meaning, rather than absence of meaning, in the finitude of this life. "[W]e should acknowledge the commitment to finite life as the condition for anything to be at stake and for anyone to lead a free life."[11] This is an interesting formulation and one he tries to support in the remainder of the book: it is not finitude by itself that provides meaning, but our commitment to it, as if we had a choice. Neo-paganism thus amounts to a re-branding of existentialism. The oxymoron "secular faith" of the subtitle he defines as just this commitment.[12] He attempts to engraft meaning onto this meaningless

7 Smith, Steven D., *Pagans & Christians in the City/Culture Wars from the Tiber to the Potomac*, Eerdmans, 2018.

8 Ibid., p. 259. Smith evidently quotes from *The Prose Writings of Heinrich Heine*, edited with a translation by Havelock Ellis, London: Walter Scott, 1887, p. 274.

9 Ibid., pp. 282-94.

10 Ibid., p. 363.

11 Hägglund, Martin, *This Life/Secular Faith and Spiritual Freedom*, New York: Anchor Books, 2019, p. 13.

12 And the "spiritual freedom" of the subtitle does not mean anything like spiritual freedom. His "spiritual" means something like personal animation in the exercise of

existentialist view by twining the commitment to finitude in death with the commitment to another kind of finitude: dependence on others. In this way, he makes activism for collectivist leftist politics the *sine qua non* for a life, including, quite explicitly, Marxism within social democracy. Hägglund recycles discredited Marxism and meaningless existentialism, attempting to weave them together to create meaning. Putting two dead things together will make neither come alive, however.

Neo-paganism continues the existentialist adoption of a mental stance toward the nothing-as-such we will speak to in chapters 19 and 20. It remains an attitude only, inasmuch as it does not provide meaning through actual gods nor give substance to mere fate. It is not a totalizing philosophy of meaning or of truth, but amounts to an indecisive live-for-the-moment animal appreciation for this life. It is existentialist because it emphasizes the temporal at the expense of the eternal; the physical real of the moment at the expense of ideals.

Genuine theism assuredly is not consistent with this attitude, however. A stark dualism exists between those who genuinely subscribe to transcendent reality, and those who do not. Religious people of the last century or so were encouraged toward a denial of this dualism so as to land in mainstream or liberal religious interpretations that were strong on certain holdover Christian ideals, like protection of the downcast or alien or oppressed, and weak on transcendent ideal and personal holiness. Those tentatively willing to throw off the shackles of religion altogether were encouraged toward a denial of this dualism so as to negatively self-identify in relation to religion; as one "not religious" or "spiritual but not religious."

There was an appropriate preservation of fellow-feeling with one's countrymen and community, in this project, but also a muddling of understanding. Inevitably, the shared public space would be a battleground for dominance of ideas. The battle was lost by religious people because the entire war was engaged on the enemy's terms. For the balance of the twentieth century, religion was in full retreat from the public sphere and was relegated to the private,[13] with occasional irruptions into public expression in the United States, as with mid-century reaction to

---

agency, and his "freedom" derives from participation in socially-formed consensus.

13 As related by Jose Casanova in *Public Religions in the Modern World*, 1994, privatization is among the means by which Christianity is quietly pushed into the closet of our minds, with the door shut softly behind.

communism,[14] and evangelical political activism in the 1970s and '80s.[15] Just as self-created purpose was a private affair within the neo-pagan and subjectivist, existentialist mode of thinking, so became Christianity. Political battles raged, of course, but proceeded according to rules imposed by the godless perspective. Increasingly, those rules shifted in accordance with identitarian and divisive and collectivist postmodernist philosophy.

Postmodernism, like its ideological predecessor, Marxism, rests upon atheism. This atheism is not incidental to the postmodern outlook or its political project. Commitment to a God-less reality is an essential element of most philosophy since Kierkegaard. Philosophy branched off into the God-less and God-minded versions, in the twentieth century. An image of two lines of thought spiraling symmetrically away from each other would be inaccurate, however. "Philosophy" denominated as such was mostly atheist and intentionally so, in the twentieth century. Philosophy which embraced orthodox Christianity took place in academic cul-de-sacs, mostly ignored in secular society, though popular writers like C.S. Lewis emerged from time to time to exercise influence, and some of them are rightly regarded as philosophers of the first order. Still, God was ignored in the most impactful philosophy after the turn of the twentieth century. The atheist premise was the first brick in the wall, so to speak, of new philosophical developments. Philosophy which excluded that first brick increasingly moved forward outside the mainstream, for the most part sequestered into sectarian enclaves. Theology has been increasingly seen as an endeavor quite distinct from philosophy, and increasingly irrelevant.

---

14   As when the phrase "under God" was added to the American pledge of allegiance in 1954.

15   As with Jerry Falwell's Moral Majority.

CHAPTER FOURTEEN

Postmodernism and Deconstruction

EXISTENTIALISM HAD ITS heyday but tiptoed a little too close to the abyss of nihilism. What was needed was a means of explaining reality that did not skitter so close. Existentialism was replaced by postmodernism. This is not to say that philosophers went to bed one night as existentialists, and woke up the next as postmodernists. Rather, pragmatism ran parallel to existentialism, in the first half of the twentieth century, and both were subsumed into what we think of now as postmodernism.

Existentialism was a project of individual subjectivism. Postmodernism is collectivist, but continues the project of attempting to explain reality without God by attenuating the inevitable meaninglessness that results. Replacement meanings emerge in the form of highly selective and distorted Christian ideals, like protecting the downtrodden. The essence of postmodernism is an overthrow of the concept of transcendent truth itself, and therefore of the necessary dualism of truth and falsity.

Both the Bible and the ancient Greek philosophers invoked the hoary old god of oppositional dualisms, in the search for truth. Objective truth was thought to be the purpose of all our ruminations about reality. In the midst of wide variation about what is true, there was nonetheless no variation in the assumption that truth was there to be discovered, rather than created. This assumption obtained throughout the early Christian and medieval period in the West. The primary reliance for direction on that objective truth was revelation and authority.

The modern era is conceived to be that within which the primary basis for the search for truth shifted to individual reason. In all of this, the presumption of an objective truth remained, however. Indeed, objective truth makes science possible, and the modern age is certainly associated with advances in science.

We can think of ourselves as being in a postmodern age because objective, "out-there" truth is no longer presumed, in much of our philosophy, and the idea of a malleable truth is manifested in Western politics and culture, as well, serving to erase oppositions that enable us to discern between competing principles so as to acquire understanding. Confidence in objective truth was eroded with criticisms of the simple idea that the truth of a matter corresponds to how things factually are. Among some philosophers, this correspondence theory came to seem less and less explanatory, and more an unhelpful tautology.

Individual-oriented philosophy of atheist existentialism would dead-end at mid-twentieth century, more or less, and God-free collectivism would burble along in the background during the first half of the twentieth century. In the leading secular philosophies of the early twentieth century, existentialism and pragmatism, the source of truth became ever more malleable. That unmooring of truth from an objective Absolute marks the transition from modern to postmodern.

The word, however—"postmodern"—is sometimes pegged to the 1960s, with publication of works by philosophers like Jacques Derrida, Francois Lyotard, Michel Foucault, and others. Nearly all were leftists and atheists, and collectivists in the sense of directing their philosophic interests to addressing what they perceived to be practical inequities and injustices of society as a whole. In most postmodern philosophy, and certainly in postmodern cultural applications, anything about a person is meaningless except in identification with subset groups within society. A hyper-collectivist approach is necessary, so it is thought, to understanding one's place in the world. Your essence lies in your group affiliation according to race, sex, social status, economic means, sexual practices, and so on. Your very existence, or presence, requires affirmation in that identity.[1] Your existence is defined by how your group relationships intersect, hence "intersectionality."

Our concern is not with surveying philosophical history, *per se*, but with the degradation or distortion or deconstruction of oppositional dualisms, resulting in impairment of individual and collective judgment. So we'll turn here to one of the postmodernist philosophers, Jacques

---

1 Lacan, Jacques, *The Four Fundamental Concepts of Psychoanalysis*, 1973 (translated to English 1978 by Alan Sheridan). See MacLeod, Adam, *Essences or Intersectionality: Understanding Why We Can't Understand Each Other*, Witherspoon Institute March 1, 2020.

Derrida.

Derrida was a post-structuralist because he framed his philosophy in terms of a critique or improvement upon structuralism. Structuralism had been in play for some time, when Derrida published in the 1960s. It is the idea that there is a structure to our thinking and ideas, especially as expressed in language, necessary to the communication of those ideas and their manifestation in culture. The structure is substantive, meaning it contains semantic content, rather than merely comprising a framework for discussion. Structuralism was explicitly based on an understanding of the binary oppositions that necessarily obtain in our individual understanding of the world, and our collective understanding—the sum of which we would describe as culture.

Structuralism provides context to language or other representation. An idea expressed in words does not have independent meaning that a person with no cultural context, armed only with a dictionary, can fully understand. Meaning is produced not merely by the definitions of words, but by their cultural context, and the cultural context of the words in their definitions, and so on; all depending on the existence of binary oppositions. One must understand the cultural context of a story or proposition or social tradition in order to fully make sense of it. To make sense of anything, one must employ binary distinctions. Structuralism, therefore, employs binary oppositions in order to provide context to stories and propositions of truth and social traditions and so on.

"Binary opposition" in today's popular culture is sometimes regarded like ragweed to be eradicated wherever it is found. But actually the concept is central to the thinking of structuralists like Ferdinand de Saussure and Claude Levi-Strauss, and Jacques Derrida recognized the reliance of structuralism on binary oppositions, finding them to be socially-derived meanings favoring established and dominant hierarchies within society. He therefore sought to bring attention to these oppositions and the way they were employed. He didn't deny their existence.

The intent of postmodernism is to uncover injustices hiding in our systems of thought, but the practical effect is to corrode our systems of thought. Binary oppositions are not the enemy. They are necessary to rational thought. Irrational thought is the enemy. Remember postmodernism is an extension of pragmatism and of existentialism. As such, it constitutes a means of finding truth alternative to assuming an objective reality of truth in the cosmos. Truth is created in action, and is therefore a social—that is to say, a collectivist—project. We are to act, and formation of truth will take care of itself. So the structuralist effort to find meaning in context, and the post-structuralist effort to deconstruct that meaning, were both truth-creating projects. That is, a binary opposition hiding the non-dominant perspective amounts to a corruption of truth, a post-structuralist would say, which the deconstruction project seeks to restore.

Truth itself is at stake, not just the validity of polemical strategies for advancing one's truth claims. Truth in the abstract is an ideal. We all have an orientation to that ideal that is so intrinsic in our everyday thinking that we're hardly aware of it. Everything we do is oriented to truth and falsity. To break down this most fundamental of dichotomies is a dangerous thing. We should approach with extreme skepticism any attempt to shift our idea of truth from an objective, "out-there" phenomenon to one internally and subjectively created and then projected onto the hyperreal evolving historical consciousness.

We have considered whether mathematical principles, including dualisms, and ideals more generally, are objectively present features of the universe, to be discovered and not created. Or, whether they are creations of human mind that are projected onto the universe, imposed on it to cause it to have order in our minds. Is it a feature of the universe that the angles of a triangle sum to 180 degrees? Or is that just something we made up for our own purposes? Do we manufacture reality, or is it there already? Do we build ideals from the ground up, or are they the means by which God develops us within the world he created? Do we generate an ideal of beauty *ab initio*? Or is beauty discovered by us? Is morality something we invent to have order in society? Or does it comprise pre-existing ideals to which we aspire? Do our aspirations consist of God pulling the spiraled ziggurat up, or does it originate with us, as stones we heave upward into our own Tower of Babel?

Postmodernism paves the way for Nietzschean will-to-power because it leaves truth up for adjudication within society. One's idea must prevail across society because of our collectivist approach to everything now, and there is no external generalized principle (like Christianity or reference to objective and absolute truth) for adjudication of dispute. We live now inside a battle that is not merely for hearts and minds to be persuaded to postmodernism as a methodology for ascertaining truth, but rather for the very establishment of what we're all expected to thereafter call "truth." There's a lot at stake.

Derrida argued from dualistic opposition by claiming one term of a dichotomy is necessarily privileged vis-à-vis the other. The very existence of the dualism creates this privilege, because either side of the dualist dichotomy defines the other. The binary oppositions undergirding our thinking include presence/absence, speech/writing, and infinite others. To remove or unmask the truths obscured by binary oppositions, Derrida would either reverse the oppositions as they appear in text or cultural understanding, or destruct the opposition itself. The first of these approaches assumes the validity of the opposition, but criticizes the privilege we assign one side of it. The second approach would collapse the opposition altogether, impairing our ability to discern between the two concepts involved. Derrida's project was one of trying to expose inequities hidden in the binary structures by which we perceive reality. As such, his entire approach is meaningless if there are no binary oppositions to attack. Without them he has nothing to deconstruct, and therefore no space to intervene into the system of thought prevalent in the world. In this way, Derrida back-handedly acknowledges the prevalence of binary oppositions. He did so on the way to dismantling them for polemical purposes.

According to Derrida, "metaphysics" installs hierarchies and orders of subordination in the various dualisms it creates. It places presence and purity over and against the contingent and complicated. We might say ideals over and against gritty facts. According to Derrida, this means privileging one side of an opposition and ignoring or marginalizing the other. The main target of his deconstruction is "the metaphysics of presence." He believed traditional philosophy to be infected with "metaphysics," by which he meant a division of ideal and real. Thus, Derrida's project also amounts to dismantling of transcendent truth.

We should pause and qualify this definition, to properly understand Derrida. The use of the word "metaphysics" is potentially confusing. "Metaphysics" traditionally refers to that which is meta to the physical; that is, spiritual. Derrida and other late-modern and postmodern philosophers reject the spiritual, however, so when they use "metaphysical" they mean only the reality of concepts attendant upon or derivative of or emergent from what is physical. So metaphysics of presence refers to finding ideals in the privileging of one side to an opposition at the expense of the denigrated other. Text (or other cultural representation) thereby creates meaning, rather than reflects it, he would say, and the resulting meaning favors present over absent representations.

This is a bit theoretical, so let's consider an example with political implications, since that's really the point of Derridean deconstruction. If we deconstruct (racial) white and black, we get this. At a minimum there is a binary which we can say produces some meaning, because white is not-black, and black is not-white. Meaning is derived from delineating the broad category "people" into categories according to the criterion of European or African ancestry. Merely distinguishing racial white and black does not by itself create differing values attached to each, however. Contra Derrida, nothing about the opposition standing alone denotes white superiority or black inferiority. Binary tension, and meaning derived therefrom, is brought to the text or representation by the reader or viewer, based perhaps on one's understanding or experience of the history of slavery and emancipation and exclusion and social strife. But that is meaning not generated merely from placing racial white and black in opposition, which is to say racism does not arise from the text unless the text overtly communicates it. That being the case, what is the point of deconstructing text to identify black/white binary opposition, and then imputing oppressed and oppressor status? It can only be for the purpose of shifting political power by racial groups, with the effect of culturally re-installing race-consciousness in place of color-blindness, which to many seems like a step backward. That isn't to say there is no racism, of course. Nor is it to say that a text or other representation might not overtly advance racism. It is only to say that deconstruction amounts to finding racism even where it may not exist, through a process of replacing an ethical metanarrative with a Marxist one, which is to say it is only a polemical technique.

What all this means is that Derrida is not adding anything to our understanding, really. If racism contributes to various social ills, those social ills should be directly the subject of our concern, rather than approaching them through the prism of race. Doing it through deconstruction of text serves a sustained critique of logocentrism, the real target of deconstruction. Logocentrism assumes a transcendent, ultimate truth, and postmodernism, as with Derrida's method of deconstruction, excludes transcendent, ultimate truth, and the God it implies. The logocentrism is to be exposed and vanquished by deconstruction of binary oppositions. The concern we should have with the approach of critical social theory, and postmodernism more generally, is that truth is relocated from objective, external, unchanging reality, to a subjectively-felt, changeable, socially-located coercive "consensus," which isn't consensus at all, but rather what is left after ongoing ideological battle. The shift from objective truth to internal and changeable truth-formation means facts don't matter, belief does. Appeal to facts is wasted effort when truth doesn't derive from facts. Truth is a created thing, therefore the effort is expended on creating it, rather than discovering it. That means a fight for dominance in formation of social orthodoxy in the public arena, rather than simple disagreement about what is objectively true or false, right or wrong.

The goal of the postmodernist approach to truth might be removal of our tendency to look down on the non-preferred half of various oppositions, but it doesn't work, and more importantly, it also removes our ability to see superlatives by means of the opposition. One removes the lows, but the highs also, moving us in the direction of muddy mediocrity. Oppositions don't just reside in social constructs. They reside in reality. The first casualty of Derrida's superstructure of belief formation is the distinction between natural physical reality and the supernatural, the first and proper definition of "metaphysics."

Binary oppositions are real, but deconstruction is an unnecessarily complicated way to criticize existing cultural assumptions. Binary oppositions are foundational to the thought processes by which we make sense of anything. They are not confined to nor spawned by postmodernists' ideas of "metaphysics." An attack on dualist oppositions in the abstract is an attack on rationality itself. Why not instead just take up the argument that an idea or people group is unjustly marginalized, rather than creating an entire super-structure to then deconstruct? We might re-engage the principle of Ockham's razor, to pare away unnecessary entities. Ockham's razor is often trotted out as a stand-in for the rather obvious proposition that we should unclutter our reasoning from unnecessary theoretical helps. This would seem to apply to post-structuralist deconstruction. Indeed, applying the razor is another instance of distinguishing one concept from another. Whether we are reducing an idea to its essence, or building an edifice of interlocking concepts, we are distinguishing among them. We all do this, all the time. It is normal reasoning. It is the way to move from an amorphous blob of intractable proto-ideas to nuanced discernment.

As with other postmodernists, Derrida is not merely trying to right individual instances of wrongs the putatively tainted oppositions reveal, like the privileging of white experience in American culture over black experience. The project is larger than that, contributing to the re-location of truth to societal "consensus." It advances what many regard as the Enlightenment Project of driving out remaining vestiges of religious superstition. Pragmatism is about what works, after all. Proponents of pragmatism and its unruly daughter postmodernism may be silent about what they work to accomplish, but not indifferent. The undisclosed end is the collectivist project. We like to say "the ends don't justify the means," but they actually do, for one who has already over-thrown objective truth. In fact, pragmatism within postmodernism can be reduced to the opposite of that time-worn phrase. The ends *do* justify the means, in postmodernism. We're used to thinking of philosophy as a search for truth, but that's not what postmodernism is. It is creation of truth, because truth is formed in action toward some other object. It's not something out there to go and discover for its own sake.

Postmodernism is a body of philosophy advancing a particular set of ideologies in the power struggle that ensues upon ushering God out of our mental image of reality. It accomplishes this by targeting metanarratives. A "metanarrative" (addressed most specifically by postmodernist Jean Francois Lyotard)[2] is a totalizing philosophy; i.e., a "comprehensive doctrine," in John Rawls' terminology.[3] An obvious metanarrative or comprehensive doctrine is religion, and postmodernism serves as an engine for dismantling religion.

There is benefit to Derrida's approach, if it enables one to re-examine ideas, words, and concepts hiding in the background of the structures of meaning in society. But postmodernism isn't merely an aid to our analytical thinking about subordinated people groups or ideologies. It is about power. Postmodernism amounts to polemics hidden inside process, and it accomplishes this by playing upon Christian-originated moral concern for the lesser-advantaged "other."[4] Someone must decide what oppositions a text or tradition represents, and what meanings are to be attached to it, and what absences are to be re-privileged as a result, and to what political end. But, as always in politics, and now in culture, the question is never the question. The question is "who decides?"

Understanding postmodernism is like reading the box-top playing instructions for an unusually complicated board game. The winner in that game will be the one most successful at spotting and shooting down ideals that, the instructions say, can only exist and be seen because they stand on the beleaguered shoulders of their unseen oppositions. But this is no game. The outcome is incorporated into law and into the constitu-

2   Lyotard, Jean Francois, *The Postmodern Condition*, Manchester, UK: Manchester University Press, 1979.

3   Rawls, John, *The Idea of Public Reason Revisited*, Cambridge, MA: Harvard University Press, 1999.

4   Christ the innocent victim, as René Girard cogently observed, becomes the basis for the new knowledge of the Gospel story, such that "the concern for victims becomes the absolute value in all societies molded or affected by the spread of Christianity." Girard, Rene, *I Saw Satan Fall Like Lightning*, Maryknoll, NY: Orbis Books, 2001, p. xix. First published in 1999.

tional structure for law, and even more significantly, in the culture that is supposed to be denuded of oppositions, but which is in fact reloaded with new postmodernist-preferred oppositions. It is about created truth rather than mere arguments, and it requires collectivism, but there is one more necessary ingredient: it is resolutely atheist. God is rejected *a priori* in most mainstream, non-sectarian philosophical thought of the last hundred-plus years, and this is certainly true within postmodernism. The godless element isn't incidental. It is necessary and self-perpetuating within the system of thought postmodernism requires. Traditional religion exists to honor God, in part because doing so builds ideals by which we live, which are founded on meaning derived from oppositions. Postmodernism is the opposite of that religious effort, which is why it can be likened to the Tower of Babel story.

The thoroughgoing collectivism of modern Western democracies, combined with the removal of transcendent Presence in our thinking patterns, combined with the elimination of external, objective, discoverable truth, means all-out ideological war. What's good and right is not determined by reference to increasingly obscure, millennia-old texts, but rather by the *zeitgeist*, a social consciousness formed by polemical philosophy and persuasion, and by enlisting political force and a new form of cultural oppression.

CHAPTER FIFTEEN

Cultural Marxism

WHAT WE'RE ABOUT HERE is identifying how truth-formation became corrupted in the postmodern age. To do that, we should understand more of Marxism—not just in its original formulation by Karl Marx and his collaborator, Friedrich Engels, at mid-nineteenth century, but in its permutations since.

Marx was offended that some have wealth, and others don't. Wealth means capital accumulation. Marx thought those with capital—"capitalists"—oppressed the lower classes whose only recourse was to work as wage slaves, alienated from the fruits of their efforts. In his view, the workers made just enough to live on and reproduce so there would be more workers, and capitalists reaped the rest of their production. He published *Das Kapital* in 1867 to decry this state of affairs, building upon his theory of socialism to be subsumed into communism.

One could say Marx essentially invented capitalism. This may sound odd because he was an arch-enemy of capitalism, but capitalism is the foil for socialism. We think of capitalism as an economic system, in the same way we think of feudalism, Marxist socialism, democratic socialism, Keynesianism, and communism as being economic systems. But capitalism is not an economic system in the same sense. The variants of socialism involve top-down centralized government management of economic affairs. It's something we collectively impose (that is, by coercion) on individuals in society to govern economic activity.

Capitalism, by contrast, doesn't involve central management. We may call it an economic "system," but there's no systematizer. It's not the product of a grand design. It's not a set of principles a collectivist authority imposes on economic activity. It's just what happens when people act freely. Whenever we hear "capitalism," we should substitute the word "freedom." No one opposes freedom, in the abstract, but they may fail to associate capitalism with freedom, and then fail to associate coercively mandated economic systems like socialism with loss of freedom. Stumbling at that first step in their thinking, they then cite features of capitalism they don't like, and imagine socialism to be an improvement.

To be sure, there are aspects of capitalism which are imperfect. It allows for accumulation of capital, which tends not only to pile up in the hands of a few, but pile up at an increasing rate. This can feel unfair, but it's the natural order of things, given that people are not all the same. To correct it in the economic sphere, we'd have to coercively take from some and give to others. That seems unfair, too, unless fairness means equality of outcomes forced by a totalizing authority; i.e., communism. This inevitably fails, when tried. Aside from inefficiencies in movement of goods and services, and disincentives to production, and reward of indolence, it requires a coercive power center, the state, which is inevitably corrupted, and requires totalitarian repression of individual selfhood. The constraints imposed by the collective inevitably repress individual distinctiveness because equalizing outcomes of economic effort (as opposed to opportunities) falsely assumes that people are essentially the same in their ability to produce. Forceful measures of repression ensue to sustain the illusion.

For many, the problem with capitalism is moral, and Christians of course should pay attention to this criticism. The criticism is that market economics reduces human interaction to monetizable transactions, pushing out other kinds of interactions motivated by a communitarian attitude of sharing and fellow-feeling and mutual concern for the well-being of our brothers and sisters with whom we live. Everything can be monetized in a market economy and increasingly even expressions of love are reduced to money, and money becomes the measure of all things. The movement of tangible things and services results from a more or less adversarial negotiation of terms of trade. Even when that element of adversarial negotiation is removed, as when a large company sells its product at one price to all, it still must compete, often fiercely, to attract those customers.

There is a sham element, too, in that the market is based on appearances, which are manipulable. Maybe you sell the best soap at the lowest price, but it could also be that you've just positioned your product into that market perception. Large companies perhaps provide more affordable goods to more people, but they do so in a separate market that marginalizes smaller providers, so that every day the gulf between Wall Street and Main Street widens, with concomitant loss of community in everyday commercial affairs. The concern is not just with the cumulative indignities of living within a prosperous market economy. The concern is that the moral vices of commodification it generates are internalized and replace those of doing justice, loving kindness, and walking humbly with our God.[1]

Is justice possible with capitalism? Kindness? Humility before God? The commodification principle means that even people are mere commodities in a market economy, wherein monetary transactions dominate. If capitalism is understood as a totalizing philosophy (in the same way religion and fascism and communism are) then we make ourselves vulnerable to applying that principle in all of our personal affairs. We're then vulnerable to descent into consumerist materialism. This would be "materialism" in both senses of the word: being motivated solely by accumulation of material things, and believing material reality is all there is. It's one thing to form our self-identity around a hierarchy of values, quite another to self-identify around consumer choices and style. In a market capitalist economy, we must vigilantly guard our hearts and minds, to preserve our humanity.

But at least it's possible to do, and as the society we live in becomes more prosperous, our options for living without privation expand, and we're more free to apply ourselves to pursuits that don't maximize income, and we're more free to resist human commodification. We can scale back market motivations as we scale up other motivations. In a society driven by market forces but also other forces, like those of religion or nationalism or racialism or tribalism or filial piety or communitarianism, people can and do live on motivations other than the market. Socialism forces a restricted, which is to say unfree, range of thought concerning how we are to live. Walking justly and kindly and humbly is outsourced to the state.

With freedom there really is a concentration of capital that occurs, and that of course means that some people have more than others. This concentration of capital happens as a result of this unavoidable and fundamental truth about human nature: we are not created equal. We read that "all men are created equal" in one of our founding documents, the Declaration of Independence, but that obviously means we equally have God-given rights and should be treated equally by the law. No one

---

1 Micah 6:8.

thought then nor thinks now that everyone has the same set of abilities. There is an uneven distribution of intelligence, industry, diligence, affability, curiosity, good looks, creativity, health, and so on. Freedom exercised by people born unequal inevitably means growing gaps in economic and other kinds of success. The gaps may be wider than we wish them to be, but the cure for this would be worse than the disease. It is imperative, when speaking of equality, that we distinguish between equality of opportunity, and of outcome. The first is freedom; the second is tyranny.

If we compare economic success to a footrace, the fastest person is going to finish much more quickly than the slowest. The competitors have equality of opportunity, but because of individual differences in ability there is inequality of outcome. They don't all cross the finish line at the same time; in fact, the range from fastest to slowest may be quite large.

This analogy is a bit too simple, of course, because in life we don't all start at the same time, and, more importantly, we don't all start at the same place. There is a relational aspect to the disparities in ability. If you're born into a family or a culture that inculcates relatively more industry, diligence, curiosity, and excellence, your starting line is going to be well ahead, compared to someone without the same advantages. Does that relational feature of our existence mean there's unfair inequality? You could say the circumstances of your birth afford you certain advantages, and those are the result of others' positive outcomes, from which you benefit. Arguably, the situation in life you're born into is not something indelibly "you," but is an unfair accident of birth, whereby you get a head start, or start behind. On the other hand, you could say the same thing of innate intelligence or affability: you didn't create those traits, either; they just came with your unique existence.

You can see why people begin to have a hard time clearly distinguishing between equality of opportunity and of outcome. And if there's no real difference, then why should you be permitted to succeed as compared to others, just because you're smarter? Or better able to get along with others? Or because you work harder? Why not tinker with a social "system," so that we all have the same degree of success or failure, regardless of our individual collection of positive and negative traits?

This kind of thinking is where socialist utopias come from. All the attempts at equalizing outcomes prove disastrous. Marxism as an economic system has been discredited because it stands in opposition to capitalism, which means it stands in opposition to freedom. Marxism as a cultural influence should also be discredited because it stands in opposition to the principle that outcomes cannot be equalized, without tyranny. Therefore, cultural Marxism is also an enemy of freedom. It operates on resentment, but freedom is ultimately a stronger motivator for human beings than resentment.

We must understand that this freedom is not just economic freedom; freedom to sink or swim on our own. Socialism is broader than economics. It requires a much narrower band of common thinking than does freedom. If we're all free to think and do what we want, there's no need to persuade, cajole, coerce, or force others into your way of thinking. You're free to disagree. But if we're not free, if we're forced to operate within any kind of collective, economic or otherwise, then our thinking has to conform, to make that artificial social engine operate. Enlightenment liberalism meant being left alone. This meant "liberation" from collectives with coercive power, which means, most relevantly to us now, the government. At the extremes, there is no functional difference between left and right. If we're concerned about creeping totalitarianism—and we should be—it makes no difference whether the gradual shedding of individual freedom happens because we're traveling a leftist road or a rightist road; Stalin or Hitler. They both lead to abrogation of the self.

There are many different ways to think about reality, certainly, but the first oppositional divide is between materialism and transcendence. All the many variations of religion and philosophy follow upon choosing between those oppositions. Marxism explicitly disavows transcendence and insists upon atheism. It is right there in the diamat—dialectical materialism—that is quite explicitly the cornerstone of all Marxist thought.

The dialectic of Marxism is also antithetical to religion. It presupposes a Hegelian historical consciousness, but solely in the realm of material things, because that's all there is, in Marxism. All of history is tied to all of the future, in this thinking. There's no taking the state of the world as a given, and working toward improvement according to ethical principle. Instead we're to work toward a new narrative we create for ourselves, and that requires razing history to the ground to build a utopian New Man. We can't advance brotherhood between races in the future, for example, on an ethical principle like equality. Instead, we think historical imperatives require re-asserting racial division as the means to dismantle effects of historical oppression. All of history is tied together and tied to the fortunes not of individuals in their moral choices and responsibilities before a just God, but by artificial people groups negotiating power by violence, threat of violence, and contrived moral shaming. Dialectical materialism excludes God and therefore excludes ethical ideals emanating from him.

Marxism was birthed in a nineteenth-century intellectual ferment of increasing skepticism about metaphysical claims of religion. Marx was strictly a materialist, and materialism stands in binary opposition to the metaphysical idealism of Christianity. Other elements of Marxist theory also stand in opposition to practical Christianity, however, so cultural Marxism can be understood as standing also in binary opposition to cultural Christianity.

Marxism and Christianity are not merely differing ways of seeing reality; they're opposing ways. Indeed, each version of reality can be understood in terms of the fundamental ways it differs from the other. Dualist idealism is intrinsic to Christianity's system of thought. Monist materialism is intrinsic to Marxist thought. These are non-overlapping visions. That being the case, we should be about understanding this opposition, to understand how it informs the world we live in.

Christianity certainly contains mysteries and paradoxes, but its central doctrines are propositional and its orthodoxy is discernible from common elements of the various confessions and creeds, despite the centuries-long process of a splintering church. A dualist idealism is central to Christianity. Heaven is understood to be a spiritual realm, "spiritual" to distinguish it from the physical realm in which we experience a movement of time and the phenomena of our physical surroundings. The spiritual realm exists apart from the physical, but at the same time in and through the physical.

Marx's dialectical materialism, by contrast, supposes there is but the physical reality into which people are born, struggle, and die. That's materialism. The dialectic is Hegel's pattern of thesis, antithesis, and resulting synthesis, repeating itself through history and producing a historical consciousness, except that for Marx this historicism had to do with material conditions and relations, rather than ideas. The key features of Marx's thought, still relevant today, are these: (1) resolute atheism; (2) a human nature that is not innately selfish, but can become so through corruptions of society; (3) an understanding of history as one long story of oppression; (4) a need for revolution to destabilize the existing bourgeois order to overcome this oppression; and (5) a resulting collectivist utopia.

It's important to grasp these essential features of Marxism because the cultural milieu in which it is applied has changed over time, though without diminishing Marxism's anti-ideal and anti-Christian pungency. Marxism isn't just incidentally atheist. Its application requires an overthrow of Christianity because, in Marx's time and still today, Christianity in the culture is thought by Marxists to serve as an instrument of oppression, fraudulently sustaining capitalism and bourgeois (complacent and non-transgressive) culture as systems perpetuating oppression.

Its application further requires an overthrow of Christianity because the perception of human nature under Marxism and Christianity are diametrically opposed. They are opposed on the concept of innate evil. A logical starting place for understanding this is the thinking of Jean-Jacques Rousseau, who influenced Hegel, and in turn Marx. Rousseau conceived an idea of freedom which involved capitulation to the collective, just like Hobbes before him, and every fascist and Bolshevik since. For Rousseau's idea of freedom to make any sense, we have to grasp that he believed people are basically good until they're corrupted by society. Christianity and the other monotheisms rest on the doctrine of original sin; in Christianity: "all have sinned and fall short of the glory of God."[2]

We sometimes muddle this principle, because we don't all do awful things all the time, regardless of religious belief. God also places his law on our hearts—the conscience. We are inclined to evil, but our doing evil is constrained by the conscience and propositional values to which we reason and reinforcement in the mores and legislation of society around us.

Rousseau's writings marked an acceleration of acceptance of the concept that people are basically good, not evil. The relevant evil here is essentially selfishness, and selfishness is something taught us, not something inborn, Rousseau held. Again, in contrast to what Christianity tells us. We can think of Rousseau as marking a cultural shift more generally, from perceiving evil in ourselves to perceiving evil only in the world around us. On this view, selfishness is the result of being corrupted by the world, so if we could fend off corrupting influences, we'd be less selfish, and would more easily blend into a harmonious communitarian collective. Rousseau's view has gained increasing currency, to the point that today, education theory increasingly centers on shielding children from the corruptions of selfishness in society. The opposing point of view is that children are born with unrestrained selfish desires, but they can be trained to embrace a hierarchy of values which makes them able to get along with others, and which gives meaning to their own lives.

---

2 Romans 3:23.

When this is accepted culturally, we all benefit by living in civilization instead of meanness and treachery at every turn.

Rousseau was influential before Marx, but Marxism depends on this view of Rousseau, that people are basically good. Marxism means seeing the world through the lens of oppressor and oppressed, and fomenting discord or disruption or even revolution to bring about a socialism which will correct it. To embrace Marxism is to embrace the idea that people will harmonize in a communitarian way, rather than selfishly, if corrupting influences like the structures perpetuating capitalism are removed. It is for this reason also that Marxism is antithetical to Christianity. The Marxist movements toward this kind of "freedom," if successful, would mean personal anomie rather than community, because oppression is *not* the main driver of history. Selfishness is human nature, correctible through adhering to objective, hierarchical, ethical principles. Selfishness is not generated externally by evildoers in power, devising schemes to perpetuate their power. Selfishness is already there in every human heart.

In the mid-1800s Marxism meant revolution to correct the alienation of the proletariat from the fruits of its labor, and the resulting socialism then giving way to communism. That narrow understanding changed because the needed revolution just wouldn't materialize of its own. It required theoretical helps along the way. Religion had an overly strong hold on the imaginations of people Marxist theorists thought should feel oppressed. Theories of diamat evolved to create and direct revolutionary fervor. Marxists after Marx regarded all forms of social organization as intrinsically political because all of them connect to the economic structure of society, and the economic structure of society is all-important in a materialist world devoid of spirit.

Ideologies on the left and right advanced through the first half of the twentieth century to culminate in the worldwide conflagration of 1939-45. Afterward, there was a recrudescence of Marxism in reaction to the right-wing ideologies which drove the bloodshed in some theaters of the conflict. Somehow, left-wing ideologies tend to be mostly invisible to postmodernists who hold them. When postmodernists speak of "ideology" or "metanarrative," they invariably mean right-wing ideology, as if Hitler and Mussolini were the only monsters and we're to consider harmless Stalin, Mao, Pol Pot, *et al.*

By mid-century, pragmatism and existentialism had combined to make truth more malleable and less objective. With that softening of objection to breakdown in hierarchical values, and with blinders to shield our vision from the catastrophes in the East, postmodernists introduced a reinvigorated Marxism into public discourse. One can think of post-modernism now as a three-headed monster, snapping away at the rem-nant of Christianity through pragmatism, existentialism, and cultural Marxism.

The oppressor/oppressed paradigm for all of political life is a funda-mentally Marxist invention, and in the latter half of the twentieth cen-tury, it became ever more pervasive. It is a strategy for bringing down bourgeois hierarchical power structures to collapse idealistic value structures within them. These included, perhaps most visibly, Christi-anity's interdictions concerning sexual morality; hence, the sexual revo-lution.[3] The sexual revolution seems odd and anomalous from the broad perspective of the history of the whole world, but it is a consequence of recent—that is to say postmodern—efforts to destabilize bourgeois society at the level of the family, where hierarchical value formation tra-ditionally began.

The Marxism reinvigorated at mid-twentieth century is not the ad-vance of economic socialism through revolution, as Marx conceived it, but rather the application of Marxist principles to re-shape culture. These are postmodernist movements to destabilize and deconstruct bourgeois cultural institutions seen to preserve hierarchical idealism as with Christianity. Apart from sexual revolution, this means relentless hype in favor of neo-pagan personal license and bohemian aesthetic to replace buttoned-down bourgeois conformity thought to sustain op-pressive structures of society.

The movement also involves division among people groups to sow dissension in the form of resentment: the original sin of Cain. If we read the text of that story closely (in Genesis 4), we see there's no reason to infer Abel did something meriting God's pleasure, nor his own success in consequence. Nor did Cain do something meriting God's displea-sure, nor his own failure in consequence. The violence erupted because of inequality. The inequality wasn't caused by Abel, nor by God, except in the sense that God created a world of highly individual people with moral agency, so inequalities of success and failure naturally result. Abel was more successful in life than Cain, for whatever reason. There was inequality because there is always inequality. Cain compared himself to Abel, and resented him. When Cain attacked Abel, he felt he was acting

---

3 Trueman, Carl, *The Rise and Triumph of the Modern Self: Cultural Amnesia, Expressive Individualism, and the Road to Sexual Revolution*, Wheaton, IL: Crossway, 2020. See especially chapters 5 and 6.

defensively, rather than gratuitously. Cain felt wronged.

This pattern of resentment frequently repeats in history, as with the French Revolution and the revolutions of Soviet Russia, China, Italy, Germany, Spain, and many other places. It has accelerated in the last century as the light of God's word has been repudiated. We grope around in the gathering twilight, wondering what became of the light. The horrors of the twentieth-century wars and dystopian regimes resulted from this ineradicable failing of human nature. But only in magnitude of scope was it unprecedented in the history of the world. We become intent on substituting man-generated meaning to replace the logos of God. These movements appeal to the worst in us, a destructive impulse that takes over like a drug, a blood-thirst not slaked until our ideals lie about us in ruins.

For Marx, the history of humanity is a history of oppression and victimhood. For Christianity, it is a history of liberation and freedom. Applied Marxism involves rigorous historicism, hence the "progressive" label and contrived sense of inevitability. Marxism's negative drivers of revolution and destabilization and transgression of religious principle, combined with rigorously anti-transcendent materialism, are central to Marxist thought. These strands of thought within social movements are sometimes referred to collectively as "cultural Marxism" because the "cultural" qualifier signifies application of Marxist principles in contexts other than the economic socialism by revolution which was Marx's chief object. Economic socialism in the West today results primarily from democratic drift to statism, rather than Marxist revolution. It is the culture which is being overhauled by Marxism.

It would be impossible to overstate the degree to which the advance of Marxist theory over the last two hundred years springs from the opposition of theism and atheism. Nietzsche alerted his fellow thinkers to the fall-out of declaring God "dead." As had others more poetically, like Matthew Arnold.[4] Having killed him in the nineteenth century, what do we suppose we have replaced him with? Carl Trueman:

> To dispense with God . . . is to destroy the very foundations on which a whole world of metaphysics and morality has been constructed and depends.[5]

Postmodernists nonetheless advanced the project. Throughout the

---

4   As in his poem "Dover Beach," 1867.

5   Trueman, op. cit., p. 168.

twentieth century and into the twenty-first through today, the goal of deconstructing the idealism reflected in Christianity became ever more explicit. Since the mid-twentieth century, postmodernism incorporated principles of Marxism according to theories of the so-called Frankfurt School, especially with regard to sexual revolution, with the result of shifting self-identification away from one's relationship to an external hierarchy of values, and toward self-creation by collapsing those values.

The last century-plus can be fairly characterized as primarily a clash between metaphysical idealism, as evidenced most particularly in the West's remnant of Christianity, and a monist collapse of that idealism into the relative and the particular, to socially-located morality and truth, as with application of Marxist deconstruction.

CHAPTER SIXTEEN

Default Materialism

WHEN CHRISTIANITY broke out of its Hebrew enclaves in the first century, it was introduced to a mainly pagan world. One reason for the rapid spread of Christianity was that pagans didn't have to be convinced there was a reality beyond everyday physical experience. They believed that already. But their gods really couldn't help them. They could deliver calamity, however (so they thought), so people conducted themselves in a manner thought to ensure peace with the gods. They planted when they were supposed to plant; maintained loyalty to the place of their gods' putative reign; and sustained social relations in accordance with the gods' supposed dictates. Their paganism was superstition, even as they sought One in whom they might "live and move and have [their] being."[1] They knew their own sinfulness, just like we do. When they heard the Christian message, it was received as the opportunity for absolution that their paganism did not afford.[2] They didn't have the messy history of Christianity at their backs, to aid them in crawling back into obscurantism and spiritual paralysis.

Still, there was an appeal to the paganism that new Christians were expected to turn their back on: an earthy and sexually free social environment which had the effect of elevating, in the imagination, the daily tie to this physical existence in the body. For that reason, there have been exceptions and setbacks to the spread of Christianity in the West, as with Julian the Apostate in the fourth century. Paganism in the form of overt worship of demiurge gods died out, however, in the

---

1 Acts 17:28. Paul is thought to be quoting a pagan philosopher, Epimenides of Crete.
2 Budziszewski, J, "This Time Will Not Be the Same," *First Things*, March 2014.

West over time, such that at the dawn of the modern era around the turn of the seventeenth century, it existed only in a transmuted form in which incipient naturalism substituted for actual gods who course the air. The twentieth and twenty-first centuries are sometimes regarded as a return to paganism—neo-paganism—because of the ongoing draw of this earthiness, to the attractions of living as though the material present were all there is.[3] Spiritual reality is vague to neo-pagans, as it was for the pre-Christian pagans, and the monotheistic view of spirituality may feel to them sterile and removed from reality.

The attractions of living as though the material present were all there is also drives the worldview of naturalism, which has coincided for much of history with paganism or neo-paganism. Those who subscribe to naturalism eschew supernatural reality altogether, rather than minimizing it or regarding it superstitiously. They hold the monist view that all of reality is natural, rather than spiritual. What is consists only in material things and the forces acting on them. All of reality is comprised of material things responding to natural forces. It is therefore nothing more than matter in motion.

Naturalism can also be described as "materialism," for our purposes. The word "materialism" is sometimes used today to mean the acquisitive pursuit of things rather than more noble pursuits of relationships and personal integrity. "Materialism" is sometimes equated with the tendency to identify with one's consumer choices; what one owns instead of what one is. But "materialism" also means the philosophical belief that physical reality is all there is; that no spiritual realm exists which supervenes upon that physical reality. One who holds this point of view would be a "materialist," or a "naturalist," the latter meaning not one who studies or appreciates nature, but one who believes that nature is all there is. Materialism, and naturalism, assert there is no supernatural; no eternal life; nothing beyond this finite earthly existence; and no God.

Materialism is the prevalent metaphysical view in the West today, but its origins are ancient. We should consider its ancient antecedents, because they are instructive to what is going on around us now. We can imagine a very early understanding of life in which one's attention extended only to the next kill and the next meal. But with even the first bellyful of meat and a warming fire and an awe-inducing kaleidoscope of stars overhead, there must have been contemplation of the fuller scope of reality, and where all this comes from, and what it all means. Still,

---

3 E.g., Smith, Steven D., *Pagans & Christians in the City/Culture Wars from the Tiber to the Potomac*, Eerdmans, 2018.

the needs of the day might have put this feeling on a shelf at the back of the mind, so that the star-gazing in the form of philosophy might have been put on hold, to be taken up again at times more convenient or by a later generation able to redeem time for these thoughts from the urgent necessities of the moment.

Even in pagan times, when gods of various kinds were thought to be swirling around all the time in a region beyond the visible, there were some thinkers who believed there was nothing to it; that no gods were necessary to understanding; that all of reality could be explained by natural processes. Epicureans held to this view, for example, upon the founding of that school of thought in about 306 BC, notwithstanding the Platonist and Aristotelean influences already prevalent and suggestive of another, greater, realm. Epicurean communities were active for several centuries, and continued to influence Western thought thereafter. Its materialism was thought to be necessitated by the idea of atomism, which traces back at least to Democritus in the fifth century BC.

Physical atomism was an early reductionist attempt: the urge to reduce reality to fundamental understandable elements. This reductionist project stands in opposition to the expansionist project of theism. When people looked around at repeating forms of matter, logic took them to the supposition that they had the same or similar fundamental constituents. The water in this river and that ocean, they thought, must be similarly composed on some invisible level. They were engaged in this-not-that binary thinking. This was thought by some to necessitate the conclusion that these common elements explained all of existence. If common elements, "atoms," explained the physical presentation of the world to our senses, there was no need to invoke gods for explanation, it was thought. An early materialist like Lucretius (first century BC) might reject the gods, for example, because atomism seems to explain everything, and "everything" is taken to mean all the physical cosmos which presents to our sense impressions. This would be especially true in the pagan age not yet influenced more broadly by monotheistic religion, because the natural/supernatural binary distinction was not yet so vividly drawn.

Of course we now know that atoms are real, and that there are apparently a fairly small number of unique kinds of atoms, barely more than a hundred, which are joined in sometimes complex combinations to constitute all that is physical. This is not seriously disputed. You might say we're all atomists, now. Does that mean we should also be materialists? Our look-back on history and science should inform us that the logical connection made by the Epicureans and other early atomists was wrong. Atomism does not imply materialism. The mistake is in thinking that matter and forces acting on it constitute all of reality. This is the mistake made by most of the so-called "New Atheists" of recent years, who argue for their conclusion of materialist atheism by simply assuming it to be true at the outset and then begging the question from start to finish.

It has not always been the case that people make a sharp distinction between the material and spiritual realms. Clearly there has always been a reality beyond what can be seen or touched, but that hasn't always been taken to require a spiritual reality. Mathematical principles, for example, are true everywhere and at all times, but we effortlessly distinguish between those principles and their manifestation in measurable physical things. The idea of a supernatural reality that is more than an ideal was extant among the Hebrews, and the seeds of this idea could be found in pagan Platonic ideals and Aristotelean *telos*. Jesus taught it explicitly, and it is crystal clear in the New Testament. It took some time for these thoughts of Jesus-followers to become prevalent across Western society, however. Clear awareness of the oppositional distinction between spiritual and natural became more prevalent following the teaching of early Christian church fathers, most notably Augustine of Hippo, writing in the fifth century.

Even as Christianity spread, however, there were from time to time resurgences of paganism or of materialism in which the distinction between natural and supernatural was collapsed. Sometimes this was in straightforward paganism with its worship of local gods, but the pagan confusion about the full scope of reality has persisted even into the modern era when Christianity was dominant. Following the medieval project of explaining Christianity rationally, Enlightenment-era thinkers who thought themselves Christian sometimes foundered with ideas such as the "necessarianism" of William Hazlitt and others.[4] Essentially, the thought was that true religion actually required a materialistic determinism, the idea that one's thinking in this moment necessarily follows the physical circumstances of the brain just before the thought. This was rightly criticized, even at the time, as an atheist proposition.

The Christian view of reality has been understood to require a component apart from the physical cosmos. It is by definition immaterial, and so speaking of it with materialist concepts like location or duration

---

4 Rée, Jonathan, *The Invention of Philosophy in English*, London: Penguin/Random House, 2019, p. 216.

fails. We have to imagine ourselves outside the boundaries of the physical cosmos, to apprehend it. Because we have to "imagine" it, or place the image of it in our minds, the immaterial realm can be referred to as that which is "unseen," as the Bible does in Hebrews Chapter 11.

In the modern era, the turn from reliance on authority and revelation to rationalism and empiricism was a trend long in the making, becoming more prevalent with the advance of science. It is not as though thinkers woke up on the first day of 1600 and decided scientific processes were the only way to acquire knowledge. We may think of the Enlightenment as commencing with Isaac Newton, but he was in turn preceded by Galileo and Erasmus and da Vinci and so on. The modern era (still speaking of the West) can be characterized as a gradual collapse of the natural/supernatural distinction; an erasure that leaves us not with the paganism of yore, but a reductionist materialism.

It is instructive how this came about. Newton was himself a devout Christian, and for generations, scientific endeavor was not generally thought incompatible with faith. It in fact isn't,[5] but the project of science requires a consistent methodological naturalism, and that has misled many to a philosophical naturalism, too. In olden days, people might have thought the explanation for gaps in our knowledge was the result of God-caused events. That presumption has been largely replaced with a materialism of the gaps; that is, whatever has not yet been explained by science someday will be, because science is the study of everything that is real, on this view—that is, physical things and forces acting on them. Many popular science writers now openly subscribe to reductionist materialism. Physicist Brian Greene, for example, would have us believe there is no such thing as a natural moral order, no free will, no purpose to the universe: "the reductionist, materialist, physicalist approach to the world is the right one. There isn't anything else . . . ."[6] Likewise Sean Carroll, who might be a brilliant physicist, but dabbles incoherently in philosophy by arguing from tautology: that there is no supernatural reality, therefore there is no supernatural reality.[7] Both hold that whatev-

5   In fact, there has rightly been substantial push-back to the notion of science as reproof of Christianity. Thoughtful commentators point out that science is more compatible with theism, than with reductionist materialism. See, e.g., Plantinga, Alvin, *Where the Conflict Really Lies/Science, Religion, & Naturalism*, Oxford University Press, 2011.

6   "String Theorist Brian Greene Wants to Help You Understand the Cold, Cruel Universe," by Jeffrey Kluger, *Time*, March 2-9, 2020, p. 22.

7   Carroll, Sean. *The Big Picture/On the Origin of Life, Meaning, and the Universe Itself*, 2016; review of same by author at albertnorton.com, "Blinkered Reality," February 9, 2018.

er is not presently understood will eventually be understood solely on principles of physics.

One needn't be a physicist, however, to believe physical things comprise all of reality. So-called New Atheist writers declaiming to us from on high arrive at their point of view with expertise in other areas. Richard Dawkins, Daniel Dennett, Sam Harris and the late Christopher Hitchens were grounded, respectively, in biology, philosophy, neuroscience, and journalism. They all adopted rigorously materialist views, though sometimes debating with one another on nuanced differences about free will and determinism and the arguable distinctions among materialism, physicalism, naturalism, and generic atheism.

They seemed to have sprung up overnight, but there have always been atheists railing against the God they don't like. Typically skeptics indulge a reactionary program, reacting against Christians' hypocrisy or credulous superstition or chauvinistic xenophobia. Enlightenment writers who were ambiguous deists, if not atheists, like David Hume or Voltaire or Thomas Paine, attacked Christianity; they did not defend materialism as a comprehensive explanation for all of reality. So with the New Atheists. They do not advance a comprehensive worldview to compete with theism on its own merits. Perhaps because doing so might provoke criticism of materialism as an explanation of reality, showing it to have far less explanatory power than Christianity.

To this day, the default materialism of the post-Christian West is not well-defined as a stand-alone explanation for the cosmos. It is more typically described by what it is not (Christianity) rather than what it is. Consequently, it fails to address, much less explain, insoluble facts of our existence, like why there is something rather than nothing, and why the something that does exist so uniquely supports life, and how the continuous upholding of the world can be untethered to any outside agency, and why human beings are so indelibly oriented to the good, the true, and the beautiful.

In the default materialism of post-Christian society, people don't typically reject God as conceived by Christians because they thoroughly weigh the alternatives and find materialism a more convincing explanation for the whole of reality. More likely, the Christian story seems to them progressively less plausible until they're down to the bare nub of a necessary creator God, and then "God" in quote marks instead, and then even that gleam of understanding winks into the cold nothingness of sterile physical reality. It is only a negation, not a philosophical construction. The project is to dismantle an understanding of reality, not to construct another in its place. Whatever one believes about ultimate reality, we're taught, it mustn't include the fable of Christianity nor the cloying hypocrisy of its adherents. It's easy to go thus far and stop, not getting to the question of what does explain ultimate reality, if Christianity does not.

Labeling the current metaphysical *zeitgeist* "materialism" or "naturalism" or anything else may seem inapt, because it isn't so much chosen as lapsed into. A person who goes along with the metaphysics assumptions prevalent in the culture might not even know what "materialism" or "naturalism" mean, in their philosophical usages. So how can they be a materialist or a naturalist? The answer is that the words may fit, whether they know them or not. It doesn't matter how people label their system of thought. It matters what it is. "Materialism" and "naturalism" are used here in order to put an affirmative label on something, rather than continuing the non-label which is only a negation of something else, like a-theist or a-gnostic or "not very religious."

Richard Dawkins thinks the existence of God is a scientific hypothesis like any other. "Either he exists or he doesn't. It is a scientific question."[8] How could that be? Every discussion of science by scientists (like Dawkins) rests on the understanding that science is about material, physical things. Science does not involve non-material reality, by definition. The anti-God argument actually goes like this: the study of material things does not prove the existence of non-material things, therefore there are no non-material things. The argument assumes the truth of materialism in order to prove the truth of materialism. Daniel Dennett is a more careful atheist writer, and is actually a philosopher rather than a biologist like Dawkins, but he makes the same foundational mistake in *Breaking the Spell.*[9]

Materialism incoherently holds that nature proves that nature is all there is. Supernatural reality does not exist because it is not material reality. X is all there is; Y is not X; therefore, Y does not exist. The premises assume the conclusion. If nature is conceived of as a closed system

---

8   Dawkins, Richard, *The God Delusion*, New York: Houghton, Mifflin, 2006, p. 48. Dawkins advocates prior restraint on free speech (Chapter 1); considers religious teaching child abuse (Chapter 9); and lays violence at the feet of religion while excusing the bridle-high materialist bloodshed of the 20th century (Chapter 7). Most importantly, he doesn't defend his own idea of reality, he merely attacks Christianity.

9   Dennett, Daniel, *Breaking the Spell/ Religion as a Natural Phenomenon*, Viking Adult, 2006.

sufficient unto itself, how can that be proven from within the system?[10] David Bentley Hart expresses the circularity of the argument this way:

> [P]hysics explains everything, which we know because anything physics cannot explain does not exist, which we know because whatever exists must be explicable by physics, which we know because physics explains everything.[11]

The fictional god which is the straw man of New Atheist writers is not the God of Christianity. The real God is unconditional; pure actuality; the source of all things; and the source of all being. This is the actual God of early philosophy and of theologians putting revelation together into systematic, reasoned understanding of God. Many atheist writers either don't understand this, or pretend God is a more manageable and imaginary lesser deity like Zeus or Apollo or Thor. The New Atheist writers are (or were) bent on attacking the kind of entities that even Christians agree do not exist. In the course of doing so, they say little or nothing about the materialist philosophy of reality they adopt in its place.

Materialism is the more prevalent metaphysical view in the West today, but it shouldn't be. If you believe the only way to detect dangerous lions is to stare out across the savannah through telescoping field glasses, you may conclude there are none present. But the field glasses don't prove the absence of lions. Lions may be present and remain undetected if they're hidden by vegetation, or nighttime, or proximity to the glasses. Field glasses are valuable but they do not show us all of reality. If we believe they do, on the atheist misconception of "faith," we might be eaten. And God is much more dangerous than a lion.

What is happening here is an attempted erasure of binary oppositions. Reductionist thinking is applied to reduce physical reality to foundational elements. There's nothing wrong with that as far as it goes; it might help us in our scientific endeavors. But it doesn't mean physical reality is all there is. The binary opposition is drawn in the wrong place, in this way of thinking. To understand all of reality, the first relevant opposition is a spirit and material reality, on the one hand, and a physical-only reality, on the other. Jumping to oppositions within physical

---

10 This was answered, for those with ears to hear, in Gödel's incompleteness theorem in 1931.

11 Hart, David Bentley, *Experience of God/Being, Consciousness, Bliss*, Yale University Press, 2013.

reality is fine, if the object is just to understand physical things, as with science. But it doesn't answer for what constitutes all of reality.

The urge to reductionism is also applied in thinking more generally, resulting in an oversimplification that amounts to a leveling-down of our ability to reason. One way to win a debate is to have a superior message. Another way is to coarsen the receivers of that message. That's why a lie repeated often enough begins to sound like the truth; why the "big lie" technique was adopted and was successful by mid-century dictators. Truth is a casualty both when the seed of a lie is cast, and when the soil in which it is cast is made receptive to the lie. So it is with metaphysical considerations.

We have acquired the habit of seeing the universe not merely as something to be investigated with a mechanistic paradigm, but as actually a machine. Since the time of Francis Bacon at least, there has been a drift to a mechanistic worldview. Darwinism initiated a significant phase of this drift. Because of the mechanistic philosophy already in place, the Darwinian proposal of natural selection fit the machine model. It seemed to support the idea that nature is merely the product of unguided mindless forces. And that is the essence of modern materialism.

CHAPTER SEVENTEEN

Darwin's Dangerous Idea

MATERIALISTS PERFORCE believe the cosmos is self-created from utter nothingness; that life sprang solely from non-life; that a person's consciousness is entirely an emergent property of the tissues and electricity of the brain; that every living thing, no matter how complex, results from unguided and undirected response to environmental challenges, with no driving life-force whatsoever; that features of man's common experience which are immaterial are nonetheless rooted in their material bodies, including ideals of mathematics and of virtue and the inexorable directedness to truth and beauty. Even the conscience and morality in general, a materialist must assume, are evolved features of mankind, and only that. There is no soul. There is no part of a person that is immaterial; therefore, no part of him that can be said to be eternal. His only way to live on, after death, is in the memory of those encountered in life in the body. There is no afterlife of any kind. Once a person dies, his consciousness simply ceases. He has no more awareness of any kind, because all awareness resided in the memory of a living brain, which has now ceased to function. After death, there is only oblivion, we're to believe.

During this life in the body, a person's conscious self-awareness is largely a mystery. It is necessarily a mystery which resides solely in the workings of the brain, however, for materialists. Materialism provides no basis for explaining subjective experience, and awareness of subjective experience, other than the neural networks of the brain processing sensory input, making rapid associations, and storing memory. All of our consciousness resides in the living brain, in the materialist paradigm, there is nothing on a level beyond that which would assist in understanding how one is not only able to think, but to think abstractly, and to think about thinking, and to exercise imagination, and to contemplate the boundaries of our ability to think. There is no goal or purpose in life, other than to survive as long as possible, and to procreate, and to provide for progeny. All of life arose from non-living material, in some as-yet unexplained way. Life became increasingly complex in variety and constitution, through the passive working of environmental challenges, extinguishing some mutations and not others. Increases in complexity of life occurred in defiance of entropic influences through self-organization of organic materials. The chief feature of biological complexity is that of information storage and passage to progeny. This information also arose and developed in living things spontaneously. Morality is an evolved thing, consisting essentially of internalized behaviors that enhanced our living socially. Our social living arrangements give rise to a sense of empathy for others, and an evolved tendency to reciprocate others' empathy for us. Ideals that are not material, like beauty, truth, justice, and loyalty, are internalized results of evolution, resulting from our social nature, as with morality. Matter, time, energy, and the laws of physics acting upon them arose spontaneously, and from nothing.

Well that's a lot to take in, for someone who occasionally senses the majesty and mystery of an unseen realm. But so what? If it's true, it's true. If truth is the goal, then it doesn't matter if we find this point of view bleak. But it just isn't true. Darwinism is a proposed explanation of biological development. Whether that explanation of biological development is true or not, it does not explain the origin of life. It does not account for the very existence of the universe or the order found within it or the reach of human consciousness or the pervasive information spoken into the world in the form of DNA, mathematical constants, and the dualistic oppositions which make the world comprehensible, and us able to comprehend it.

Many who attempt to refute the existence of God say things like: "if God created everything, what created God?" It is a silly question, because to be coherent, it would have to make God into something not-God: another contingent being like us, or the imagined fickle demiurge servitors of fate conceived in the pagan era. Even aside from that convenient re-sizing of God, it is puzzling that materialists make an argument against the existence of God from this infinite regress. From a physics perspective, wouldn't that leave an insoluble conundrum? What *did* create the first thing? An endless regress of causes would mean there is no actual beginning. An infinite regress is therefore equivalent to nonexistence. But things do exist. So what is the point of the infinite regress argument?

All finite things are always, in the present, being sustained in existence by conditions they cannot have supplied for themselves, and they together comprise a universe that, as a physical reality, lacks the supernatural power necessary to exist on its own. None of this dependent, conditional reality is reducible to an infinite regress of contingent causes. There must be an unconditioned reality upon which all else depends. That unconditioned reality is, by virtue of being "unconditioned," not finite in any spatial or temporal sense. Philosophers and theologians have called this unconditioned reality God.

Anselm of Canterbury (1033-1109) articulated the ontological proof for the existence of God: "That than which it is not possible to conceive anything greater." This was not the first time this idea was expressed, however. It was expressed, for example, as an already obvious statement in the sixth century by Boethius, in his *Consolation of Philosophy*.[1] That entity, the actual God, is not a being among other beings, and not even the greatest possible of beings, but is instead the fullness of Being itself, the absolute upon which all else depends. It is meaningless to say that Being lacks being, or that Reality is not real. By analogy suggested by David Bentley Hart: "It makes perfect sense to ask what illuminates an object, but none to ask what illuminates light." In the same way: "It makes perfect sense to wonder why a contingent being exists, but none to wonder why Absolute Being 'exists.'"[2]

If you start with a philosophical commitment to the rejection of any supernatural reality, and then undertake to explain the origin of things, you're likely to gravitate to the explanation that fits that philosophical commitment. In other words, one may be an atheist first, and exclude valid evidence of supernatural truth because of that prior commitment. It's often said, we must follow the evidence where it leads. That's a valid principle. We should do so not just in science, but in every endeavor. Indeed, that is the essence of reasoned, rational thought. We sometimes deviate from that principle, as when theists cling to questionable Biblical interpretation, or when atheists reject supernatural reality because they think it's not apparent in the natural world. We must be wary of putting on blinders.

Philosophers sometimes channel their thoughts on these subjects

---

1 Boethius, Anicius, *Consolation of Philosophy*, c. 524.

2 Hart, David Bentley, *Experience of God/Being, Consciousness, Bliss*, Yale University Press, 2013.

by considering whether mind prevails over matter, or the reverse. By the word, "mind," is meant that which is non-material, and which creates the material. The mind of God is the obvious meaning, in this context. The opposite view, that matter precedes mind, yields conclusions like that of Francis Crick, when he wrote:

> You, your joys and your sorrows, your memories and ambitions, your sense of personal identity and free will, are in fact no more than the behavior of a vast assembly of nerve cells and their associated molecules.[3]

We might well ask: if what he is saying is true, how could he know it? The assertion itself is just the result of all the unguided physical processes up to the moment he wrote it, so there is no reason to take it as "true." This sort of nonsense is what results when we assert that matter produces mind, rather than the other way around.

The proposition that matter nonetheless produces mind is why Daniel Dennett presents evolution as "Darwin's Dangerous Idea." He wrote that Darwin "was offering a skeptical world . . . a scheme for creating Design out of Chaos without the aid of mind."[4] He meant that Darwin's ideas are dangerous because they upend the top-down conception of the physical world as originating in the Mind of God. Evolution is thought to be an illustration of the principle that the opposite is true: that mind evolved from matter, therefore thoughts result from undirected, mindless, purposeless process.

To make the jump to eliminating the need for a creator, one has to overlook the distinction between the development of life on the theory of evolution, and the creation of life. Whether evolution is the mechanism for development of life or not, the existence of a mechanism does not negate a creator of the mechanism. The existence of laws of physics do not negate a creator of those laws. The existence of a mechanism for biological variation over time as a result of mutation and environmental constraints does not negate a creator of the mechanism, or of the life for the mechanism to act upon. For natural selection to be true, there had to be something there to be naturally selected. Evolution does not, by itself, negate God.

One would hardly see this in reading materialists who ascribe creative force to the laws of physics, and personify them in the course of

---

3 Crick, Francis, *The Astonishing Hypothesis*, New York: Touchstone, 1994.

4 Dennett, Daniel, *Darwin's Dangerous Idea*, New York: Simon & Schuster, 1996, p. 50.

their explanation, thus shifting subtly over to a creator for the mechanisms they contend have no creator. The forces of physics are the "blind watchmaker," according to Dawkins' analogy. The genes of the body take on purpose and intent when they are referred to as the "selfish gene."[5] Routinely, books describing unguided evolution use purpose-driven words and concepts like "selection" and "adaptation" without clarifying that no selecting or adapting happens. Rather, selection (or, more accurately, deselection) and adaptation are the passive *result* of purposeless physical processes, according to the theory.[6] Evolution requires the existence of a fine-tuned universe, in which to operate, but there is no naturalistic explanation for that. The laws of physics must be in place for evolution to work as theorized, but there is no answer to the question of where those come from. There is obviously some life force, or motivating driver for survival and procreation that is necessary to the evolution process, but neither is that explained. The point is that, if true, naturalistic biological evolution by itself is a long way from disproving a supernatural reality imparting a *telos* to the process.

When understanding of the structure of DNA was developed at mid-twentieth century by James Watson and Francis Crick and others, this was thought to be another *ah-ha!* moment for naturalistic evolution. The emphasis should not be on the physical process, however, as fascinating as that is. The emphasis should be on the fact that DNA is about information. Every cell of the body carries this wealth of information for its own operation and that of the individual's progeny. This is real semantic content, carried directly in the body. Perhaps it evolved, but if so, it evolved as an information-generating and information-distributing function of living beings. The implication is that information turns out to be most fundamental to the reality we know. Information is a product of Mind. If there is no supernatural reality at all, then the information is self-generating, just as living things are thought to be, and as the existence of all physical things is thought to be. But that can't be correct if information in DNA, and in mathematical constants of the universe, and in dualisms, and in mathematical principles more generally, is a real, "out there" fact of reality. It exists in the universe we know, not merely as concepts in our mind. It points to and constitutes the ideals which are not self-created nor human-created, but God-created.

All that said, there is indeed a sense in which Darwinism is "dan-

---

5 Dawkins, Richard, *The Selfish Gene*, New York: Oxford University Press, 1989.

6 E.g., Mayr, Ernst, *What Evolution Is*, New York: Perseus, 2001.

gerous." It is dangerous because it leads us down a false path of conceiving all our ideals as human constructs. It encourages us in the belief
that mankind mentally constructed and then projected ideals onto the
world, starting (but not ending) with mathematics. If we take it to disprove God and to affirmatively prove materialism as an explanation of
all of reality, then we've bought in to a ground-up human construction
wherein mankind is the sole author of everything that is good or beautiful or true, and of every ideal. Mathematics would be just a game we
play to amuse ourselves, fitting it by chance to the wonderful but accidental orderliness of the universe. It would have to be the case that we
built from the ground up the obvious hierarchy of internalized ideals
we have, and continue to build toward those to which we aspire. And all
this with no explanation of why.

CHAPTER EIGHTEEN

Political Freedom

W E'VE TRACED THE IMPACT of certain essential dualistic realities to understand how attempting to collapse them fails. We should approach the tensions between oppositions as opportunities to better understand reality, rather than trying to wish them away. Binary oppositions create tension which produces meaning. Naturally we want to resolve tensions because they are a form of conflict, creating uncomfortable dissonance if unresolved. We can resolve tension by choosing one side of the opposition over the other, or by finding a way to transcend the opposition altogether. What we can't do is simply extinguish it.

We might attempt to extinguish the opposition between us and God, for example, by denying God's very existence. We could alternatively try to mentally erase the self, by stepping outside the individualist self-perception, and into the collective. This rather obviously compromises individual freedom, but we might deny this by devising alternative ways to define freedom, rather than embracing the fullness of a person's individual significance before God. There are real-world consequences to attempting to collapse the individual and collective oppositional dualism in this way.

The freedom we're talking about is personal in nature, as opposed to collective political freedom such as America acquired upon its break with England. The point of personal freedom is not social isolation, but rather social and economic independence. This kind of personal freedom is necessarily a two-edged sword. It necessarily involves opportunity for both success and failure. If one is truly free from collectivist interference, as with government regulation of one's individual undertakings, then one must also be free to fail. Attempts to ameliorate failure through collectivist action necessarily result in diminished freedom.

The two-edged nature of freedom is a crucial point. It is of course human nature to maximize gain and minimize loss, but risk and reward must go together. Minimizing risk means minimizing reward. As we build in collectivist safety nets to minimize loss, we reduce the concomitant prospect for gain. Collectivist activity thus has the effect of reducing both the highs and lows of human experience, reducing us to a muddled mushy middle instead of witnesses to the stark contrasts that inhere in genuine freedom.

This can be seen in individual economic endeavors. In a society unconstrained by collectivist regulation, the economic engine is mostly untaxed and therefore most capable of creating wealth. But regulation exists to avoid risk, so a balancing takes place. We give up potential for gain in the form of higher salary or entrepreneurial profit or pursuit of non-monetary goals like art or literature or leisure. We get in its place a more secure return from our quotidian pursuits. We might consider the balancing that takes place to be an acceptable trade-off. What often goes unconsidered, however, is that the trade-off is not just between security and potential for financial upside. The trade-off requires cashing in some personal freedom.

The economic systems in which this analysis is most relevant include those prevalent in Western societies today, most of which are at some point on a spectrum between radically unconstrained free trade, and undiluted socialism. The liberalism that has come with the modern age has meant greater individual participation in government, through the vote, but this is not an unalloyed good, from the standpoint of individual freedom. We're used to thinking of the liberalizing trend from monarchy to democracy as enhancing freedom, but we are in an age in which the individual vote is so miniscule, arithmetically, that the real power is in moving large blocks of vote in the public "conversation." Without shared commitment to individual independence, that contributes to non-stop ideological struggle. Government is the usual instrument of collectivism in this age, and we've become used to thinking of almost any issue as appropriate for government action. Government is looked to for resolution of a range of issues that would never have been considered within the province of government just a short while ago. Most modern states have some form of government involvement in health care, to pick just one example. Usually this is justified by a belief that everyone in a prosperous society "should" have access to health care, but of course that could be said of food and housing as well. And why stop there? We've seen a snowball effect in the range of public economic activity, because we've become inured to it. We no longer stop to consider the cost in loss of personal freedom.

Western societies have mostly enjoyed prosperity, when we're not destroying ourselves with war, and this prosperity has the effect of clouding our ability to discern a loss of freedom. We don't know how much more prosperity we would have enjoyed, had we not taken up socialism to the degree we have. We do know, however, that for most people the collectivist vehicle, the state, can pick up the tab, spreading the cost, for a range of goods and services that were formerly provided through private initiative. Because of general prosperity, those who retain relative independence from the state can carry on without sensing their independence much compromised. The cost in terms of freedom seems negligible on the margin. We give it up one grain at a time, but in total we're profligate with our freedom, inching forward steadily to totalitarianism.

One of the costs we likely don't see at all, if we're net payors rather than net takers in socialist economic activity, is that the net takers have already given up significant freedom. They're past a tipping point at which they become captive to the State. Their choices in life are hemmed in by collectivist decision-making. If you're an American in this situation, most of your economic life is decided for you. Once you begin eating at the public table, so to speak, the menu is selected for you and it becomes nearly impossible to break the cycle of dependence. A captive class grows, and its members suffer even more loss of personal freedom than do the net payors.

The trend is to economic socialism, and this requires a command economy rather than an economy operating on decentralized, individual and freely-made choices. The command economies of deliberate socialism have all been unmitigated disasters. Nonetheless, we trend again toward economic socialism, but now more gradually and through exercise of the franchise in democracy, rather than through misguided Marxist revolution. We should expect the result to be the same, however, ultimately. The same loss of prosperity, and the same loss of freedom, vis-à-vis the State. Socialism depresses economic prosperity, enhances hegemonic centralized power, and diminishes personal freedom. We're not voting it in as an economic system complete unto itself. Western nations didn't wake up socialist one day. Instead we vote it in incrementally, one measure at a time. Each measure seems an acceptable trade-off of freedom, if we even think of it in terms of freedom at all. The freedom trade-off is least obvious to net takers, and as that class grows, the move to socialism accelerates. Today there are even overt calls for socialism, called by that name. Given the history of the last 120 years, this should be unthinkable, but we have to relearn the hard way.

Socialism is an obstacle to finding God. It is a collective muddling of the highs and lows that must attend life as created by God. Christians on the political left push socialism because they believe it advances the interest Jesus taught us to have in the well-being of our neighbor. Capitalism means greed and socialism means love, they believe. But capitalism, if uncorrupted by government, means maximal freedom and prosperity; while socialism means stagnation, tyranny, and decline.

A Christian can be rightly concerned with his own and others' well-being, but not with another's greater wealth. Envy is ugly. We tend to think of socialism as spreading wealth to have-nots, but in doing so we imagine wealth to be property of the collective, thus de-emphasizing that it involves taking from people who perhaps have more. The only question, really, is the perennial political question of "who decides;" in this case, who decides how to spend the dollars in the hands of the person who earned it: the person himself, or the government. Charity is a virtue, to be encouraged. Charity is about giving to those who "have-not." The Christian ideal of charity is stood on its head, however, once the "charity" becomes involuntary. We should ask ourselves whether exercising the vote to take things from our neighbor is really consonant with Christian ideals. Rather than eliminating injustice, socialism would seem to create it.

Politically, we should consider freedom as an end unto itself, rather than a means to something else. Freedom is acquired through liberation from constraint. Freedom and constraint are a dualism in which each defines the other. Most of us in the West today live between those extremes. We convert our time and effort into money in order to exchange it for things we need or want. We live inside mixed capitalist and democratic socialist systems which present a tug-of-war between individual freedom and State-sponsored security.

Once freed from constraints, one acquires "liberty." Historically, the constraints were understood to be collectively-imposed: the aristocracy and the established church, for example, in the French revolutions of the late-eighteenth and early-nineteenth centuries. The trend toward reclaiming personal freedom from these collectives is what is meant by "liberalism." We must distinguish the confusing use of "liberal" in the

United States, however, so let's call the traditional understanding "classical liberalism."

If we look back over a span of hundreds of years, we observe lives lived inside social constraints that we would today regard as unacceptably rigid. The removal of those constraints came about through development of ideas of natural rights, and the idea that politically, no person has inherently greater worth than another. We could look to John Locke (1632-1704), for example, for early articulation of these ideals. Individual freedom was the object of the ensuing (classical) liberalizing movement. In Europe the Reformation broke the exclusivity of the Roman Catholic Church, and very quickly denominations arose for differing expressions of conscience and doctrinal consistency.

In short order, any religious adherence became optional. While authority from the collective, established Church was shifting to individuals, the power of hierarchical aristocracies faded and was replaced by the rise of nation-states. As greater representation in government came about, the collectivist power center became the State, rather than aristocratic lords and the established, aristocracy-supported church. Thus, over time, the collectivist institution from which an individual would be considered "liberated" was primarily the State.

In this way, classical liberals were those who regarded the State as being potentially adversarial to individual rights, so that the State had to be constitutionally limited. A classical liberal is one who promotes individual autonomy as against the authority of the State. A person who meets that description in the United States today would be called a "conservative," perhaps a "libertarian," and would stand in opposition to those on the left confusingly called "liberals." The rise of the nation-state combined with the decline of the church and near-extinction (in the United States) of the aristocracy has meant that power not exercisable by individuals has become progressively more concentrated in the State. And so today the institution from which one should protect one's freedom is, primarily, the State.

There is push-back available on this notion, however, even if one accepts the premise that individuals are in a state of antagonistic tension with the collectivist State. What about private centers of authority? How about giant corporations and absurdly wealthy individuals who can fund advocacy groups which in turn affect politics and culture? How about culture and partisan news media which are effectively advocacy groups unto themselves? These aren't to be shrugged off. They may have more officious impact on our day-to-day lives than does government policy.

A couple of features of these private concentrations of power, however, make them of less concern than power reposed in the State. One is that they are limited in their ability to coerce. An essential difference between private and public (that is, government) undertakings is that the State has the monopoly on the legitimate use of force.[1] Individuals hanging on to their autonomy have freedom to resist the entreaties and manipulations and lies of non-government entities. This consideration ought to make us think carefully, however, about the various kinds of public/private partnerships that have proliferated like kudzu in recent years. If there is to be collective power of force over individuals, it should be tightly contained within government, where we have a shot at keeping an eye on it.

A second consideration is that these private sources of pressure on individuals are a necessary corollary to an essentially capitalist system. Capitalism is the least-unfree economic system available. It is criticized widely, and not without cause, but the criticisms are typically rooted in an assumption that wealth is a collective asset, and its disposition something in which we all have a voice. The (usually) unspoken assumption of critics is that private capital is unfair; that private leveraging of capital produces return far in excess of the value of one's labor. Essentially, a reversion to a ground-up Marxist valuation of labor, rather than top-down market valuation. The criticisms are not based on freedom, or lack thereof.

A legitimate criticism of nominal free-trade capitalism lies not in business competition, but in the ways we allow it to be compromised, as in our unprincipled intermingling of private and public entities as in most Western nations today. Private enterprise takes on attributes of coercive power concentration when it borrows coercive power from the government, in public/private partnerships of various kinds, and willing industry regulation, and "too-big-to-fail" public bail-outs. This inevitably expands the unequal application of law, and shifts government's coercive power to private capitalist undertakings, thus removing by degrees what justifies capitalism in the first place: individual freedom.

---

1   This idea is sometimes attributed to Max Weber, in his lecture, "Politics as a Vocation," 1918. The principle appeared in earlier works implicitly, such as Thomas Hobbes' *Leviathan* (1651) (describing in theory what we would now call a fascist state). The principle has greater currency with the rise of the nation-State in the eighteenth and nineteenth centuries, because prior to that, force deemed legitimate was also exercised by private entities such as feudal lords, the Church, and individuals pursuing common-law rights of retaliation.

There is an unhealthy tendency already toward this kind of freedom-limiting intermingling. Large companies such as those traded on public markets want stability and protected markets, if they can get it, and a way to get it is through more regulation, paradoxically. Big businesses can afford legal compliance departments and the limitations of regulation, and they go along with it because in exchange they get stability, protection from competitive incursions from other big business, and protection from small business competition that can't carry the necessary fixed cost. Regulation is the law; it applies to a business's competitors, too. If you are a car dealer who wants to have Sundays off, but you want your competitors to stay closed on Sundays, too, what do you do? Petition the government to require all car dealers to close on Sundays, that's what. This simple vignette illustrates a mentality pervasive in the business world, once the public/private opposition is blurred. It gives competitive advantage to big companies, not little ones that are unable to avail themselves of such risk reduction by government entanglement. As public/private partnership and regulation increase, small businesses suffer in comparison. Big government in bed with big business leaves small business on the sidelines, and individuals merely consumer units inside the government/big business machine. This erodes the virtues of free trade capitalism, starting with freedom.

Why is this allowed? Partly because we make decisions on the margin, without re-thinking first principles. We take each step thinking of only the last step, without considering what road all these steps are on. We get far down the wrong road this way, and lose the ability to remember why we're on the road in the first place. But another reason is that collectivism and atheist materialism take us there. Starting with the given of corrupted capitalism, the advance to socialism is made through "democratic socialism" rather than through the old-school Marxist revolution. Socialism doesn't have to be called "Marxism" to be the inevitable destruction that goes with economic and political collectivism.

The tension between collectivist action and the desire for personal autonomy can be partially mediated through Constitutional and parliamentary procedure to recognize that one's individual rights mean something more than having a single, equal, voice in the direction of the State as an expression of collective will. We think of the founding fathers of the United States as geniuses because they embarked on a grand experiment in which individuals retain freedom, rather than forming illiberal institutions constraining people in ways similar to what had been experienced up to that time in Europe. In actuality, the American experiment was a natural next step in the developing liberalism of the West. It was a grand experiment because it involved unprecedented individual freedom. In 1776, the United States was devoted to principles of classical liberalism.

Those principles do not obtain today. The vote is thought to be for purposes of steering the direction of the State in the collective exercise of collective will, rather than for limitation of the State in favor of exercise of individual will, as at the founding. The vote is thus reduced to a gesture of participation in the direction of that collective will, rather than preservation of individual will. This has been the trend-line for the history of the United States since its founding on (classically) liberal ideals: a gradual entropic unraveling of its key founding principle.

The individualism at the nation's founding has been overridden by collectivism. In the culture, this mostly takes the form of political correctness, the result of a Rawlsian[2] view of how we're to engage with one another, delimiting acceptable public discourse to views within a narrowing range of leftist orthodoxy, particularly with regard to the "comprehensive" doctrines of religion. This has the effect of institutionalizing a false neutrality concerning religion, which means secular, materialist, humanism has pride of place in the public square. Political correctness is not confined to culture, unfortunately, because it is in many respects enshrined in the law of the State.

The idea that freedom resides in turning one's autonomy over to the State is called fascism. The Italian fascist dictator Benito Mussolini in 1919 proclaimed:

> Liberalism denied the State in the name of the individual. Fascism reasserts the rights of the State as expressing the real essence of the individual.

Fascism seeks to meld individuality into the State collective. Mussolini again:

> The Fascist conception of the State is all embracing; outside of it no human or spiritual values can exist, much less have value. Thus understood, Fascism is totalitarian, and the Fascist State—a synthesis and a unit inclusive of all values—interprets, develops, and potentiates the

---

2 Rawls, John, *The Idea of Public Reason Revisited*, Cambridge, MA: Harvard University Press, 1999.

whole life of a people.[3]

Fascism is the extreme deification of the State,[4] but collectivists seem unable to see it. The word "fascism" is used by them for something else entirely. Here it is as articulated by one Aleksandar Hemon:

> Fascism's central idea . . . is that there are classes of human beings who deserve diminishment and destruction because they're for some reason (genetic, cultural, whatever) inferior to "us."[5]

This formulation is unfortunately not an outlier, but is a reasonably approximate definition of fascism even today by people on the left. This is a serious misapprehension. Fascism is about power, not bigotry. Fascism is actually the relinquishment of individual self-governance in favor of the state, not merely the noxious constraints of little minds. On the political left there is a preoccupation with the relatively less important elements of xenophobia and racism, and an insufficient concern with power.

To take the Nazi example, of course the racialist ideology was odious, but fascism had to be fought at the expense of millions of lives because the ideology gained momentum under Hitler, as head of an increasingly powerful state. The many millions of military and civilian deaths in the European theater of World War II resulted from the exercise of power, not the stunted imaginations in which the racialist ideology took root. People can think what they want. But when groupthink takes over and manifests in the State, it acquires tanks and planes, and war must ensue, if there are opponents who love freedom. It is the collectivist groupthink that is the problem, not the remaining elements of the ideology that is

---

3 Mussolini, Benito, *The Fundamentals of Fascism*, 1935.

4 A political prisoner of Italian fascism, Carlo Levi, spoke of those in Fascist state authority this way: "they were all unconscious worshipers of the State. Whether the State they worshiped was the Fascist State or the incarnation of quite another dream, they thought of it as something that transcended both its citizens and their lives." About small-f fascism and the official kind: "[I]t is probable, alas, that the new institutions arising after Fascism, through either gradual evolution or violence, no matter how extreme and revolutionary they may be in appearance, will maintain the same ideology under different forms and create a new State equally far removed from real life, equally idolatrous and abstract, a perpetuation under new slogans and new flags of the worst features of the eternal tendency toward Fascism." Levi, Carlo, *Christ Stopped at Eboli*, translated by Frances Frenaye, 1945.

5 Hemon, Aleksandar, *Fascism is Not an Idea to Be Debated, It's a Set of Actions to Fight*, Literary Hub, November 1, 2018.

its subject matter. This should be obvious from basic facts about the same world-transforming conflict. A competitor to Nazi ideology was Stalinist communism. Leftists were sympathetic to the ideology which informed it, but as with Nazism, it wasn't the ideology of coercive collectivism in the abstract that was the problem, it was the corruption of truth and resulting concentration of power in the State. We didn't fight a hot war with communism, at the time, because there was an uneasy alliance. But Stalinist communism was a Cold War adversary because of its concentration of power in the State. The West's concern, legitimately, was with the U.S.S.R.'s missiles, not trade union activism in places like Bolivia.

The problem isn't individual attitudes about how we relate to others. The problem, as always, is power. Classical liberalism was about checking power. The current US ideology of "liberalism" retains collectivism and tries to cleanse the wayward human heart of hate and greed. That's fine, as far as it goes, if it proceeds on individual initiative that cannot command coercion. But it is not fine when the coercive power at hand, the State, is invoked to accomplish it. This is the sentiment that drives collectivist illiberalism. Fascism's central idea is not border walls nor exclusion of immigrants nor racism, implicit or otherwise. Fascism's central idea is concentration of power in the State. And so is the socialism or communism to which collectivism in modern times takes us.

Fascism is therefore no different in its most important respect than the dictatorships thought necessary in communism, which gave us Stalin, Mao, and a host of other tyrants at the heads of disastrous totalitarian States. None were about to give up power to complete the ideal of Marxist utopian historical evolution. Extreme left and right meet at loss of individualism and its replacement with collectivism. Decentralized, individualist autonomy entropically gives way to centralized, collectivist control. This has been an inexorable trend in the reversal of classical liberalism into the illiberalisms of the twentieth century. It happens because collectivists misperceive the operative dualism. When unprincipled political leadership comes to power in a republic, it can then turn that weaponized State into an engine of tyranny. A particular idea of misuse of State power is presented and accepted as the culprit, and not the State power itself. The collapse of the individual and collective dualism in favor of collectivism enables and therefore results in tyranny.

We should be concerned when we see trends that move us in this direction. Those trends exist now. Socialism of thought is a function of postmodernist thinking which relegates truth to something made, rather than discovered, and consequently, to removal of God from reality. This is consequential to individual freedom. We are constrained by cultural norms, and this has always been true, but in recent decades it has taken on a more virulent form, being more constraining and monolithic, and accompanied by opprobrium and ostracism. There have always been norms of behavior and thought in modern classically-liberal societies, but the band of acceptably polite opinion has typically been broad and accommodating of significant heterodoxy. There is now a new form of puritanical thought which is increasingly intolerant. There are certain received opinions that are the "right" way of thinking, and dissenters from this orthodoxy become objects of obloquy. This is political correctness, which in essence disposes of disagreement *ad hominem*, rather than addressing the merits of dissenting points of view. If you don't mouth certain approved shibboleths, your point of view will be disregarded as improperly motivated, outside the bounds of polite conversation, and you yourself will be ostracized. The principal method for dealing with dissent from left-liberal orthodoxy is to de-platform or "cancel" or otherwise discredit the dissenter, rather than addressing the dissenting point of view on the merits. The effect is creation of a collection of acceptable thoughts, policed by the mob.

It's interesting to think how almost the entirety of German society in the 1930s engaged in the groupthink necessary to put into power Hitler and his party, with all of its extravagantly materialist and pagan and racist ideas. How could that have happened? Likewise, how could a twisted culture of distrust and suspicion so overtake the political and daily life of the communist Soviet Union, with many in gulags and many millions more simply killed? What power must have been associated with the cult of Mao such that people stood by while millions were murdered and many millions more died in famine? How could this happen? A *hundred million* non-combatants dead, an amount about equal to a third of the entire population of the United States today. These episodes of history, plus many more that could be cited, demonstrate the power of society-wide groupthink that can take us far away from any civilized standards of right and wrong.

And yet we tend not to be on the lookout for it when it happens in our own back yard. It can happen in the United States just as surely as it happened in Cambodia and Romania and Venezuela and Cuba. Socialism of economics is only part of the story. Socialism of thought is the more pernicious and dangerous. Today's political correctness is tomorrow's occasion for thought-police correctives. The nations of the

West today are not immune.

If we are wise, we look on these episodes of mass delusion and consider how to avoid falling into a similar trap. What is the source of our understanding? The approbation of our peers, or a more foundational basis for evaluating right and wrong? The danger of collectivism is that it can shift our attention from ferreting out truth and decanting falsehood to sniffing the air for what society tells us must be so. Just because everyone else says it's true, doesn't make it so. This used to be plain homespun wisdom, but now it is disregarded because our epistemology actually leads us to the opposite conclusion: that right and wrong is what the herd says it is. We have drifted away from truth resting on a foundation of immutable God to a shopping mentality for choosing delectable truths from a carousel of truthy offerings.

CHAPTER NINETEEN

Nothing

ALL THAT IS, IS CONTINGENT on God's existence. If there were a collapse of all not-God material, and thought, and ideals, we would have, apart from God, nothing. What is this nothing?

Imagine you're on a tour in a deep cave. The tour guide directs you and those with you to find a comfortable place to stand, or lean, and get ready for the sensation of total darkness. Then he switches off the lights. The darkness is so complete you imagine it to have density and weight. You experience for the first time not merely darkness, nor deep darkness, nor a different kind of low-level light, but the entire absence of light. It would be a mistake to think of the cave as merely different-ly-lighted than other places, wouldn't it? Nothing in this environment would inform you about the properties of light. It is not just a dark place. It is the absolute of darkness.

In the same way, there is a Nothing that is the absolute of noth-ingness. We can call it Nothing, with a capital-N, to distinguish true and complete Nothing from all the ways we think of "nothing" that is actually a something. Space is something. It consists of particles and has mass and contains forces including those forces which give it shape. Thoughts are something. Theories and mental connections and rational processing, even if considered apart from physical material like brains with which they are associated, are nonetheless "something" rather than Nothing. Ideals, too, are something. The ideal of a triangle doesn't phys-ically exist anywhere; that's what it means to be an ideal. But as an ideal, it is still something. The sum of the angles of the ideal triangle will al-ways be exactly 180° because that's what a triangle is. This, along with all mathematical ideals, and other ideals like virtues, are something. The oppositions apparent in the universe, and mind able to comprehend them, are something, not nothing. So Nothing—the absolute—excludes all these. It's not just darkness and quiet. Not just a thoughtless void. Not sense-deprived mind folding back on itself. Nothing is an absolute.

We have a hard time imagining such a Nothing because even in trying to imagine it, we make it a something. A feature of something-ness is that it can be thought of as a thing unto itself. Absolute Nothing is entire absence, so there's nothing even to attach the thought to. We can speak of it as theory only. Nothingness is a metaphysical concept, like spirit. Both Nothing and the supernatural, spiritual "realm" (for want of a better word to describe the domain of the spiritual) are distinct from the physical, or "natural" world. From the realm of space- and time-bound physical things, it is difficult to conceive what lies beyond or apart from it.

If there were Nothing, that would be reality, though there would be no one including God to understand it as such. Let's call that version of reality A. If there were a spiritual realm supervening upon a physical cosmos, that would be another version of reality. Let's call that reality B. If there were a physical cosmos of material and forces acting upon the material, but no spiritual beyond, then that would be another version of reality. Let's call that reality C. These three visions of reality are mutually exclusive. Only one can actually describe reality. This might seem an obvious point, but it bears emphasis. We have the ability to hold alternative theories in the mind at once, precisely because we think in oppositions, but that doesn't mean both theories are right, or partially right, or that the truth is somewhere in between. When the subject under consideration is "reality," each of the competing theories is all-encompassing, necessarily excluding the others. In a binary way we can understand: one theory must be true, the others false. If A is true, B and C aren't. If B, not A and C. If C, not A and B.

There is much debate over the origin of physical things, in philosophy and theology and science. Theists argue the "something-from-nothing" problem of the atheist position. The argument goes something like this:

Theist: There has to be a God because the universe of physical things could not have created itself.
Atheist: We know from Darwin that biological things "create themselves," so to speak, in that they evolve without a creator, so there is no reason to think the same isn't true for all physical things.

Theist: That is not a disproof of God's causation. The nothing you say everything came from cannot produce a something.

Atheist: You don't understand quantum mechanics.

Theist: Nor do you, if you think it answers those problems.

Atheist: Quantum mechanics suggests indeterminism, so it's possible.

Theist: Even if quantum mechanics applied on the scale of an incipient universe, it wouldn't mean something came from nothing. It would only mean something came from something else.

Atheist: Nothingness is something else.

Theist: You don't understand the concept of Nothing.

Atheist: You don't understand the problem of closed-mindedness.[1]

The problem in this kind of back-and-forth is a failure of agreement on terms, possibly unwittingly. It's not easy to mentally conceive the reality A, of true Nothing. We're used to thinking of nothing as being the absence of particular somethings. If you look for your coat in the closet but the closet is empty, you might say "there's nothing there," but of course something is there. We think of the atmosphere as being nothing, but of course it contains nitrogen and oxygen, without which we'd be dead in minutes. Outer space seems like a lot of nothingness, but it is full of particles, electromagnetic radiation, magnetic fields, neutrinos, cosmic rays, dark matter, physical forces, and so on.

It is of crucial importance to grasp the concept of true nothingness, what is called here capital-N Nothing. If there is a God, then he was there in a non-physical realm as the agency for creation of the physical universe. If there is not a God, and there was Nothing, then there would have to have been a spontaneous transition from that Nothing reality (A) to a physical-only reality (C). That is impossible. Something can come from something else, but something can't come from Nothing. Even if it were a mere phase transition of some sort, there would have to be some precipitating agency or event; some cause, but Nothing excludes that possibility because the causative agency would be a something. This A to C transition would be impossible because it would involve replacement of one reality (the Nothing reality, A) with a completely different,

---

1 This is a nice version. It sometimes sounds like this: Creationism is frothing with risible fallacies. Creationists are dolts. They make zombie arguments. Creationists or their arguments are unthinking and mindless, tired and drooling, relentlessly shuffling along, impervious to reason, intelligence or debate, and desperately ugly. This is how Adam Rutherford describes skeptics of Darwinian evolution. Rutherford, Adam, *A Brief History of Everyone Who Ever Lived*, The Experiment, 2016. "Closed-mindedness," as in this imagined exchange, might really only mean a desire not to remove valid dualistic oppositions.

irreconcilable, mutually exclusive reality (the physical-only reality, C) with no intervening agency or external force whatsoever because that's what Nothing means. This cannot be merely an unexplained phenomenon we'll figure out through science, someday. It is a philosophical category mistake having nothing to do with science.

What category? The categories are formed by dualisms: Nothing and something; Nothing and the barely-there something we mistake for Nothing; this concept of reality and not those; and of course, God and creation. We might think of Nothing as the ultimate oppositional antithesis of God, especially if we grasp the nature of God in the philosophy of physical causation as the ultimate, purely actualized, uncaused-cause.

In truth, the universe could not have come from Nothing. It might have been preceded by no physical thing, but that is not Nothing. God was there. In fact, God was necessarily there, even if he is perceived as merely a philosophical ontological necessity. Reality B is the one that actually exists: physical stuff and a spiritual realm. There had to be a causative agent of some kind to make the reality substitution of the stuff-filled universe we know, from the nothingness before the Big Bang.

Confusion over Nothingness is more common than you might think. Smart people sometimes stumble because they don't recognize the dualism of Nothing and something. Victor Stenger, a physicist, seems to wade into this problem with eyes open, but still manages to discard absolute Nothingness because it doesn't serve his argument against God. He asks:

> How do we define "nothing?" What are its properties? If it has properties, doesn't that make it something?[2]

The question might suggest he's on the right track, but no. He confuses "nothing" with "something" by first confusing Nothingness with mere simplicity. The dualism of simplicity and complexity only applies to somethings, however. They have no place in Nothing. For Stenger, the simple something he imagines can be unstable: "It would likely undergo a spontaneous phase transition to something more complicated, like a universe containing matter."[3] The problem is that only somethings exist in phases. Something can go through a phase transition and be something else, as when water freezes, or hydrogen and oxygen com-

2 Stenger, Victor, *God—The Failed Hypothesis*, Amherst, NY: Prometheus Books, 2007, p. 132.
3 Ibid., p. 133.

bine to form water. Nothingness is not a "phase" of anything. Only a something can transition, spontaneously or otherwise. Stenger really only abandons the very concept of Nothing, by mentally collapsing the something/nothing dualism.

Physicist Lawrence Krauss wrote a book in which he set out to solve the something-from-nothing problem, called *A Universe from Nothing/Why There Is Something Rather Than Nothing*.[4] As with Stenger's, Krauss's book turned out to be only a speculation about how something might have come from something else.[5] His "nothing" wasn't really Nothing:

> [S]urely "nothing" is every bit as physical as "something," especially if it is to be defined as the "absence of something." It then behooves us to understand precisely the physical nature of both these quantities.[6]

This makes no sense at all. He might as well have said "non-existing things are every bit as existing as existing things." Krauss's[7] and Stenger's[8] militant atheism may have overridden their reasoning faculties necessary to preserving the something/nothing dualism. Their arguments for atheism require dumbing down ideas, concepts, and words,[9] by attempting to eradicate ineradicable dualisms.

Despite all that, Krauss's explanation is inadvertently helpful to understanding how our own reasoning can become clouded when we try to understand absolute Nothing. Krauss equated nothingness with "absence of something." Absence and non-existence are not the same, but we might nonetheless internally conflate them. Absolute Nothing is not mere absence of something, because if we think in terms of absence, we think in terms of the something(s) not present. This matters especially in the context of internal and subjective consciousness and cognition. An "absence," in my thinking, suggests emptiness of the thing I consider not present. The state of absence in the abstract is mentally a something, therefore, rather than true Nothingness. The absence or emptiness or

4 Krauss, Lawrence, *A Universe from Nothing*, New York: Altria, 2013.

5 See Albert, David, "On the Origin of Everything," *New York Times,* March 23, 2012.

6 Krauss, Lawrence, *A Universe from Nothing*, New York: Altria, 2013 preface p. xxiv.

7 Krauss, Lawrence, "All Scientists Should be Militant Atheists," *The New Yorker*, Sept. 8, 2015.

8 Stenger, Victor, *God—The Failed Hypothesis*, Amherst, NY: Prometheus Books, 2007 2007.

9 See Feser, Edward, "Scientists Should Tell Lawrence Krauss to Shut Up Already," *Public Discourse* (Witherspoon Institute) September 28, 2015.

incompleteness or negation easily elides to a vague somethingness with unrecognized or invisible or unacknowledged form and content. It is an internal dissonance that is left from unsuccessfully attempting to collapse an oppositional dualism.

We are quite capable of holding in the mind such a negation while continuing to conceive the dualism we attempted to collapse. It's as if the position vacated by the negation were reserved, in a manner of speaking. If you have a reserved parking space but there is no car in it at present, it's occupied by "nothing" though the empty space remains a something in your mind. A potentiality for a particular purpose, at a minimum. An empty space in which your car could be parked. The space is therefore not true Nothing. We think of absence as if it were the negation of presence, but then conceive the negation of presence as something rather than Nothing. The negation—of a thing or a concept or God—does not yield Nothing, in our imagination, but a vacancy that can be filled. In this way, we arrive at the nothing-as-such, which we regard as Nothing though it is a something existing as a vague cloud or shadow in the mind.

This constitutes confusion of dualisms, in which we drift from the dualism of existence and non-existence to that of presence and absence. Existence and presence are a dualism of dualisms. Absence is not the same as entire non-existence, because the thought conceives a something (which is absent) rather than Nothing, which precludes mere absence. We come to believe in nothing-as-such when we remove something and fail to see that the negation does not work a Nothing.

The nothing-as-such is a subjective psychological absence or void we may allow to be embedded in our thinking. We create and employ it in order to sustain an illusion of freedom in personal autonomy. The purpose is to try to erase barriers that confine. What we perceive as barriers include necessary choices to be made among oppositions. They are the constraining structures that must be engaged, to live a successful life, but engaging those structures requires effort, care, and some unavoidable anxiety. Any success in life is going to require affirmatively engaging the innumerable choices before us, and navigating well the results, rather than wishing away the constraints oppositional this-not-that structures impose.

Paradoxically, having no choice in some instances seems like more complete freedom. One feels "free" in doing nothing if there are no oppositional this-not-that decisions to make at every turn. The freedom you feel if you vacation at the beach is largely the result of unstructured

time. Choice-making can be overwhelming.[10] Pervasive oppositional choices are the framework of a life constrained by having to choose
among personal guiding principles and moral choices and calculated
risks. If you were born a serf in feudal Europe or a slave in early America, your constraints would be severe and your choices concomitantly
circumscribed. This is not a preferred state of affairs for anyone, because
we want freedom, but freedom means more choices, and choices do not
necessarily correlate to happiness. In our more complicated world, we
can choose to abort a child in order to have freedom, by pushing into
the mental background dualistic realities about existence/non-exis-
tence, and presence/absence. By mentally referring to this vague nothing-as-such buzz, we can imagine away freedom-inhibiting oppositions,
such as choices which hinge on moral value, or personal rather than collective responsibility. The nothing-as-such is a psychological disposition
enabling us to hold more than one point of view at once, even if they are
in conflict in the reality formed by oppositional ideas. An absence rather
than a presence seems to defy the oppositional barriers or limitations
that would otherwise obtain. We adopt this levelling mental construct
to avoid what we may come to regard as a tyranny of oppositions. Of
course, it's not real. The oppositions in reality remain. But the nothing-
as-such, existing more as a buzz in the mind, we might say, rather than
an identifiable thing with texture and shape, is an individual psychological means of avoiding the oppositions, because we feel them to amount
to limitations which might impinge on personal autonomy.

David Bentley Hart identifies this tendency in the modern outlook.
He writes: "To be entirely modern (which very few of us are) is to believe in nothing."[11] While people do believe in this or that thing or idea,
they have a radical, underlying faith in "the nothing," or "nothingness as
such." It is rooted in a desire for freedom, but results in nihilism:

> Modernity's highest ideal—its special understanding of personal au-
> tonomy—requires us to place our trust in an original absence under-
> lying all of reality, a fertile void in which all things are possible, from
> which arises no impediment to our wills, and before which we may
> consequently choose to make of ourselves what we choose. We trust,
> that is to say, that there is no substantial criterion by which to judge

---

10   To the point they do not make you any happier; quite the opposite. In connection
with consumer choices, consider Schwartz, Barry, *The Paradox of Choice*, Harper Perennial, 2004.

11   Hart, David Bentley, *Atheist Delusions/The Christian Revolution and Its Fashionable
Enemies*, Yale University Press, 2009.

our choices that stands higher than the unquestioned good free choice itself, and that therefore all judgment, divine no less than human, is in some sense an infringement upon our freedom. This is our primal ideology. In the most unadorned terms possible, the ethos of modernity is—to be perfectly precise—nihilism.[12]

The unspecified "nothing" we adopt when we reject God is not really nothing. It is a kind of nothing-as-such, an unspecified collection of beliefs normative in the culture. No one rejects Christianity and thereby wipes their belief slate entirely clean. And yet, people seldom reject Christianity to affirmatively embrace a competing belief system. Instead they remain engaged by the negation, with the beliefs they've repudiated, so they're not fully conscious of the metaphysics that occupy the place they think of as "nothing." This is part of that nothing-as-such that occupies what is mistaken for void. It is a belief in something unidentified, unspecified, and vague, an absence that seems to be freeing, a belief space we can move into and inhabit without commitment. It might be thought of as a kind of ultimate freedom, because it is thought of as "nothing." That nothing-as-such does not constrain us or make demands upon us. It doesn't even require that we grapple with what that something-we-call-nothing really is: an open-ended desire for unquestioned freedom in all things, as if it were possible to live without any constraint whatsoever. This is a relationship with the idea of nothing as if it were a vacuum in the mental space of somethingness. We don't want to grant that it occupies some mental space, as a something we only call nothing, because doing so would cancel the magic. We would feel compelled to give that feeling a name, and the frame on which we've staged our illusory freedom would collapse.

We want maximal freedom and consider any constraints on personal autonomy to be impairment of freedom. But constraint is not a genuine opposition to freedom. Constraints are necessary to build anything, including physical things. Constraints are also necessary to build a hierarchy of ideas, ideals, values, principles, including the abstract reasoning necessary to perceive the real God. Imagine you set out to lay a sidewalk along the street in front of your house. What's the first thing you do? You prepare the surface and then install forms to mold the concrete, perhaps into squares. Then when it's poured, you trowel the surface smooth. When dry, you remove the form. Then you have a level and aesthetic sidewalk instead of blobs of concrete to trip over.

---

12 Ibid., p. 21.

The forms and the trowel are constraints on the concrete, necessary to construct a useful sidewalk instead of a mess. In the same way, we use structural forms in all manner of physical improvement. Scaffolding, fasteners, cutters, equipment to isolate or separate; in fact, everything we do to improve our living or working environment results from application of constraints to materials in the environment.

The same is true for ideas. We have freedom to think and to develop ideas and concepts for every purpose under the sun, but it is of little value if it is unguided by education, by acquired principle, by understanding missteps and valid conclusions of others, and by grasping the practical purposes for which we engage in thought. These are constraints on our thinking, and yet are essential. You teach your child not to touch a hot stove, but that's a constraint on his freedom. You want him to learn from you, but any teaching effort is in fact a form of constraint on his freedom, including the inculcation of ideals and principles. Constraint is a necessary element to guiding our exercise of moral agency. We instruct ourselves and the next generation on moral principles to guide the proper exercise of moral agency. Those principles are a form of constraint, enabling us to make moral distinctions in behavior, and to distinguish good from evil.

These various constraints on freedom are preferably learned and internalized and thereby self-imposed, rather than imposed externally by an authoritarian State or opprobrious conformity-driven community, or the cultural coercion of political correctness. The constraints on maximal freedom exist to build and serve an elaborate hierarchy of principles, values, and ideals, on which civilization is based. That civilization in turn symbiotically provides an architecture of constraint for the individual, humanizing him and opening the door to a broad vista of possibility in moral and intellectual reasoning, and to thriving practically in life. In this way, constraints serve a larger and more expansive kind of freedom. It is a mistake to balk at any kind of containment of maximal moment-to-moment freedom. It is a mistake to reject all authority by which constraints erected in love are imposed.

And yet we do. There is an ongoing push and pull in societies between, on the one hand, destruction of freedom-inhibiting forms, and on the other hand, overbearing construction of them. The right balance requires the solvent of love, which is why families are better builders of humans than the State or cultural collective or village ever could be. A child obeys his mother if he trusts her constraints are for his good. A man accepts the authority of the State if he trusts its constraints are rightly principled. A person embraces the teachings of God's prophets if he grasps the love by which God's mercy overrides his justice.

The push-back against forms of constraint on maximal personal freedom can take the form of this nothing-as-such or buzz of negation by which we overthrow objective truth and morality, finding them to instead be self-manufactured, or collectively manufactured and coercively imposed, and time-sensitive rather than eternal, changeable rather than unchanging. Once we depart from truth understood as that which corresponds to the way the world is, we also depart from the trans-historical nature of truth. What is regarded as "truth" is derived only from the power structure and the interests which inform it, as do our conceptions of right and wrong. Thus, goodness and truth have no independent authority, but are contextual to time and culture. Clearly, this view excludes eternality of truth and of morality. Nothing can be true nor false at all times and all places; nothing can be right and wrong in every context. Moral relativism coincides with this slippery redefinition of "truth." Foundational principles are removed to allow for more imagined freedom. Truth retains the meaning necessary as a baseline orientation for all our mental efforts, by which we can make sense to each other, but is otherwise open to negotiation, which means disputation. Morality likewise continues to be conceived as common to all, but at the same time, open to ongoing evolution in the culture. Inconsistently, truth and goodness become placeholder words for shifting concepts, like using "x" in basic algebra. This misuse or reinvention of words, and the concepts they represent, can occur also with the word and the concept "nothing," which we then employ as a stand-in to buffer the absoluteness which should attach to true Nothing. Freedom is not absolute, but we want it to be, so we embrace a buzz of nothing-as-such negative energy in place of the absolute and therefore constraining aspect of truth and right and wrong. This is an emotional negation resulting when our instinct for freedom overcomes our apprehension of absolutes, when we attempt to transcend inevitable constraints on our existence by buffering the self with the buzz of emotional negation.

The erosion of idealism and of a coherent concept of truth corresponds to the nothing-as-such residing in our muddled postmodern psychology. It can happen like this. As we grow, we acquire awareness of our separateness from those who love and care for us in infancy. A sense of estrangement from others follows. As we grow into adulthood, we experience an increasing awareness of estrangement from the family, and likewise of our independent distinctness from society. That sense of estrangement may induce a kind of repudiation, such as we feel most keenly in the angst of adolescence. This often takes the form of teenage rebellion, in which the adolescent is tortured by that sense of alienation and feels he must finish the job, so to speak, sundering the family ties that formerly bound him in bonds of love but also restraint. We naturally hope the rift is not permanent, but it could be. The break might lead to a lifelong posture of negation with respect to authority, including the authority implicitly asserted in the understanding that truth and morality are absolute, and extant in the world rather than formed subjectively by us.

Rejection of values, customs, and norms feels necessary because they impede the sense of liberation. The resulting posture of negation represents, in Roger Scruton's words: "a refusal to accept any external authority and a rejection of every value, every custom, every norm which impedes the 'liberation' of the self."[13] As with individual adolescent angst, so with the movement within society more generally, toward the false sense of liberation:

> This arrest of the soul in the posture of negation is worthy of study, since it is at the root of much that passes for philosophy in a modern university: from Marxism to deconstruction, the modernist philosopher has occupied himself with proof that there is no authority, no source of law, no value and no meaning in the culture and institutions that we have inherited, and that the sole purpose of thought is to clear the way for 'liberation.'[14]

This "arrest of the soul in the posture of negation" should be understood by us, because a society infected with this buzz of negation does not merely grow out of it and put aside childish things, like an individual might. Instead it burns, pillages, and destroys, as we have seen in the awful summer of 2020, until the earth is scraped clean of those vestiges of civilization that were so long in the building. Nothing is to survive, in the new dispensation, including most especially the Christian metanarrative. This is nothing short of individual and collective nihilism. Martin Gurri commented this way, on the riots of 2020:

> The protests I have studied have had speed and agility but little depth.

---

13 Scruton, Roger, *Modern Philosophy/An Introduction and Survey*, New York: Penguin, 1994, p. 460.
14 Ibid.

The same slogans appear around the world: "I can't breathe," "Silence is violence," "Black Lives Matter." Beyond the slogans, we hear the same calls for generalities like "racial equity" or "social justice." Beyond that, there's nothing—no agreed-upon proposals to achieve these ideals, no organization, no leadership, no coherent ideology. Any hint of a positive program would likely shatter the movement into its component war-bands, so revolt has come to mean an exercise in pure negation, in the repudiation of the status quo without an alternative in sight. At this point, the question of nihilism becomes impossible to avoid.[15]

As always in the history of mankind, we want freedom, and that desire precedes much of our substantive understanding of reality. That is to say, we hold that desire first, and engage reality over the medium of that desire for freedom. If we hold in our minds a buzz of something-called-nothing which seems to give freedom, we may hold that notion ahead of strict logic about what nothingness really is. We may feel, for example, that moral constraints of yesteryear ought to be replaced with "nothing," because we desire freedom, skipping right past the fact that we have merely chosen another moral construct. We may overlook that we've landed at a faux-nothingness with regard to morality.

If there can be a nothing-as-such, then it feels like there can be a blank space left, when religion is removed. When people say they're atheists, they tend to think it means only that they haven't adopted any of the religions known to them. They believe in the absence of something, they would say. They believe in "nothing." That's obviously false, however. If someone believes that material reality is all there is, that is just as fundamental a belief about reality as the belief that something like God exists behind and through the material reality we perceive.

Though this conceptualizing of nothing-as-such has its roots in a desire for freedom, it means also that we fail to see true Nothing, and therefore fail to see the metaphysical concept actively in competition with both theism and materialist atheism. True Nothingness is a metaphysical concept because it is accessible only to our imaginations. It must be "imaged" in the mind, because the mind is connected to the body in space-time. Nothingness is imperceptible from the position of life in the body because life in the body is something. Nothingness is in that respect like spiritual reality, what the Bible refers to as the "unseen,"

15 Gurri, Martin, "Everything Explained," *City Journal*, Summer 2020, see https://www.city-journal.org/2020-riots-protests.

because spiritual reality, like true Nothingness, is beyond the physical platform from which we do the perceiving. A consequence of the inability to conceptualize true Nothingness is that it prevents us from grasping the impossibility of shifting from true Nothing to physical existence without the intervening agency of a Being outside both.

Another consequence of confusing nothing-as-such with true Nothingness is that we fail to see that there is actually content to the nothing-as-such. It's not a nothing. Because it's not a nothing, it's a something. We might think of it as a chamber of absences within physical reality, which like a vacuum draws into itself and collapses dualist distinctions among the good and the true and the beautiful which should constitute the edifice of our lives. The distinctions are thus smudged between good and evil; truth and falsity; beauty and ugliness. Thus this something-as-nothing, which we mistake for freedom, tears down instead of building up.

CHAPTER TWENTY

God and Creation

A SIGNIFICANT EXAMPLE of how this nothing-as-such confusion can work is in obscuring our ability to apprehend the existence of God. Because we live in a post-Christian society suffused with Christian suppositions about morality and spirituality, and a language similarly suffused with theist and specifically Christian concepts, we don't greet the God proposition as if for the first time. We're all quite familiar with the idea of a Creator God who is said to have made the heavens and earth, and who makes certain claims on mankind. Many reject the God proposition, obviously. That is typically a negation only, however, rather than an affirmative embrace of a reality in which only physical forces and things exist.

Why does this matter? Because it is not merely an alternative way of saying the same thing. That is, saying (perhaps only to oneself) there is no God is different than saying what is true about all of reality. The first is a negation of one assertion about reality—that it is God-created. The second is an explanation of reality unto itself. The negation is how atheist belief is usually expressed: a-theist, rather than materialist or naturalist or physicalist. It is stated in terms of what it isn't, rather than what it is, as in: "I'm not religious" or "I don't believe in God." We invite self-confusion when we say what we are not and what we do not believe, rather than what we are, and what we do believe. People do this anyway because they mistakenly approach the God proposition as if it were a proposed reality add-on, instead of an entirely distinct understanding of the nature of reality.

The nothing-as-such is at the heart of negatively-stated beliefs, as when an atheist insists his is a non-belief only, rather than a coherent

189

set of beliefs unto itself with all the usual oppositional limitations that entails. This belief in nothing-as-such, or the something-called-nothing, is sometimes affirmatively argued by those who stridently reject Christianity. The nothing-as-such that is really something is adopted as the basis for belief in "nothing." It is cast as if it were no belief at all. The late Christopher Hitchens argued, for example, that "Our [atheists'] belief is not a belief."[1] A.C. Grayling presents his atheism as a mere "privative thesis," meaning essentially the same thing: absence of affirmative belief in God, rather than an affirmative belief unto itself.[2]

People who say this sort of thing seem to mean atheism is belief in nothing, while theism is belief in something. But obviously an atheist holds beliefs about reality. He just doesn't say what they are, perhaps not even to himself. We're left to assume it's the physical reality we all know, but with God subtracted. The problem is you can't just subtract God and have a coherent explanation of reality remaining. Innumerable assumptions requiring transcendence remain. Transcendent truth continues to do the heavy lifting of explaining the evidence before us, even as we adopt a posture of negation with respect to it. How can we live with the dissonance of assuming transcendence while denying transcendence? One way is by calling the new belief a non-belief, or a "privative thesis." In this way, the actual materialist version of reality goes unexamined and unexplained.

Eventually the concept of transcendence leaches out of the language we use, to the effect of dumbing us down further. Formerly religious words take on non-religious meaning, and words necessary to navigating a pluralistic society are used to squeeze out the richness and variety of individualism into a collective monism of reductionist materialism and its accompanying despair, nihilism, and totalitarianism. "Faith," for example, used to mean confidence in spiritual truth. Now it means believing without evidence. "Love" used to mean acting on God's demonstration of love for us. Now it means emotionally affecting. "Tolerance" used to mean respecting another despite difference in belief. Now it means sameness of beliefs. "Spiritual" referred to the reality running through and beyond the physical world. Now it means contemplative. "Redemption" meant reconciliation to God despite sin. Now it means finding one's worth in self. "Soul" meant the eternal element of self. Now it means groovy. "Transcendent" pertained to spiritual reality beyond

---

1 E.g., Hitchens, Christopher, *God is Not Great/How Religion Poisons Everything*, Atlantic Books, 2009, republished 2017.

2 Grayling, A.C., *The God Argument*, New York: Bloomsbury, 2013, p. 132 et. seq.

the natural world. Now it refers to something really special. With these words thus drained of their potency to express elements of spiritual reality, we're left with no words for transcendent spiritual reality. With no words for them, the concepts themselves become more elusive. The ideals collapse.

Let's think further on this notion of nothing-as-such. We wake up and look around and take in the sights, sounds, smells, tastes, and feel of the world around us. We take in credible information about other places and times. We consciously and continuously draw conclusions from all this. We conclude that material things occupying space and time are real. We don't just deny the reality of our sense impressions. We don't say we're "agnostic" about material reality. And so we don't say there's "nothing."

And there is more "something" than what presents to our sense impressions, isn't there? We are able to consider, for example, that all those sense impressions come to us over the medium of our consciousness. In the form of thinking, certainly, but also this kind of something includes our being aware that we're thinking, and aware that other people are similarly self-aware. It is bringing intentionality and order to the bombardment of sensory impressions. This is a recognition of the utterly subjective and irreducible nature of individual experience, and of the internality and privacy of our unuttered thoughts. Awareness of the inviolable self. That is beyond the material reality that presents to our senses, but it, too, is undoubtedly real. It's something.

Likewise, the quandary we entertain of how there could ever be anything material in the first place. Not merely the current explanation of how mankind might have originated; not merely the current theory of how living things came from pre-biotic matter; but how could something have arisen from nothing? From *nothing*? And if there was always something, how could there always have been a something? Where did it come from? We're inured to the experience of sense impressions, but if we pause and consider the newness of each sense impression, and the astonishing fact of existence of material things, how do we lay that aside and carry on with a conviction that things just are? Likewise, the ideals that we prize most in the abundance of our life experience: beauty, wisdom, justice, compassion, fairness, and the surprising observation of their presence in us and in others—are ideals of everyone around us, too. Instead of seeing them collapsed, we should be witnessing the ideals built up by our appreciation of the transcendent.

Imagine two mutually exclusive ideas, A and Z. Assume the law of

192 ⌘ *Dangerous God*

non-contradiction, as is necessary in binary reality: A is not Z, Z is not A, and together A and Z comprise the only two possibilities concerning the subject matter. If we disbelieve A, that means we must believe Z. Muddled thinking might cause us to focus on our non-belief in A, however, rather than affirmative belief concerning Z. This is a roundabout way to try to collapse an inconvenient binary. We might describe our rejection of A as being only non-belief in A, rather than affirmative belief in Z. We might come to think of non-belief in A as being belief in "nothing," rather than belief in Z. We would then be prey to confusing that "nothing" with neutrality on the question of which is true as between A and Z. That is not neutrality, however. That is just adoption of Z without acknowledging it.

Now suppose A stands for theism, and Z stands for materialism. Materialism means that reality is comprised entirely of that which is bounded by space and time; there is nothing beyond the physical. Theism means there is material but also an immaterial, supernatural reality, a reality beyond the physical. By definition, and by the law of non-contradiction, theism and materialism cannot both be true. They are each defined in opposition to the other. They are mutually exclusive. Theism and materialism also comprise all of the possibilities on the subject matter. Either there is a reality transcending the physical which includes the physical, or the physical is all there is. All of reality = A, or all of reality = Z.

Muddled thinking results from adopting a spurious nothing-as-such outlook to attempt to collapse oppositional boundaries, so that we may focus on our non-belief in one point of view rather than the resulting affirmative belief in its opposite. That is the result of mentally erasing the distinction between them, consigning both parts of the dualism to the illusory black box of nothing-as-such. This is how one can come to think of his view as only non-belief in God, rather than affirmative belief in a physical-only reality. In this way, we equate non-belief (as with non-belief in God) with belief in "nothing," rather than a God-less version of reality.

Another consequence of substituting a vague something for true nothing is that it handicaps our ability to understand just how the physical something-from-nothing problem is dispositive in favor of theism. If we understand that all the somethingness of the universe came from true nothing, we are better able to understand the dilemma. One metaphysical view, true nothingness, is suddenly replaced with a mutually-exclusive metaphysical view: matter as all of reality. And this supposedly happens with no outside agency to cause the shift. That is simply impossible—physically, mathematically, logically, philosophically. That impossibility is obscured, however, if we think of the "nothing" not as true nothing, but vaguely as a mysterious void, the way we might think of space. Perhaps in all that mystery there is a way matter could just pop into existence, we may think. But the moment we do that, we've imported something—a mysterious something, but something—into what is purportedly nothing. Moreover, if we label as "nothing" that which is something, then we have no word left for the concept-former-ly-known-as-nothing. Our ability to understand the dilemma of true Nothingness is thereby obscured from our own comprehension, and the impossibility of the something-from-nothing problem (without God) is left unexposed.

Materialists typically attack the theist's claims, and theists under-take to defend them. It's seldom the other way around. Theists seldom attack the incoherency of the materialist point of view. Why is that? One reason is this habit of stating the materialist position in the negative, as with "a-theism." Materialists say there is no God, and then set out to disprove him, rather than saying matter in motion comprises all of reality, and then set out to prove that. This would be a very good strat-egy, if it were adopted intentionally rather than being taken up in this manner through the accidents of history. With this technique, one can criticize the claims of Christianity without having to explain the facts of existence and consciousness and revelation and so on. Added to this, one can seize upon the point of agreement—the fact of natural processes within the physical cosmos—to attempt to make miraculous deviations from them seem ridiculous. Though it's a good strategy for advocacy of the atheist position, it is bad strategy for the pursuit of truth, because once Christianity is debunked, we're still left without explanation for al-most everything we know. How did physical things come into existence? How can human consciousness, the interval over which we "know" any-thing at all, be explained in purely material terms? How do we account for miracles, if scriptural revelation be true, and how can we account for scriptural revelation, if what it relates is false? In all of this questioning, why do we assume there is a truth, and that it is obtainable by us? Why do we attach significance to beauty, and virtue? How do we manage from thought to thought by physical process only, devoid of pre-existing logos, or semantic content?

Christianity on the merits of its doctrines alone, in isolation, dumbs us down by leaving unaddressed, much less answered, the questions everyone has. The question is not whether Christianity is true, yes or no. The question is what explains the reality we know? And the first thing that must happen is to properly understand what "reality" even means. If we suppose it is the physical cosmos, only, then we've assumed the answer before beginning the inquiry. Whether the physical cosmos is all there is, is the very thing we're trying to figure out. It's not the starting point on the path to shoot down Christianity. Putting Christianity in the dock without undertaking to explain reality without it amounts to finding Christianity false by assuming it to be false. It is utter nonsense but is the method employed in countless atheist polemics of recent years.

This approach also has the effect of looking to science as the only way of knowing anything. Some go so far as to justify their agnosticism on the grounds that science has not proven there is a God.[3] This is puzzling because science is only about physical creation. Science explicitly assumes naturalism, for purposes of prosecuting the empiricist scientific project. It does not speak to whether the assumption is right. It can't say anything about whether there is something beyond empirical experience.

This is a throw-back to the philosophy of positivism, or "logical positivism." Thus, Alfred Jules Ayer wrote in 1936:

> We shall maintain that no statement which refers to a "reality" transcending the limits of all possible sense experience can possibly have literal significance; from which it must follow that the labours of those who have striven to describe such reality have all been devoted to the production of nonsense.[4]

So you're producing nonsense if you're engaged in theology, ethics, aesthetics, or metaphysics. Positivism employed the empirical verification principle of science, but applied it to all of reality. It meant reality can only consist in what is measurable to our sense impressions. But this means truncating immaterial reality from consideration *a priori*. This philosophical movement, positivism, had its moment in the sun in the first half of the twentieth century. It reinforced a materialist view of reality, of course, but also contributed to the divorce underway between

---

3   Here's an example. In a book review for *The Wall Street Journal* on October 26, 2019, John Horgan wrote: "I am not a multiverse denier, any more than I am a God denier. Science cannot resolve the existence of either, making agnosticism the only sensible position."

4   Ayer, Alfred Jules, *Language, Truth, and Logic*, Dover, 1952, first published in 1936, first chapter, first paragraph.

philosophy and theology. Positivism persists today implicitly in the polemical works of the so-called New Atheists, but in philosophy more broadly is largely discredited.

We can imagine a conversation or a formal debate that proceeds with the God proposition on trial, so to speak, but that's not the only way this tactic is employed. It's actually implicit in the very structure of our society. We're told that for the sake of politics or politeness, we're to stay away from matters of religion. Public matters should be "neutral," though that turns out to mean conducive to materialism and hostile to religion. Religion should be "private," though that turns out to mean that materialism exclusively is to be the common currency; the *lingua franca*, the spirit of the age.

This substituting of the concept and of the word "nothing" allows us to think that we can reject Christianity (or any other belief system) and replace it with nothing, when in fact we're not replacing it with nothing, but rather with something else. Belief in a vague "nothing-as-such" elides to a false subjective neutrality. It encourages us to focus on the thing we don't believe, instead of grasping what we accept uncritically in its place. It can blind us to the materialist paradigm we then unthinkingly embrace, rendering us unable to see it for what it is, nor to subject it to the same scrutiny as the Christianity we rejected.

A consequence of this self-deception is that the merits of the competing versions of reality are not weighed side-by-side. We become lulled into deciding the existence of God is implausible, without considering the plausibility of reality imagined as God-less. One can reject God without considering the holes that result in the map of the physical reality we experience. If there is no God, then how does anything exist? How do we resolve the otherwise unresolvable dualisms of mind and body, of good and evil? How is human consciousness to be explained? How do we make sense of the ubiquitous provision of meaning in DNA, in mathematical relationships, in the oppositional dualisms by which we think rationally? This is not to say one must answer these questions before rejecting God, necessarily. There will be unanswered questions whichever way we turn. But perhaps the combination of known, unknown, and unknowable renders the God-infused reality more plausible than the God-less reality, if they're both given full consideration.

Negation prevents us from seeing this. One can say "I'm not very religious" or call oneself agnostic as a way of avoiding the problem altogether. It's a rather lame way of affirming one's commitment to following the default drift of society. It makes possible the adoption of a vague sense of neutrality on the God question, not recognizing that the absence is really a presence. The passivity of not affirming any set of beliefs concerning the God proposition really means God is unimportant, which means reality is what we see less the God we don't, which means the God-less reality is operative. One decides by not deciding. But this may not be apparent because of the habit of negation. The habit of negation results from mentally erasing existing oppositional dualisms to erect a nothing-as-such, which feels a little bit like freedom, but is freedom of an illusory sort.

The false neutrality we can drift into by this errant habit of thought amounts to erasure of God by self-deception. Why would we do this? Because God is in opposition to us in a very real sense we'd rather not think about. He judges us. Yes, he loves us; he provides for us; he has a plan for us; and all these things are true. But he judges us. If we can have his provision of material blessings and rational competence and the richness that inheres in the oppositions of good and evil, love and hate, virtue and debasement, and so on, but not God himself, maybe that's better, we may feel. Because of this, an attractive thought might be that we can be rid of him just by denying him, without really thinking through how to disentangle him from reality. Even in our imagination, he is ineluctably intertwined with the physical reality we know. But not if he simply doesn't exist. So if the thought of God is just too oppressive, there's little incentive to work this out intellectually, in the usual way we make sense of things. Rejecting God is largely a matter of emotional disposition, for most who reject him.

God does not empower us to simply remove him from reality, however. He's still there, whether we like it or not. He judges us as part of this fundamental opposition of God and his creation. The Christian story of Jesus is so important because it is the other shoe to drop, so to speak. God doesn't simply create us, judge us, and that's it. He doesn't create a reality in which we die and then he tallies up the merits and demerits. He (alone) is able to reconcile the oppositions of justice and mercy, and Jesus is the mercy side of that dualism. God is going nowhere. He ceases to exist only in our imagination. The lion is loose. We are reconciled to him only on his terms, and his terms are redemption in Christ.

CHAPTER TWENTY-ONE

Religious Liberty

T HIS TENDENCY to negation plays out in the culture, combined with other trends which have the effect of diminishing the hierarchy of ideals on which civilization is based. We are witnessing the deconstruction of ancient metanarratives which were formed by a logocentric understanding. This tendency to negation is exacerbated by confusing the political model of secular religious neutrality with an unattainable and illusory personal neutrality concerning metaphysical views. We want the public square to be secular, but that ends up meaning public discourse is cleansed antiseptically of any whiff of religion, with a result that is not neutral at all, but rather a specially-enforced adoption of materialism as the state religion. In the zeal to avoid establishing one religion at the expense of others, we adopt instead a metaphysical outlook that repudiates all religion. We're still free to worship as we please, in theory, but in reality the state establishes this hostile competitor. Culturally we default to that perspective, especially as the state expands into ever more formerly-private areas of life, bringing its religion-purging program with it.

The United States was founded on certain fundamental principles, including limited government and religious freedom. Limited government is in the very structure of the Constitution, but the principle is largely abandoned now. Religious freedom meant not sponsoring one religion at the expense of another, or interfering with private exercise of religion. The Constitution embodies these principles in the First Amendment:

Congress shall make no law respecting an establishment of religion, or prohibiting the free exercise thereof; or abridging the freedom of speech, or of the press; or the right of the people peaceably to assemble, and to petition the Government for a redress of grievances.

The idea behind the "free exercise" clause is that the exercise of religion is to be free from interference by the government. The idea behind the so-called "establishment" clause is that the government is not to establish a religion that is the official religion of the state, or to sponsor one religion at the expense of another. Though conventionally called the Establishment Clause, it is more accurately a "non-establishment" clause.

A significant body of case law interprets the proper application of these clauses in actual practice. That case law is, like the Constitution itself, the law of the land. In 1947, the United States Supreme Court established the theory of neutrality with respect to religious matters, in the case of *Everson v. Board of Education*. The court based its analysis on the presupposition that the state was to be "neutral in its relations with groups of religious believers and non-believers."[1] This might have made sense in a day when society seemed to be organized into conveniently identifiable religious camps, with atheism an outlier so remote that its significance to constitutional jurisprudence could be ignored.

In *Zorach v. Clauson*, the Supreme Court in 1952 acknowledged that Americans at the time were primarily a religious people, and that some accommodation to their spiritual needs by the government was necessary; that to do otherwise would show a "callous indifference to religious groups" and "That would be preferring those who believe in no religion over those who do believe . . . [W]e find no Constitutional requirement which makes it necessary for government to be hostile to religion . . ."[2] Although rare passages like these suggest that non-religion would come under the same scrutiny as religion, that has not proven to be the case. Instead, the Supreme Court seems to be looking for secularism-as-religion to be as obvious as Christianity or Judaism, for purposes of First Amendment analysis. The public-school prayer and Bible-reading cases included the Supreme Court's decisions in *Engel v. Vitale*[3] and *School District of Abington v. Schempp*,[4] in 1962 and 1963 respectively, in which the neutrality principle was embedded in the decree that laws passed by

---

1   330 U.S. 1 (1947), p. 18.

2   343 U.S. 306 (1952), p. 335.

3   370 U.S. 421 (1962).

4   374 U.S. 203 (1963).

legislatures must "neither advance nor inhibit religion."[5] At that time, vocal atheists were still such a minority that they had little political clout.

The Supreme Court adheres to the common-law principle of *stare decisis*—the following of precedent—but in times of rapid social change, slavish devotion to *stare decisis* may undermine another of the Court's purposes, which is to apply the Constitution to specific cases. It is sometimes said that the founders had no concept that one day atheism would become a prominent worldview, but is that really so? Weren't they under the immediate influence of many Enlightenment thinkers who thinly disguised their atheism in ostensible deism? Thinkers like Rousseau, Voltaire, David Hume, and Thomas Paine? Perhaps Benjamin Franklin, during the relevant years? Thomas Jefferson was said to have simply excised from his Bible inconvenient passages about supernatural reality.

And yet, when a renewed challenge to the domination of Christian theism came along in the twentieth century, justices instituted a principle of theoretical neutrality that could only have resulted in establishment of naturalism as the default metaphysical worldview for American jurisprudence. The school prayer decisions necessarily embodied the principle that elected officials were not to concern themselves with the religious or spiritual well-being of the citizenry. What they mean is that children are to attend state schools every working day without any acknowledgement of their own religious beliefs or those of their family. Children properly conclude that if religious beliefs had any real importance, they would not be scrubbed entirely from their every-day school experience. Journalist and author Peter Hitchens, writing about his similarly secular school environment in Britain, wrote of his own experience:

> Christianity was not implied in every action and statement of my teachers, whereas materialist, naturalistic faith was.[6]

And:

> The use of the majestic word 'laws' [of nature] curiously turned the mind away from speculation about whose laws they might conceivably

---

5 *Lemon v. Kurtzman*, 403 U.S. 602 (1971).

6 Hitchens, Peter, *The Rage Against God*, New York: Continuum International, 2010, p. 31. On the secularization of Britain more generally, see Gilbert, Alan D. *The Making of Post-Christian Britain/A History of the Secularization of Modern Society*, Longman, 1980.

be, or why they might have been made. Science, summed up as the belief that what could not be naturalistically or materialistically explained was not worth talking about, simply appropriated them.[7]

The U.S. Supreme Court reiterated the flawed neutrality analysis in 1971, in *Lemon v. Kurtzman*.[8] The decision assumes there is such a thing as a purely secular point of view that floats free of any conception of the existence or non-existence of the supernatural; of spiritual reality; of God; and of the movement of God in the affairs of men. The state is precluded from sponsoring any spiritual metaphysical view, but not from sponsoring a materialistic metaphysical view, so in effect it establishes materialism: the belief that there is no supernatural. While religious views on ultimate questions and on human nature are neither "advanced or inhibited," in effect their irreligious counterparts are. The default position had to be materialism, the one metaphysical view that does not overtly bear the "religion" label.

The *Lemon* test has served as the touchstone for Establishment Clause issues since 1971. It institutionalized religious neutrality as the paramount principle that was previously latent in Establishment Clause jurisprudence. The *Lemon* test was again applied in 1987 in *Edwards v. Aguillard*.[9] If the purpose of a state statute was to endorse religion, the high court held, then there was no need even to go to the remaining elements of the *Lemon* analysis. But how are we to decide what constitutes "endorsing" of religion? What it means in practice is endorsement of the primary metaphysical competitor to religion. The goal of neutrality in the law is elusive, because the default neutrality is simply another metaphysical position, materialism, which is now favored above all other metaphysics points of view, as a result of being falsely labeled neutral.

Alongside these decisions, there have been a few that seem to acknowledge that atheist or materialist beliefs are comprehensive beliefs about ultimate reality just like those of religion. In *Torcaso v. Watkins*,[10] the Supreme Court declared emphatically that government could not require a person "to profess a belief or *disbelief* in any religion" (emphasis added), quoting its earlier decisions, *McCollum v. Bd. of Educ.*,[11] and

---

7   Ibid., pp. 31-32.

8   403 U.S. 602 (1971).

9   482 U.S. 578 (1987).

10   367 U.S. 488 (1961).

11   333 U.S. 203 (1948).

Everson v. Bd. of Educ.[12] So it would seem that affirmative beliefs in any religion are off-limits to government regulation, but so also the absence thereof. The competing beliefs in *Torcaso* were God and atheism, but the court chose to counterpoise "belief in God" to "those religions founded on different beliefs." Then, by way of footnote, it gave examples: "Buddhism, Taoism, Ethical Culture, Secular Humanism and others."[13]

Secular humanism was, around the time of this decision in 1961, a phrase coming into use among Christians to describe, reasonably accurately, the burgeoning dominant worldview in American society. A short-lived tug-of-war ensued, and Christians lost. Their bid was to see secular humanism categorized in the same way as orthodox Christianity, for purposes of constitutional analysis. A few Christians at the time understood what was going on. The landscape of metaphysical views had been changing, and changing more drastically in the twentieth century, to the point that the polite fiction of America as a Christian nation no longer held sway, and this would be further reflected in constitutional analyses. Among Christians, this was not an effort to promote secular humanism and its underlying naturalism to equal status with Christianity in the hearts and minds of people. But it was a bid to do so for constitutional analysis, because thus far "secular humanism" was regarded as a neutral position of metaphysics, and by that subterfuge given preference in constitutional jurisprudence.

Non-belief was referenced in an Establishment Clause case in *Epperson v. Arkansas*[14] in 1968, in which the Supreme Court required the government to be "neutral in matters of religious theory, doctrine, and practice. It may not be hostile to any religion *or to the advocacy of no-religion*" (emphasis added). Although there are references to the Establishment Clause's application to atheists as well as theists in *Everson* (1947), *Zorach* (1952), *Torcaso* (1961), and *Epperson* (1968), there has not been a case in which the Establishment Clause was used to prohibit the government from sponsoring non-belief. To the contrary, non-belief has been effectively the default "neutral" position.

Vietnam-era conscientious objector cases provide some insight into judicial attitudes toward the claim of religious freedom when the "religion" is something other than traditional belief in God, or gods. In *United States v. Seeger*, the Supreme Court avoided distinguishing between

---

12   330 U.S. 1 (1947).
13   *Torcaso*, p. 495, n. 11.
14   393 U.S. 97 (1968).

traditional theistic believers and nontheistic believers, by formulating a test based on whether a person's belief was "sincere and meaningful" and whether, for that person, it occupied a place "parallel to that filled by the God of those admittedly qualifying for the exemption . . ."[15] Was this a way of extending conscientious objector status to belief systems other than that of Christian pacifists? Or was it a recognition of a constitutional principle already present, to the effect that non-religion has the same standing as religion? It's difficult to say. It is likely that the Justices in *Seeger* were bending to the *zeitgeist* of the times rather than trying to maintain strict fidelity to a baseline principle of the Constitution.

So what happened in later cases? Why do the courts not accept the principle of cases like *Torcaso* and recognize that materialism should not be given preferential treatment among the array of potential metaphysical beliefs? Simply put, it is a matter of convenience, because such a recognition would get in the way of the fiction that there is a neutral position we can all subscribe to in public education and public discourse. In this way, the courts leave materialism expressed as secular humanism as the presumptive equivalent to neutrality, so that it acquires the privileged place of being the default system of beliefs in the law.

The untenability of the neutrality principle as a matter of constitutional law has not gone unremarked by legal academics. Law Professor Stephen D. Smith, for example, has written on the subject in carefully reasoned tomes, including one with the unfortunate but accurate title *Foreordained Failure*.[16] But to be fair to the jurists, it's a difficult knot to untie. Widely disparate belief systems co-exist under our Constitution, and the government has become over time ever more intimately involved in affairs that were previously entirely private. As with people in their private musings, jurists think of religion as a presence and materialism as an absence. A negation of spiritual truth stands in for neutrality because it seems necessary that it do so, practically.

Usually when atheists try to justify their beliefs without reference to materialism or any other set of doctrines (other than, of course negatively, vis-à-vis theism), the result is a confused mess. Thus Phil Zuckerman, in his *Living the Secular Life*.[17] He believes "religion is definitely not the only avenue for people to live good, meaningful, or inspired lives." That's an interesting formulation. It's as if we first decide how to

---

15   380 U.S. 163 (1965), p. 176.

16   Smith, Steven D., *Foreordained Failure/The Quest for a Constitutional Principle of Religious Freedom*, Oxford University Press, 1995.

17   Zuckerman, Phil, *Living the Secular Life*, Penguin Books, 2014.

live good, meaningful lives, and then choose the reality necessary to get us there. This requires an elastic "truth." And why "inspired?" Other religious words are sprinkled here and there, too, words like "spiritual" and "transcendence." This borrowing of religious words is an effort to rake back meaning for life, after it's been given up. Religious concepts are borrowed to imbue to irreligion the depth, purpose, and nobility that religious concepts have. The starting point for Zuckerman's treatise on how to live as an atheist is his insistence that atheists are not without morality. In his view, the chief Christian objection to atheism is that atheists have no source of morality. It isn't. The chief Christian objection to atheism is that it is not true.

What Zuckerman and those who think like him don't see is that the problem of morality is not that atheists lack morals, but that they believe their morals are tethered only to their conscience, and as Zuckerman rather startlingly puts in print, that conscience is both unique to each person, and made up of the combination of influences upon that person's life. Every man is a law unto himself, but every man's law is developed from the *zeitgeist*. This is about as clear a postmodernist statement approving moral relativism as one can make.

CHAPTER TWENTY-TWO

Christian Unraveling

W E THINK WE'VE TAMED God. He was a bit too wild, so we domesticated him to make him manageable. He's the God of Niceness, now, and we imagine he subscribes to the platitudes we devise for ourselves to make life seem more safe and secure. He's quite malleable, too. We imagine he doesn't interfere with all our jostling for what we say he stands for. We don't like fighting with our neighbors, so can't we just all agree on a few basic things and then attach those things to the bulletin board of our social living? Be nice, number one, and don't offend. We're to be "tolerant," redefined to mean accepting of anything. We're to find no moral shame, except in failure to put away moral discernment about the world around us. God wants it this way, we tell ourselves. He functions only as a solvent for harmonious social living. Getting along with others is to be our first priority. We can't have God interfering with this project, like a wild lion disrupting our camp. We need him caged, so we can admire him or ignore him in safety. Then we can work on shaping him into our own image. He works for us; it's not the other way around.

What we're afraid of is the Absolute that is God. He created the physical cosmos from nothing, and that by itself is a statement not just about the origin of the physical surroundings we know, but of his undiluted omnipotence and pure actualization. What God overcame, in this act, was true nothingness, devoid of anything but himself. Not just seeming emptiness, like space, but true nothing, a metaphysical reality accessible to us only in the imagination. Even in the true nothingness of physical things, there was God, the agency by which all came into being. This describes the Absolute, not merely a thought experiment about the

204

beginning of things. There is God, and then there is creation: everything else that is not-God. This is a first and fundamental dualism, by which we begin to make sense of anything.

It has been well-documented that the actual beliefs among those in the pews are not orthodox Christian. Many, if not most, deviate from traditional creeds in large ways and small, notwithstanding what gets recited on Sunday morning.[1] Moreover, the prevalent deviations from orthodoxy are identifiable as coherent systems of belief unto themselves, and not fairly described as Christian.

Basic Christian orthodox belief can be reduced to these essentials: the true reality in history of Christ's incarnation, ministry, and resurrection; the trinity, the virgin birth, the forgiveness of sins, and the possibility of eternal life by identification with Christ in his death and resurrection. It includes a belief in the divine inspiration and authority of a particular set of sacred scriptures, the Old and New Testaments. It includes adherence to the moral vision encoded in the Ten Commandments and developed from it.

That one has to first pause and articulate basic Christian orthodoxy highlights one of the reasons for the development of personalized heresies. Churches now seldom even adhere to the idea that there is such a thing as orthodox doctrine, or, if they do, that it should be asserted by the church with the expectation that it be followed. We no longer live in an authority-driven environment, with the doctrines and traditions of the church constituting the authority. Instead, we live in an environment of self-sovereignty in which we evaluate discrete truthy propositions to accept or reject like we would apples at the fruit market. We take the church's role to be a vague kind of spiritual leadership, rather than one of prescribing orthodoxy and identifying heresy. For the individual in the pew this seems like license to adopt whatever set of beliefs he thinks reasonable, taking into account such doctrine as he understands, but also the priorities of the culture around him.

Except it's worse than that. Even in a church that actually presents orthodoxy, the individual process of reason we might expect to follow doesn't really happen. What people really do is take the teaching as a proposal and mix the proposed doctrinal points into a stew with emotion, expedience, and self-interest, and then stir that around until the resulting concoction is one they feel they can live with for the moment. We live in a thoroughly consumerist culture. We're indoctrinated into a

---

1 See, e.g., Douthat, Ross, *Bad Religion/How We Became a Nation of Heretics*, Free Press, 2012.

belief in self-sovereignty in our choices, even our selections of truth-formation, and our selection of truth tends to be based on criteria other than objective and absolute truth. We don't just feel we have freedom to decide what is true. We feel we have freedom to select also the criteria for what makes something true in the first place. That freedom derives from the illusory nothing-as-such attitude. Choice precedes truth, so the means of formation of truth is also picked from among choices on offer.

We are very attached to this perception of self-sovereignty, so much so that we don't see the whole game is rigged. We choose, but the "market" for our choices is prescribed for us, like slop is chosen for pigs. The tin crown we wear comes at the cost of objective truth. Because we are sovereign, truth itself is not. Truth is among our subjects, we feel, and it must bend to our will. Matters we call "true" must live more or less happily with the other matters we put in our "truth" shopping cart.

What has happened over time, say in the last three generations or so, is that the interaction between the churches and the churched has shifted to accommodate this reality. The realm of choices over which we regard ourselves sovereign includes not just doctrines, but presenters of them, and churches within which they are presented. Congregations shift constantly, as church leaders and congregants gravitate to more congenial offerings. Over time, a rough match develops between the house of worship, on the one hand, and the worshipers who find a home there, on the other. Just as individuals abandon capital-T truth in favor of whatever they pick up in the buffet line, so the buffet operator adapts to the shifting winds of his community in addition to his own shifting and sliding choice-making.

There are families of heresies that infect churches large and small, in America. They are metaphorically the demons not yet cast out, and they sometimes join with others until they are legion within a church. Being a mega-church or a celebrity pastor does not seem to operate as a corrective on blatant departure from authentic Christian belief. Perhaps just the opposite. It has become painfully obvious that many accommodationist theologians have steered churches under their influence away from the dangerous God to a safe neutered substitute inoffensive to secularist ears.[2] Such churches accommodate themselves to secularist ideology while holding back a thin historical veneer, including custom-

---

2 This occurs under many traceable influences, but consider for example the direction provided in Cox, Harvey, *The Secular City*, Princeton University Press, 2013 (first edition 1965).

ary rites and practices such as the repetition of creeds no one actually believes. This is typically referred to as liberalization of churches, but people are not "liberated" from anything but the potential opprobrium of their secularist betters. Quaint old notions like transcendence, virgin birth, bloody death, sacrifice, propitiation, and a just God who forgives through the death and Resurrection are all just analogies, or metaphors. What survives from the grand orchestra are only minor keys played out of tune: cheerfulness, niceness, a regard for the underdog, and other pagan-acceptable bromides for nice human interaction. This is usually accompanied by uncritical acceptance of secular collectivism, which means progressively less independence from the state, which will without hesitation take away religious liberty if the church doesn't continue to behave like the paper-trained puppy it has become.

Apart from this significant "liberalizing" trend, there are, at least in America, a surprisingly large number of wealth-and-success teachers and followers. So-called "prosperity theology" is interestingly rooted in go-get-'em American optimism, but is not recognizably orthodox Christian. Aside from being a departure from what the Bible actually teaches, this way of thinking is pernicious because it moves our attention from eternity to the here-and-now. This is a shift of focus alien to that of genuine Christian belief. Perhaps for that reason, the fundamental elements of identification with Christ in his death and Resurrection exist in the background as incidental ornamentation.

In the last few decades, several strains of beliefs have developed with a Christian reference, but which are more aptly described as God-within-us beliefs, borrowing rather too freely from Eastern monist conceptions of the character and nature of God. A common thread seems to be a slight or partial glimpse of spirituality, with greater spirituality dependent upon feeling rather than reason, and experience rather than propositional doctrine. The idea in these churches seems to be that God resides solely within the soul of man, and that sin and death and evil will ultimately be reconciled rather than defeated. The most convincing manifestation of this trend is what some have aptly dubbed "Moralistic Therapeutic Deism," a more realistic name for what many self-described Christians in America actually believe. It loosely and ambiguously holds there is a God-force necessary for creation, and a background myth that can evoke emotion, but is otherwise concerned only with ongoing self-care through pop psychology and morality rooted in societal consensus rather than ultimate Authority.

Extreme fideism, too, might be considered a heresy, because it is accurately described as "belief in belief," rather than belief in Christ. It is the assertion that "ya just gotta believe," not only failing to come up with any reasons why, but actively disavowing the need to do so. Certainly, revelation is a justification for faith, but it is not justification entirely exclusive of rational thought as well, as many Christians or ostensible Christians seem to believe. The "faith alone" doctrine—salvation based on Christ's work and not our own—is twisted to mean that reason is to have no part in the formation of faith in the first place. This results in a regrettable dumbing-down of Protestant theology and an atmosphere hostile to intellectual development of apologetics to adequately respond to atheist criticism.[3] The tendency of ostensible Christians to grasp tenets of Christianity (usually selectively) on the basis of anti-intellectual fideism creates an affirmative obstacle to faith. It is a substitution of belief in belief for belief in Christ. This is not lost on observers who subscribe to a God-less vision of reality.[4] Extreme fideists are not merely ignorant and hapless and a step removed from genuine faith. They are affirmatively anti-witnesses to Christ.

We might even find heresies around other sources of self-identity that are not in and of themselves harmful, such as loyalty to one's country or to communal cultural expectations, or to some other tribe. If you don't cringe at displays of patriotic fervor in church, you may have fallen partially victim to this way of thinking. We can be unreservedly enthusiastic about American founding ideals, for example, but it is a grave error to conflate that localized and temporary source of enthusiasm with our worship of almighty God, maker of heaven and earth.[5]

One more form of heresy should be mentioned, though it is of recent vintage, at least in more conservative churches. The intellectual center of Christianity is allegiance to God-authored ethical principle above all,

---

3 Consider, in this context, Noll, Mark A. *The Scandal of the Evangelical Mind*, William B. Eerdmans, 1994.

4 E.g., Dennett, Daniel, *Breaking the Spell/Religion as a Natural Phenomenon*, Penguin Books, 2006.

5 See Hitchens, Peter, *The Rage Against God*, 2010. On his way to defending religion, Peter Hitchens first identifies some of the ways it has been pushed to the background in modern culture, faulting Christian religion for failing to stand firm in it. He discusses what he describes as a civil religion, composed of patriotism and certain cultural expectations, which he identifies in the Britain of his youth with a cult of worship of Britain as victor in World War II, and Churchill essentially as its prophet. That civil religion was, he says, a counterfeit of the real thing, and that counterfeit of civil religion for actual religion still circulates, especially in the United States. He blames Christianity for letting itself be confused with love of country and the making of great wars.

and certainly above mankind-authored social trends like cultural Marxism. Obviously racism should have no place in Christian belief or practice, and we're to overcome tribal or racial barriers in our love for others. But that principle is in service to other, greater principles. Perhaps the single best illustration is the parable of the good Samaritan.[6] Which of the men was a neighbor to the injured man? The "other," the Samaritan, one separated in the minds of Jesus's hearers by long-standing religious and racial conflict. But there's something more fundamental to this story. What made the Samaritan a good neighbor was that he had compassion for the injured man. The ethical principle is that compassion, not the overcoming of other-ness. In fact, the hate Jesus's hearers might have felt for Samaritans served to give special emphasis to the ethical principle involved. It wasn't a story about racism, it was a story about the primacy of compassion. It shouldn't be controversial that we are to "seek the things that are above, where Christ is, seated at the right hand of God." We are to "set [our] minds on things that are above, not on things that are on earth."[7] We shouldn't make group power the criteria for adjudicating social outcomes, but rather apply God-imparted values and objective truth in everything.

These trends in institutional Christianity did not irrupt without warning through a faithful religious fabric of society. Christians in the West have collectively abandoned half Jesus' admonition that we be "wise as serpents and innocent as doves."[8] The innocence part is managed well enough; it is obedience to the god Niceness. The problem is that we jettison the wisdom part. If we open our eyes a bit, we'd see the trends on a larger scale. We are ever watching with blinders on, seeing only a sliver of time. We may experience the causes and effects of ideas across society during our lifetime, but unless we purpose otherwise, we'll see them in isolation and highly colored by our own prejudices and presumptions. We may fail to see historical connections of ideas because they are blurred together or never emergent in our understanding in the first place, with history in little GIFs that don't connect, failing to provide the kind of historical sweep that comes to us from zoomed-out readings of history, bracketing large expanses of time.

Abetting this failing is an inability to understand the ideas in play. This isn't a matter of merely shooting down bad ideas that may pose

---

6 Luke 10:25-37.

7 Colossians 3:1, 2.

8 Matthew 10:16. The Catholic-approved Douay-Rheims 1899 American Edition uses "shrewd," rather than "wise," which may be more fitting to the thesis here.

a threat to Christian orthodoxy. The touchstone, as ever, is truth, and the ideas in opposition to Christianity must be weighed and evaluated against a standard of ultimate truth. In some instances, we may find in heterodoxy ways of seeing that are a help to our understanding of God in his relationship to the world. We're not to close our eyes, but to open them wider. It is not as though the ideas within Christian orthodoxy are perfectly clear and obvious, either. We are, after all, trying to make effable that which is ineffable. But it is a mistake to develop a wonderfully deep, nuanced understanding of reality under the governance of God, as revealed most particularly in his Advent in the person of Jesus, without also becoming adequately versed in the mistaken conclusions about reality that abound all around us, and which develop over time in ever more pernicious secular doctrines that debilitate and defeat the vulnerable. We are to be both innocent and wise in how we receive the world. Wise as to specifics of materialist and pagan philosophies, innocent of their corruption.

There are still Christians left, right? If most of society is past a tipping point of appreciating objective truth, why can they not look over to their Christian neighbors and understand? If they were to weigh the God proposition, why wouldn't Christians' lives make them see the hierarchy of ideals emanating from God, so as to reason out his necessary existence? There are a combination of reasons why Christians don't look materially different than their neighbors, but the main one is simple: we drift with the culture, rather than the whole counsel of God, and so we don't illuminate the path to God, for others. If we are mired in the moral and truth malleability of the present day, we no longer grasp the hierarchy of ideals pointing us inexorably upward. It's as if this hierarchy, requiring as it does the absolute, were a ladder, and the ladder has been kicked away. Some Christians hang on by their fingertips. Many drop away. It's no wonder we see a resurgence of fideism, because that's all that's left when the ladder of reason founded on objectivity collapses. Church-raised children leave the church as soon as they're able. Some return, but the percentage isn't good. Some from outside feel the existential dread of purposeless materialism, after busyness and narcotic entertainment prove inadequate distractions. They may reach for God, too, as a result of the intuition they open themselves to, that he must exist. But many, many don't. The West is now only philosophically Christian, in the sense that thoughtful people recognize Christian influence in so many of their thought patterns. But that's not unity with Christ in his death and Resurrection.

We are thinking beings. Thinking is a progression to truth, requiring handholds and footholds on real and objective rungs. Church leaders should certainly be aware that the ladder has gone soft or missing in secular society around us. No church program can make up for its lack, unless it's a program passionately intent on rebuilding our understanding of objective, and perforce transcendent, truth.

Churches too often fail even to attempt to explain doctrinal competition to Christianity. Even if we get a correct vision of God's story unfolding on Earth, we fail to correctly perceive the world's story at odds with it. We get the yin without the yang. These forces are in opposition to each other; neither makes sense without understanding the other. We may get the Gospel and have some vague sense that there's something that stands in opposition, but usually it's trivialized and misrepresented as the normal temptations every person has, rather than the identifiable evil systems of the world. We don't correctly grasp the principalities and powers[9] with which we do battle. They push and pull against the Gospel at various points, each in dynamic tension with the other. We operate on one side and turn a blind eye to the part moving in opposition, the countervailing philosophies of this world.

We don't fail in this spectacular way in other endeavors. We don't try to understand the movement of a muscle of the body in isolation, without also understanding the other muscles with which it operates in tension. We don't engineer an edifice to stand alone, without considering the gravity which would pull it down. We don't try to understand life, without also understanding death. Whole systems of corrupted thought are arrayed against us, not just the quotidian personal peccadillos we're supposed to manage. But churches tend to ignore those systems of thought, those principalities and powers.

Here's one of the more typical ways this works. You believe yourself to be a Christian. You faithfully take your family to church, year after year. The church is all they've known. As the children grow, they become more independent. That's the goal, after all. You're training them for adulthood, not perennial immaturity. Becoming independent means encountering influences other than Mom and Dad, and teaching other than what they get in church. A very large percentage of young people older than twelve or thirteen drift away, progressively further from the

---

9 Ephesians 6:12, KJV. The KJV is quoted here for the "principalities and powers" language which still has some hold in our culture. The verse is rendered differently in modern translations. In the ESV, for example: "[W]e do not wrestle against flesh and blood, but against the rulers, against the authorities, against the cosmic powers over this present darkness, against the spiritual forces of evil in the heavenly places."

one-sided teaching they've been getting in church. They witness one hand clapping and rightly see this as nonsensical. Often, they abandon church altogether as soon as they are able, perhaps early in college. In most cases, they're lost long before that, even as they go through the motions at church. We think we're filling them with a Christian perspective on life, and we foolishly think that's sufficient. It's not. It's like cultivating a rare green-house plant that won't survive the harsh conditions into which it must inevitably be transplanted. We bring up children in an antiseptic bubble that prevents them from building antibodies they will need, when they eventually encounter the world in full.

The principalities and powers we're to be alert to are not merely spiritual. That is to say, though they're spiritual, they operate through the physical. We can't see or hear spiritual powers, but we can see their manifestations in the physical world, just as we can see the manifestations of wind, riffling tree leaves, but not the wind itself. If you were the devil, what would you do? Probably tempt people to impurity, such as with adultery or drunkenness or covetousness, but that might backfire. It's not as effective, in the long run. Churches are full of adulterers and drunks and people who feel themselves entitled, and not all of them are oblivious to their sin. A more subtle and elegant way to destroy a human soul is to provide a competing systematic philosophy, perhaps one that borrows selectively from the Christian milieu with which the victim is familiar.

When that young person walks away from the faith during his freshman year in college, possibly forever, we should understand why. If soldiers are dying all over the battlefield, does it not occur to us to understand the enemies that felled them, their location and tactics and weapons? It certainly should. Especially if those unwitting soldiers are our children. And yet, year after year we go on arming our very own children against the temptations of the body, ignoring the temptations of the mind. We don't prepare them for the manifold corruptions in their natural desires for meaning and significance and acceptance. We fail them.

God revealed himself to us in the created physical reality and also in the narrative that constitutes our Bible. In describing God to us, his prophets repeatedly stressed the Absolute-ness of his nature. "[A]s far as the east is from the west, so far does he remove our transgressions from us."[10] This is poetic language, but it is more. It is a statement of the

---

10 Psalm 103:12.

Absolute, because it means the removal is ongoing forever. We read that Jesus said, "Get thee behind me, Satan,"[11] but a more literal translation of the Greek would be something like this: "Be gone from my authority, and keep on going, behind me, out of my sight, Satan."[12] Again, it's a removal that is ongoing forever. The same gulf exists between heaven and hell. Between them there is a great chasm fixed, so that no one can cross from one to the other.[13] We are to understand that heaven and hell are fixed polarities. They are removed from one another absolutely in the same way as good and evil, light and dark, presence and absence, existence and non-existence—oppositions that create tension and therefore meaning which infuses the world, and ushers us to ideals, and ideals of those ideals, and ultimately to God, if we are willing.

Many have an intuition that we do church wrong because we fall into worshipping the pastor, or invoke sentiment in music in false validation of belief. Or hear sermons we don't understand or for which context is a blank slate. The structure is institutional and may seem inauthentic, causing us to intuit that it takes us off course from the wildness the Gospel demands of us. This idea was at the heart of the Reformation and the many little reformations since. But it also has the effect of splintering us into tinier and tinier divisions, until we become a division of one, and so feed a competing intuition that the church is literally the church of me. Our relationship to God is to be unmediated and unattenuated in a way contrary to what we tend to make of it inside institutional religion. We long for authenticity, but come to perceive institutional religion as inauthentic because it is separated from the Author.

On the other hand, we seek fellowship, in combination with that authenticity. And in addition to fellowship, we seek simple help. We don't ascend the mount of Zion solo; it just doesn't happen. Religious institutions are like ladders, without which we might not get the first step off the ground. We grope after the ineffable and the untouchable and the authentic, and devise all kinds of mechanisms to get to it. We need ladders, and ideally we would get to the top of them and step off into starlight. Too often we don't, because we confuse the church institution with God himself. We're even subtly admonished not to get off the ladder; to stay safely inside churchy religiosity, so we can interact with the dangerous God in a way we feel is safer; that is, from a distance.

---

11 Matthew 16:23, KJV.

12 Matthew 16:23, translation by Wuest, Kenneth, *The New Testament: An Expanded Translation*, William B. Eerdmans, 1961.

13 Luke 16:26.

If we sense all this about institutional religious practice up front, or grow up inside of it, we may recoil at its unnecessary constraint or confusion of mission and therefore reject it, never stepping up to the first rung of the ladder, and therefore never getting to the starlight. We're always devising ways to distance ourselves from the scary roaring lion that is God. We use church like the circus uses cages. Some of us are more sensitive to the flim-flam element of churches and stay away, or run away when we've finally had enough, and consequently never get off the ground at all, and never have a hand in helping others climb, and never reach the starlight ourselves.

The choices are stark, though. We're in a train station, on the platform for just a moment. We're constantly reminded to mind the gap. It's the gap from this life to the next, from the platform to the train. We all get on a train. And then we go one way or the other.

CHAPTER TWENTY-THREE

Knowledge and Belief

DO YOU KNOW YOUR birthday? If yes, how? You certainly weren't aware nor knowledgeable enough on that day to have acquired this information from first-hand observation. Someone told you. And then re-told you and re-told you, probably. You take it to be true because there obviously was an actual day of birth, and it occurred on a date on the calendar, and there is no reason for others to lie about what that date was, and this tidbit of information was likely delivered to you in love. Most people consider knowledge of their own birthday to be as nearly certain as a thing can be, yet there is no knowing experience of the event or the date associated with it.

Extensive areas in our architecture of knowledge develop not from direct experience, but from accumulated re-tellings we have no reason to question. We have certainty about a broad range of things unsupported by first-hand empirical observation. About events of history, for example, including history before we were even born. We hold facts and relationships and ideals and concepts to be certainly true, because we believe them corroborated and cross-corroborated by the broad architecture of knowledge we are constantly adding to and revising as we live. A great deal of that architecture is constructed on top of previously acquired knowledge. I may know about an event or concept or fact, let's call it A, which is well-accepted in the architecture of things I already know. We can think of it as an architecture because the body of knowledge we have is not simply linear, such that fact A leads only to B, which leads only to C, and so on. A might corroborate P and Q but not B. The things we learn are counted as knowledge if they are corroborated in this multi-dimensional architecture.

It is multi-dimensional in the sense we mean for space-time, but added to that are dimensions of meaning, wherein the veracity of one bit of knowledge is determined by mentally cross-referencing it with other bits of knowledge. We observe the sun rise at a point on the horizon we call "east," but we also know the sun only seems to rise in the east, because the earth actually turns toward the sun. We have knowledge of that because we also hold as true that scientists pursue truth about physical things; they do so in good faith; there is valid scientific support for a heliocentric solar system; and so on.

Another dimension to add to the architecture of knowledge is certainty. We don't subscribe to every fact or concept with equal certainty. We factor degrees of certainty into how much reliance we place on a fact or concept in forming other conclusions. We can think of these degrees of certainty in terms of probability. If you're 100 percent certain of one thing, and it corroborates another, you might assign high probability to that other, depending on how it connects with other nodes in your architecture of knowledge.

But let's make an important distinction. A proposition is not true just because we have a high degree of certainty about it. If we encounter a new idea or proposition and conclude it to be true because it coheres with other things we believe to be true, that doesn't make it true. We could be mistaken. The cohering idea persuades us to a conviction of what is true objectively; it does not become true because it coheres. This is an important distinction, because if you continue to hold truth claims to an objective standard, you'll be open-minded about whether your belief is mistaken. You'll be able to distinguish between belief and knowledge. This process is distinct from the truth-formation theory of coherentism.

In at least one sense, knowledge is relational. Specifically, correspondence between subject and object. By "subject" is meant you, if it's your own knowledge or belief under consideration. By "object" is meant the external reality corresponding to that internal subjective knowledge or belief. This dualism is necessary to grasp, because confusion results without it. If you look out your door and observe water falling from the sky, you may thereby acquire knowledge it's raining. You may take it as a fact, stored in your bank of knowledge, that it is now raining. Your nearly one hundred percent belief in the rain proposition corresponds to facts in your external environment. But suppose some additional facts. Though water is falling from the sky, there's partial sunshine. The ground is wet nearby, but not obviously wet further from the house.

And, your cousin has been pranking you all morning. He could be on the roof with the garden hose, because that's just the kind of thing he would do. Your certainty in the rain proposition might drop to fifty percent. Here's why this is worth mentioning. If your certainty is fifty percent, that doesn't mean it's raining half the time. It either is or it isn't. If the weatherman says there's a fifty percent chance of rain, that doesn't mean you get half wet. Your subjective belief, whether at fifty percent certainty or one hundred percent or any other level, may not correspond to what is externally true. There can be a disconnect between belief and reality. We can hold false beliefs.

It sometimes happens that we come to realize a firmly-held belief is just wrong. This can be unsettling, because the error affects other parts of our architecture of knowledge. It's not just the one fact involved. It's all the other facts and concepts built around it. The discovery of a false belief warrants a review of how one came to it, not just to avoid another mistake, but also to identify other beliefs that do not align with reality, and remove them, as necessary, from the architecture in your mind. You've likely experienced this, and if so you're aware this may occasion a substantial re-wiring of your understanding of reality, depending on how significant the belief was; that is, how thoroughly embedded it was in the architecture of knowledge you've built from evidence. Our orientation to truth[1] requires this of us.

Suppose you discover in adulthood that the man who reared you as your father is not your natural father. This is more common than you might suppose. We protect children from hard truths, as we should, and then there's a difficulty in deciding when—or if—we should remove that protection so they're relating truthfully with the world. Learning this would change many fundamental beliefs about the relationships between you and your mother and "father," and theirs with each other, and by extension the relationship of men and women in general. There would emerge in your mind also a new but shadowy net of relationships between you and unknown others in the world.

While beliefs can be false, knowledge cannot be. A false belief within one's architecture of knowledge does not invalidate all one's beliefs, but it must be removed, and the architecture re-formed accordingly. The distinction between knowledge and belief is the distinction between objective reality and subjective appreciation of that reality. One forms beliefs about what is objectively true, and those beliefs can be held with

---

1 See Norton, Albert, *Intuition of Significance*, Resource Publications, pp. 81-88.

greater or lesser certainty. Believing something doesn't make it true, however. Objective reality doesn't adjust to my misapprehension of it.

This may seem obvious, stated in the abstract, but it's actually not so uncommon for people to make just this mistake. It's what we do, for example, when we speak of "my truth." Colloquially that might mean something like "my opinion of what is true," but more and more it expresses that there is no objective truth, that we can all create our own. That is, that there is no real distinction between belief and knowledge. This is dangerous, because it is a first step toward self-delusion. We may have different opinions about what is true, and have different beliefs accordingly. But we should not differ on the beginning premise that there is but one truth. It is a dangerous thing, individually and collectively, to attempt to breach the dualism of truth and falsity.

More cautions about belief and knowledge are in order. First, "belief" is not an adequate stand-in for truth. An appeal to one's "belief" instead of objective truth can be only an assertion of rights in contrast to other asserted rights in a post-truth world.

Second, there can be a difference between a code to which one subscribes, and one's actual subjective beliefs. You may "believe" in a set of religious tenets, for example, because you align yourself with the institution of religion which promulgates them. But unless they are internalized through a process of learning them, understanding how they fit together, and most of all accepting them, they are only vague and wispy shreds of thoughts. They're more like a pledge of allegiance.

Third, belief can be minimized as a matter of personal subjectivity, if there is no absolute standard of truth. God's existence is sometimes argued to require "exceptional proof," for example, because it is only a matter of internal belief. But what about the claim that the universe is self-created from nothing? That's not "exceptional?"

Fourth, unfair polemical use is often made of the distinction between beliefs and knowledge. For example, beliefs are relegated to mere opinions, anecdotes, and emotion-driven standards for evaluating experience, while knowledge is "that which is scientifically proven," a nonsensical statement because science is not the measure of all knowledge. Some kinds of knowledge are beyond science altogether, obviously. So why would someone say this? Because the subject matter of science is physical reality, and people who say this already believe there is only physical reality. If only evidence relating to physical reality is admissible, then only physical reality can be part of our knowledge. Therefore there is no spiritual reality, and no soul, and no God. See how that works?

Imagine you're on trial for murder. Your DNA was found on the murder weapon at the scene. The prosecution insists this is all the relevant evidence. It's physical. It's there. Anything else is just argument. So all the evidence points to you being the murderer. You're guilty, right? Well hang on. Is the jury not allowed to consider evidence of facts beyond those at the physical scene? Like where you actually were at the time, and the provenance of the murder weapon, and the possible motivations of the real perpetrator? Well of course. There are all kinds of possible innocent explanations for the presence of your DNA. You might have also been a victim, for just one example. It would be absurd to bracket the evidence by the criteria that it must be physical and present.

So if we put the question of God's existence on trial, let's not corrupt the fact-finding process in the same way. We don't call evidence which is not the subject of science "irrelevant" and exclude it on that basis. The subject-matter of science is the physical cosmos. To consider only what science reveals is to suppose the physical cosmos is all of reality, but that's the very question we're trying to answer. This kind of logical fallacy is so ubiquitous (on the question of God's existence) that many people who consider themselves open-minded about religion nonetheless call themselves agnostic, because they think science has not proven nor disproven God's existence.

To say that faith is belief without evidence is frankly ridiculous. What is "evidence?" If you have free rein to define "evidence" any way you choose, you're guaranteed to win any debate. Faith is not a repudiation of evidence, but rather a call to accept all the evidence. The object of religious faith is unseen[2] reality. The evidence of that unseen reality includes revelation and reason. Revelation is the physical world that is seen, and the logocentric aspect of it, and the words of the prophets, and the proofs of the prophet and Christ, Jesus. Reason is what we do with the evidence mentally. The purpose of all evidence is to point to or away from a proposition of truth. The Bible expresses much about reason applied to evidence, to increase faith in something that is true but not necessarily obvious to our senses. It is to the effect: *here is positive evidence of heaven transcending the natural world. Now believe.* Far from being asked to disregard the evidence, we're asked to accept as true the evidence set plainly before us, and not to disregard it just because it points to something other than itself.

---

2 Hebrews 11: 1 and 3: "Now faith is the assurance of things hoped for, the conviction of things not seen . . . By faith we understand that the universe was created by the word of God, so that what is seen was not made out of things that are visible."

The natural world forms the boundary of our sense impressions. It is what water is to fish. We would understand the skepticism of a fish about the existence of some environment apart from water. But there is reality beyond the water, for the fish, and there is reality beyond the natural world, for us. God has spoken to us to say: accept from the evidence that this "Beyond" reality is true. When we evaluate evidence by the process of reason, we attach lesser or greater weight based on its competence and its strength of relevance to the proposition under consideration. We all do this, all the time. We make fine distinctions between similar propositions by placing them in binary opposition, to discover what is true. This is normal human thinking. It is not unique to one sub-class of humans, such as those who reject God, or those who accept him. Reason describes the mental process by which every human being assimilates and evaluates the evidence around him.

The Christian story has Christ ascending bodily into the heavens, forty days following his Resurrection. The Ascension is a figurative bridge from this physical reality, to a Beyond whence he came, and to which we go. The Ascension, along with the Incarnation, and for that matter the Resurrection, are events by which we are given to understand there is some other part of reality, which in our time- and space-limited ways we can only think of as another "place." We call this heaven, or a spiritual realm, to which Jesus has returned, and from which he will re-appear in his time.

But maybe it's all just a story, we might think, with the supernatural Beyond existing only in the debunked imagination of credulous people who cling unreasoningly to ancient myths for comfort. Whatever happened, the modern thinking might go, it does not really evince some other "place" beyond the physical cosmos we know and continue to discover. The Ascension might thus be regarded as symbolic language for the earthly end of an admirable person, Jesus of Nazareth.

A necessary corollary of this putting-by of literal belief in the Ascension, as with other details of Christ's earthly ministry, is that faith means belief despite a lack of evidence. That has become the standard trope, in fact.[3] People suspicious of binary oppositions nonetheless place faith

3 Martin Hägglund makes this mistake in *This Life/Secular Faith and Spiritual Freedom* (New York: Anchor Books, 2019). The "secular faith" of his subtitle employs the concept of faith as belief based on a decision to believe, instead of evidence. He means faith—in that sense—in one's own decision-making about life purpose. Along with many other "New Atheists," Sam Harris also makes this error, in *The End of Faith*, W. W. Norton, 2004.

and reason in such opposition. Faith and reason are not a dualism that actually presents an opposition, however. To the contrary, faith in God, and in his manifestations in the Christ and the Holy Spirit, depend on reason, just like any belief anyone forms about anything. There aren't two kinds of belief, one for science and one for religion. The false dualism of faith and reason is advanced because it is necessary to dethroning a God who might be dangerous, and who is therefore scary to the complacency and comfort we desire more than truth.

Imagine you were there on the day of the Ascension. It is easy to do, because we have a trustworthy written narrative of the event, along with the deep explanatory backstory, which reaches back to the very fact of existence. That backstory shows us that the One who ascended is a person like us, but who, unlike us, is also one (in a way we imperfectly grasp) with the uncaused-cause of all creation. Upon completing an essential part of his mission here, he receded back into the great Beyond whence he came, leaving us an intangible Helper, what Christians call the Holy Spirit. The facts of the Christ's sojourn with us, and even of his Ascension, are significant evidence of the reality beyond the time- and space-bound physical reality that is our temporary home.

CHAPTER TWENTY-FOUR

Faith

WHAT IS GOD TELLING us when he says we are to believe in him? God speaks to us through the "book" of his physical creation, but also through the literal book handed down to us by his prophets and by theologians developing the canon from prophetic writings. This is the Bible. There are other forms of revelation, but the Bible is the most helpful to us in trying to understand what "belief" and "believe" really mean. Do they mean mere intellectual assent to God's existence? Do they mean some sort of reliance on that truth? Do they mean some changed mental position with regard to how we are to live? Do they imply some sort of risk on our part?

A good place to start is with Abraham. Abraham is central to all the monotheistic faiths: Judaism, Christianity, and Islam. A story told in Genesis[1] shows us Abraham's willingness to go through with the sacrifice of his son Isaac, had God not intervened and substituted a ram to be sacrificed instead. Given the great cost of Abraham's obedience, we infer a near-absolute certainty on his part concerning God and his ultimate authority. Abraham had been promised progeny as numerous as the stars in the sky,[2] and yet he was directed to sacrifice Isaac, the child of God's covenant[3] through whom God's promise was to be kept. We don't have access to Abraham's internal thoughts or emotions during this time, but he probably understood that God had the authority to

---

1 Chapter 22.
2 Genesis 15:5.
3 Genesis 17:21.

raise Isaac from the dead.[4] Abraham "believed in the Lord,"[5] and as the story of Isaac's near-sacrifice shows us, clearly this belief was something more than mere intellectual assent to the evidence he had of God's existence. Moreover, we're told that Abraham's belief was credited to Abraham as righteousness.[6] This does not signify mere approval. It signifies that Abraham's faith was counted as righteousness though he, like all mankind, was not righteous as God requires. Righteousness was instead imputed to Abraham on account of his, Abraham's, faith. That imputed righteousness meant reconciliation with God, who is just. Justice requires punishment for any departure from righteousness. The Bible's teaching is that God does not abide even the slightest derogation from his own full righteousness; therefore, imputed righteousness means something takes the place of actual righteousness. That something, we learn, is faith.

In the Christian New Testament, Abraham was counted as a hero of faith, a person of old who by faith "received [his] commendation," and this in order to illustrate what faith is:

> [T]he assurance of things hoped for, the conviction of things not seen. For by it the people of old received their commendation. By faith we understand that the universe was created by the word of God, so that what is seen was not made out of things that are visible.[7]

God's existence and his interaction with the cosmos as the Bible reveals is also a thing hoped for. It is a "thing[] not seen" because it is distinct from the physical reality we directly observe. It is created, and created by the "word of God," the Logos, which means semantic content, meaning, spoken into the world, and not merely by "what is seen" or "things that are visible."

We're not left guessing what faith is. Jesus taught quite specifically about faith, meaning specifically belief in God as revealed in the scriptures before Jesus, and by Jesus himself, as later recorded in the New Testament. The New Testament's references to belief are not merely about intellectual belief in a necessary God, as we might conclude from philosophy or an open mind about what science tells us. The references

---

4 Hebrews 11:19.

5 Genesis 15:6.

6 Ibid., see also Romans 4:3, in which Paul refers to this passage of Genesis in explaining justification by faith.

7 Hebrews 11:1-3. Abraham as an illustration of faithfulness commences at verse 8.

to belief are also about the spiritual realm and God's actions in history—physical space and time—and about how God reconciles unrighteous people to himself as he did with Abraham. "Belief" in this context therefore means not just the existence of God, but the existence of God as he is revealed to us in the Bible.

A way to go about trying to figure this out is to find variants of the words "belief" and "faith" in the Bible, and look at their context. Oftentimes, the words are paired with other concepts in such a way that we can draw inferences about what belief and faith really mean. The discussion of Abraham's faith—his believing God—can be contrasted with the many descriptions of insufficient faith on the part of the Israelites. Again and again God's good care of the people is recited, and then contrasted with their faithlessness, with the consequence that God's "fire was kindled against Jacob; his anger rose against Israel."[8] Why? "[B]ecause they did not believe in God and did not trust his saving power."[9] Not believing in God is one thing. Not trusting his saving power is quite another. But these two statements aren't presented in contradistinction. They're presented in conjunction. They are different ways of saying the same thing. Belief in God doesn't just mean intellectual assent. It means trusting his saving power.

But now we've introduced another word, "trust." Trust implies a change of position in reliance upon the belief. Faith, hope, belief, and trust are all partial descriptors of the kind of relationship we're to strive for. The Christ performed miracles in order to induce belief,[10] but not just airy acquiescence to the proposition that he was who he said he was. He healed a paralytic, for example, as proof of his sovereignty with the Father, by coupling the act with a pronouncement that the man's sins were forgiven.[11] Only God can forgive sin, so saying this would be blasphemy, were it not true in the case of Jesus. Interestingly, he did this not just because of the paralytic's faith, but the faith of those who brought the paralytic to him. They, like the one to be healed, were taking affirmative action based on their hope. They risked ridicule and disappointment, at a minimum, to do so.

---

8 Psalm 78:21.

9 Psalm 78:22.

10 The examples are too numerous to mention by way of footnote, but a prominent example is the raising of Lazarus from the dead, when Jesus prayed to God and specifically said he did so for the benefit of those standing nearby. The act of raising Lazarus from the dead was to give us warrant for belief in the truth of his message. John 11: 38-45.

11 Matthew 9:2.

Often in the New Testament only "belief" is mentioned, and not faith or trust or objective facts of reliance on belief. It's necessary in each instance to understand what is said in context, and to compare it with other instances in which belief is discussed, in order to come to the inescapable conclusion that belief means something more than just being factually persuaded to a proposition. Jesus asked two blind men whether they "believed" he was able to give them sight. "Yes" was the only answer, that we know of, though this followed their beseeching him: "Have mercy on us, Son of David."[12] We don't know what else transpired among them on this occasion, nor what Jesus subjectively knew about the state of the men's hearts. At a minimum, however, they say "yes," and acknowledged Jesus as the foretold descendant of the great King David.

In the story of the disciples freed from a Philippian jail after Christ's Ascension, we're told the jailer was so impressed with events that he converted. His question was actually not about "belief" at all, but "What must I do to be saved?"[13] It was to that question Peter and Silas answered: "Believe in the Lord Jesus, and you will be saved, you and your household."[14] We don't get more explanation here as to what "belief" entails, but this occurred after a miraculous event in which Paul and Silas were freed to walk out of jail, had they chosen to do so. The jailer would have taken belief to mean more than the kind of intellectual assent afforded to us on the basis of a 2,000-year look-back to facts not made personal to us as they were with this jailer, whose life was probably at stake.

Jesus similarly forgave a woman who ministered to him while he was visiting a group of Pharisees, the church leaders of that day, about whom we can infer some degree of hypocrisy and judgment. Much can be gleaned from this event, but for our purposes, what does it say about faith? "Your faith has saved you; go in peace," Jesus said to the woman. [15] That's it? Mere belief? No, her many sins were forgiven on the strength of her expressions of love for Jesus.

"If you have faith," Jesus said, "whatever you ask in prayer, you will receive."[16] Indeed, his hearers would be able to uproot a mountain and cast it into the sea "if [they] have faith and do not doubt."[17] Now we see faith coupled with a negative characteristic: doubt. Doubt is a vague,

---

12 Matthew 9:27-29.

13 Acts 16:30.

14 Acts 16:31.

15 Luke 7:50.

16 Matthew 21:20-22.

17 Matthew 21:21.

cloudy sort of thing, that can cast a shadow of variable intensity upon what would otherwise be utter certainty. What is Jesus prescribing? Absolute certainty unclouded by any trace of doubt whatsoever? The answer lies in the nature of the task he provides. It's difficult to conceive God desiring removal of a mountain into the sea, so it's difficult to imagine complete alignment with God's will to provide the necessary power to accomplish this feat. But it is certainly illustrative. A thing impossible to achieve is nonetheless achievable, if one is prayerfully acting in concert with God's will, and the degree of confidence in that supernatural power is utterly unclouded by doubt. We don't live utterly unclouded by doubt, however, and so we don't go around tossing mountains into the sea. Jesus is completely right in what he taught, as always, but he's urging us to aspire to ever more pure faith, undiluted by doubt.

The book of John contains more spiritual allusion and recognition of the mystery of our communion with God than do the more matter-of-fact Synoptic Gospels. When Jesus began explicitly preaching, he urged that people "repent and believe in the Gospel."[18] Mere belief is here coupled with "repentance." What is that? It means turning from sin and turning toward right and proper conduct for flourishing in life and in the afterlife. It does not mean merely turning to a principle. It means turning to a Person, to God. The belief Jesus referred to is in himself and his message of salvation, but he deliberately coupled abstract belief with affirmative conduct, repentance, indicating the deep-rootedness of that belief. A deliberate turn from the attractions of this world, and toward the eternal view of reality.

It's worth pausing to consider why the abstraction of "belief" must be coupled with affirmative conduct. It has to do with the fuzzy nature of belief in contradistinction to knowledge. Knowledge requires no action to make the knowledge true. It's knowledge. But belief is an internal and ephemeral thing. It is a lit candle wavering in the air. If it remains lit, it illuminates the room. If it is snuffed out, all is in darkness. Belief can be false, as we considered. But what can a false belief illuminate? Elaborations on the falsehood, perhaps, but never truth.

Among the most instructive of passages on this point—of what "belief" means in full—is the story of Nicodemus, found in chapter 3 of John. Nicodemus first addresses the most basic form of belief, that Jesus "is a teacher come from God, for no one can do these signs that you do

---

18   John 1:15.

unless God is with him."[19] This is mere intellectual assent to the proposition that Jesus is who he said he is. Is that enough? Evidently not,
because Jesus doesn't respond by saying "that's it, buddy, you're in the
club." Instead he said that "unless one is born again, he cannot see the
kingdom of God."[20] Here we read about the effect of faith in full—spiritual birth to go with natural physical birth—but not necessarily about
what constitutes that faith. We are reading about a spiritual component
to mere belief, and spiritual things are ineffable. We come to understand
by hints and allusions and oblique references, because that's all the language we have for understanding something that is out of reach in this
life. The Gospels are written to help us try to see the unseen.

This story about Nicodemus is followed by the oft-repeated John
3:16: "For God so loved the world, that he gave his only Son, that whoever believes in him should not perish but have eternal life." This verse
is perhaps attractive because it seems to demand so little of us. On the
surface it suggests we merely believe Jesus is real. But in context, clearly
more is required: a spiritual birth, which we can take to mean a developed consciousness that we are spiritual creatures, too, and we can aspire
to the ideals the Bible teaches, or live life as though it were meaningless.
We have agency. People seldom turn to ideals just because they're ideals.
We don't recognize higher aspirations and adopt them because they're
helpful to us in the abstract, in an existentialist sort of way. There has
to be a reason to move from the pleasure/pain self-interest paradigm of
mere physical animals. We move from it in recognition that God is real
and that what we do in this life matters in the next.

This idea is further borne out in the passages in which Jesus likened
our union with him as being like food to our flesh. We "drink his blood"
and "eat his body," at the Lord's table, to recognize the inseparable union
of body and spirit in him.[21] Similarly, we are taught to be united with
him just as the branch is to the vine. This is an analogy that tells us we
wither and die, spiritually, if we are not joined to him in some indissolu-
ble way. We are to "abide" in him, and he will in us.[22] We can be repulsed
by this spiritual merger, as many were in the day Jesus was among us as
a man.[23] Or, we can accept it as a small picture of how spiritual birth in
this life can come about.

---

19 John 3:2.
20 John 3:3.
21 John 6:47-51.
22 John 15:1-11.
23 John 15:66.

Christ asked, as recounted in John chapter 5: "How can you believe, when you receive glory from one another and do not seek the glory that comes from the only God?"[24] This is yet another way of looking at what that something in addition to mere belief might entail: "glory." We all seek it all the time. We seek it from people around us. We can disavow God altogether and still be routinely in the business of seeking acclaim or recognition or respect or at least acknowledgement from our fellow man. We wither in isolation. But without God, what is the point? It is ultimately God's approval we are to seek. This is a meaning of glory that escapes us, in this life, if we have nominal belief in a story but no relationship with God. Jesus admonishes us to reach for gold and not settle for tarnished brass.

In this passage of John, Jesus even points his hearers back to the teachings of Moses, because he wants them to see that God is engaged in a long process of revealing himself through his chosen people, and acceptance of this revelation is necessary to accepting Jesus as the culmination of that unveiling. Faith doesn't mean just belief in Jesus, even as a manifestation of God one time, who taught well and then left us. Instead, it means belief in the entire revelation of God before its culmination in the life and earthly ministry of Jesus.

In Paul's letter to the Romans,[25] we read that "everyone [not Jews only] who calls on the name of the Lord will be saved." Paul is quoting the Old Testament prophet Joel.[26] This is a different formulation for "belief" than we see elsewhere. This implies some active movement rather than cerebration that could be entirely internal and unaccompanied by conduct in conformance with the belief. What does it mean to "call on the name of the Lord?" In Joel, it referred to those who will escape travails to be poured out on Earth, the "wonders in the heavens and on the earth, blood and fire and columns of smoke. The sun shall be turned to darkness, and the moon to blood, before the great and awesome day of the Lord comes."[27] In the Romans passage, Paul is saying that the natural progression of history will be that the word of God is to break out of its Jewish delivery into history before the day of the Lord, and Christ's message was part of that process. Thus, to "call on the name of the Lord" seems to mean crying out to God to be saved, an active and passionate

---

24 John 5:44.

25 Romans 10:13.

26 Joel 2:32.

27 Joel 2:31-32.

act rather than merely passively accepting that the story must be true. It is not mere belief that brings salvation, but rather this act of "calling upon" God. Paul presents this as a progression, in which the object is salvation, not merely belief, but of course belief must precede the act of calling upon God.

This idea of "calling upon" God—meaning something more than mere belief—is inferable from the fact that mere factual belief alone does not save, because even the demons believe in God.[28] Demons are not restored to God by virtue of this level of belief. Long before Christ, pagan philosophers like Plato and Aristotle believed in a necessary creator-God, much like the deists of the Enlightenment period acceded to the necessity of God without buying into his being active in the world. But this limited scope of belief is not sufficient to bring salvation. The only reasonable inference from the New Testament is that the references to belief, even without further description, meant something more than this deist conception. The trouble with this sort of meager faith is that it doesn't evoke any kind of change. No repentance, no walk with God, and no good works based on the belief that he exists as he is revealed to us. The "faith without works" passage of James[29] reads pretty clearly that mere belief is not enough; it must be manifested in some positive way by one's acts in conformance with those beliefs; "works," as James would say. Otherwise, you have no assurance to go with intellectual assent.

So we don't have salvation by works, but instead by faith. At the same time, faith without works is meaningless. So what saves us? It has to be that faith saves us, as the Bible reiterates countless times, but in our subjective experience of faith, something more than merely intellectual assent to the truth of the story is required. Not faith plus works, because that simplistic formula is foreclosed many times in the Bible.[30] Rather, good works should be among the voluntary and cheerful acts we undertake because the faith is already there. But how are we to distinguish between works undertaken as if to replace faith, and works undertaken in response to faith? This isn't as easy as we might think, if we listen to glib and ill-informed sermons, and then try to put these precepts into practice. Human beings don't separate out motives that readily, and it ought to be crystal clear that even with the Helper, the Holy Spirit which is the spirit of truth in us, we don't have crystal clear discernment as to

28 James 2:17.

29 James 2:14-26.

30 E.g., Ephesians 2: 8, 9. The book of Romans speaks most eloquently to this point, including especially chapter 4.

what is going on inside us as we act so as to have salvation. In this age, the inner light we have is incomplete; we "see in a mirror dimly,"[31] and it makes sense that if we are not blessed with a cosmic blinding unmistakable personal revelation like Paul was, we go about trying to "confirm [our] calling and election"[32] by affirmatively practicing what we know to be right and virtuous, thus shoring up our degree of confidence in the truth of the unseen. By invoking God's grace, we can become enabled to "make every effort to supplement [our] faith with virtue, and virtue with knowledge, and knowledge with self-control, and self-control with steadfastness, and steadfastness with godliness, and godliness with brotherly affection, and brotherly affection with love."[33] This practice is the means to "confirm [our] calling and election," because with the successful practice of these qualities we cannot fail to have entrance into the eternal kingdom of Christ.[34]

What happens without this belief? Well, an absence of salvation; a failure of reconciliation with God, who is just. But it doesn't happen because we're being punished by God for not knuckling under. To the contrary, this eternal failing is the default position. It's what happens if we do nothing. We don't go to hell because God sends us there. Hell is our normal and natural destination because God is real and he is just. Jesus diverts us from that destination, but only if we are united with him. Just what constitutes that unity is the subject of the "belief" we are examining.[35] God's wrath doesn't attach to us upon rejection of Christ, or upon our death without having accepted him. God's wrath was there already.[36] We have moral agency, but we exercise it imperfectly. We're diverted from the consequences of God's justice through faith.

This is an important point to grasp, because an ongoing criticism of Christianity in the culture is that God is not worthy of our acknowledgement, let alone worship, because, it is thought, he sends us to hell if we don't love him. That idea gets traction with many people. Putting aside the problem that we don't get to second-guess God, the criticism seems to call into question his very existence, because this idea of pun-

31   1 Corinthians 13:12.
32   2 Peter 1:10.
33   2 Peter 1:5-7.
34   2 Peter 1:8-11.
35   Why would God's reality have us in the tense position of desperation over meaning to our lives, and of stretching internally to find it through faith? What is he preparing us for?
36   John 3:36.

ishment doesn't seem to square with his goodness. This is faulty reasoning, however. The problem is ours, not his, and it's a problem of our
misunderstanding, not God's character. God doesn't punish us. Quite to
the contrary, he gives us the means to avoid the consequence natural to
us all.

We live with tension concerning belief because that buzz of tension
is meaning arising from the binary oppositions of truth and falsity; certainty and uncertainty; the transcendence of God and his immanence.
"Belief" seems to be synonymous with salvation in some places in the
Bible, but in other places the context clearly indicates that the "belief"
called for is more than mere assent. We are told that "whoever believes
in the Son has eternal life," for example, but in the same verse (John
3:36) "whoever does not obey the Son shall not see life, but the wrath of
God remains on him." There are only two ways to go. This might be the
ultimate binary opposition we face: heaven or hell; eternal life or death.
These alternatives are in entire contradiction; there is no overlap and no
outcome not included in these two oppositions. Life requires belief, so
we would expect death to mean lack of belief, but that's not what this
verse says. It says disobedience to Christ means death. Belief, therefore,
means obedience. If you actually believe, you will obey because of the
enormity of the subject matter of that belief. If we say we believe but
don't grasp the true dangerousness of God, we won't have any semblance
of obedience, and our purported faith is a lie.

And yet, obedience to the Son cannot be perfect, so as to support
perfect confidence in salvation. This seeming either/or passage doesn't
give us a clean either/or after all, because we know that notwithstanding
a desire for salvation and therefore a desire for obedience, we nonetheless will fail. All have sinned,[37] and second birth in Christ does not eradicate all sin, even if it does give us power to overcome sin in the same
measure as we have faith. We imperfectly invoke that power, hence the
need to make the effort to put on the virtues that add to our confidence
of salvation by faith. The very structure of the Bible, admonishing us to
virtue and not just belief, attests to the idea that we are to act on our own
agency, not just sit back and wait for the motivations of faith to kick in.
We're not automatons with an on/off switch activated by assent to the
truth. This "obedience" element of belief means that belief is more like a
gradual volume control knob. As Hebrews 11 seems to suggest, faith lies
on a spectrum of confidence, and our task is to go about turning up that

---

37 Romans 3:23.

volume during the course of our lives.

We began with the faith of Abraham, and the later reference to Abraham's faith recounted in Hebrews. The book of Hebrews goes on to provide more insight into what belief means. "[W]ithout faith it is impossible to please [God], for whoever would draw near to God must believe that He exists . . ." So far, so consistent, but the remainder of this verse is that the belief must include the specific belief that God rewards those who seek him.[38] Again this implies acceptance of God as he has been revealed in scripture, meaning both the scripture available to those writers—what Christians call the Old Testament—but also the New Testament, then being written on the foundation of the Old.

After these statements in Hebrews, we get a whole list of "by faith" pronouncements, in which heroes of old evidenced faith. This is not about their subjective state of mind, but rather their conduct in reliance on belief, which strongly supports the inference that their belief in God and his promises was deep and compelling, not merely acceptance of theory without practical living consequence. And more than that, it was reliance on future events which may not (and did not) take place in their lifetimes, including especially the coming Christ.[39] So when the events of "belief" are recounted in the New Testament, they were related to people who knew these promises from of old, and saw them played out right in front of them in the person of Jesus. Theirs was not a dry intellectual exercise of propositional belief. We should understand that the belief we're reading about involves much more.

One more thing at least should be said about "faith" before moving on. In the discussion thus far, "faith" is used to mean belief in strong degree, "the assurance of things hoped for, the conviction of things not seen."[40] We've been considering the struggle for greater faith, for the Christian. But now we should distinguish a meaning the word does not have. It does not mean belief without evidence. To the contrary, the entirety of the New Testament we have been considering is a presentation of evidence to support belief, to be combined with evidence from our reason and observations about the world and history and human nature.

There is potentially a form of confusion, however, because sound Christian doctrine holds that understanding follows belief. "The fear of

---

38 Hebrews 11:6.

39 Hebrews 11:4-40.

40 Hebrews 11:1.

the Lord is the beginning of knowledge,"[41] we read. Christians some-times speak of understanding "with the eyes of faith," and so on. A Christian unable to articulate the evidence supporting his faith might throw up the hands and say "you just gotta believe." This is most unfor-tunate, when it happens, because it fuels the criticism that faith means belief without evidence.

The word "faith" really has two common meanings in the modern West. One is the evidence-supported form of intensifying Christian be-lief, discussed here, and the other is any belief that is evidence-free. This latter meaning is common in secular usage, to suggest that willing some-thing to be true is sufficient to make it true. We might say, for example, that we "have faith" our favorite sports team will win, not because of its stats to date, but because we wish it so.

Why is this understanding of faith important? What difference does it make? Is God urging us to this so our lives will be better, or is there eternal significance to it? If we believe in God, we believe in objective truth and the reality of other ideals, and we know something of love so as to relate well with others. God loves us; he wants our lives to be better; and belief in him will make our lives better. So it's conceivable that the point is just to make our lives better. On the other hand, why hell? Why aren't we all just saved? Why are so many fundamental questions unan-swered? Why doesn't God just take visible form while we're in this life, and remove all doubt? I hear you, you're saying he did do that, but that was a long time ago, by our reckoning of time. And some people think he could have done a better job of it. We're quick to judge God, but get upset that he judges us.

Why does an afterlife with God turn on the ongoing tension we have now, as Kierkegaard noted, and the tension being resolved by faith? Why does God put us in this deeply puzzling environment for a short while, made in his image with moral awareness, but with animal lusts and ap-petites, too? Why, why, why? If we understood some of this, would we be better off? Or would that prove to be catastrophic in some way we can't imagine? What is the point of our having such limited understanding of eternal things, in this life?

These are legitimate questions, and they don't amount to shaking one's fist at God. Just by asking them, we're not imagining he doesn't exist, or that the tidbits he's disclosed aren't true. We're just acknowledg-ing the fact that we're saddled with deep mystery for reasons that are, at

41 Proverbs 1:7.

present, known to God alone. Faith doesn't just mean accepting the story and what it tells us of our relationship to God. It also means accepting him in the face of all these questions and trusting that his reasons for withholding answers are good enough because they're his. Your child knows you don't burden him with things he's not ready for. He trusts you even in your silence. So it must be with God.

The best inference is that faith now has significance in the afterlife, though that's about all we can really say about it. It is best for us to turn our attention to what faith consists of, given that it's more than mere intellectual assent. Clearly it is something internal. We trust God if we act in a way we wouldn't if we didn't trust him. We don't live two parallel lives, one trusting and one not, so we can compare them side-by-side. How do I know if I'm living by trusting God? It doesn't make sense that I would devise some outlandish thing to do just to see if, with his help, I can pull it off.

Or at least it doesn't begin there. Where it begins is appreciating the enormity of what we say we believe in. We're saying there is a whole unseen reality running in and through this quotidian existence and separately too; life is not actually limited to the time and space which gives this life in the body form and shape. God rules there as well as here; or "there," with quote marks, we should probably say. At the end of this life, I walk through a door and enter this wonderful "place" figuratively having streets of gold, but only if I have faith now. Moreover, this life is unimaginably short, in comparison, and what happens here is inconsequential but for how it affects whether I go through that door. So who cares whether I accumulate stuff and have prestige or power in this life, since God tells us those things are meaningless there? This life is the blink of an eye, and I am but a vapor.

So the thing we're to manage, if we have faith, is our motivations for what we do in life. It doesn't mean you don't become educated. It doesn't mean you don't save money for a rainy day. It doesn't mean you don't plan for your future. It doesn't mean you don't use talents, money, influence, prestige, and power as you may have—benignly, of course. It's about what motivates you in these things. If what you want is to grow in maturity with the Lord, seeking him constantly and becoming every day more in his likeness, that's success. That's exercising faith. Being motivated in this way may put you in a "professional Christian" ministry life-path, but maybe not. Having faith is a daily process of checking your motivations, so that every day you act "diligent[ly] to confirm your calling and election."

CHAPTER TWENTY-FIVE

Dangerous God

GOD IS SCARY BECAUSE he is such an all-or-nothing proposition. We accept his offer, or we remain spiritually dead. We'd be more comfortable if we could soften the edges of this extreme binary opposition. We may try to do this with the story of Christ as mediator. We might picture Jesus meek and mild carrying us to safety like hapless lambs. This might seem to ameliorate the harshness of imagining ourselves "sinners in the hands of an angry God"[1] who wields his "terrible swift sword."[2] The oppositional extremes of life with God or death without remain, however. Christ's intervention transcends this opposition; it does not eliminate it.

What happens when this body dies? How can we not consider it? The mortality rate is one hundred percent. Are we snuffed out with no more awareness of anything, forever? Or do we live on? And if our awareness continues on, what do we experience? Are all of us reconciled to God or only some of us? The intuition of significance that is heightened at the time of a loved one's death must mean something about this life, especially given the alternative: it is all pointless and then we die. Our life as we experience it now must have some sort of significance to what happens next. It must be the opportunity for relationship with our Maker. Death really is a significant event, but not because of the frightening superficial animal anticipation of permanent death. It is significant for the reason that it is the end of the opportunity for relationship with God while he is yet unseen.

---

1 The title of a sermon delivered by Jonathan Edwards in 1741.
2 *Battle Hymn of the Republic*, by Julia Ward Howe, 1862.

We are called (though we may not listen) to see beyond physical reality now, to what lies behind it all. We have an opportunity to respond to our intuition that what is beyond is greater than what we experience now. We are to use our imagination—not to embrace a fiction, but to have in our minds an image of a reality that presents no direct visual image to us now. Our intuition of unseen reality lends a feel of enchantment to this life, and also a feel of *gravitas*, of consequence. Without that enchantment of the world, we're left with that question posed by Camus: why not just kill ourselves, if there is no consequence or significance or "heft" or *gravitas* or purpose or meaning to this life?

Is this intuition of an unseen reality just a product of my wishful thinking? And the news of God transcending from there to here, in the person of the Christ, is that also wishful thinking? The point of the Gospel story is that we're not left only with intuition, with trying to put in our mind an image of something not seen, yet more real than what is seen. The story is of God breaking through to us, so that we have more to go on than intuition. Of course, we can reject that whole story, but the intuition remains unless we have the specific intent to suppress it. That intuition is a prompt to which we should respond. Even if to do so, we have to get past distasteful experiences with people who yammer on about a God they don't understand and who are themselves showy, hypocritical, and mean.

We also have to get past the objection we're tempted to entertain that it can't be fair that this story—the Gospel—is necessary to finding God because some people haven't heard it. Who are we to say what's fair? Why does the Bible say that even those who haven't heard it are without excuse?[3] Consider the Book of Job. It was the earliest thing written in the entire Bible. Earlier than Genesis. Earlier than the explicit Old Testament prophecies of a coming physical presence of God with us. Even in Job, it's explained not only that creation screams the existence of God, but that God is our Redeemer in the flesh, among us in the body, a physical affirmation of what we know to be true in a non-physical realm running in and through and beyond this physical reality.[4] Our intuition does not lead us only to a distant God who will be visible to us in the also distant by-and-by. It leads us to the bridge from seen to unseen, that is Jesus, Christ and Redeemer.

In the end, lying alone on our deathbed—because we are alone,

---

3 E.g., Romans 1:20.
4 Job chapter 19.

that's what it means to be on our deathbed—we may say we're alone with God, and we would say it that way because all that fuss about a misunderstood or mangled purported Gospel presented by deeply flawed men is stripped away from us and we're left with the certain knowledge that God is. This idea of a Jesus "meek and mild" is such a lie. People don't typically reject the Gospel story because they become convinced by anti-metaphysical arguments. They reject it because it addresses a scary subject, and its adherents are so darn goofy. Better to tune the whole subject out, many feel. People with a Christian cultural background don't typically turn directly from nominal Christian to atheism. They first turn from Christian to what they imagine as neutral, deluded that such a neutrality might exist. They're trying to avoid the subject, and they're abetted in doing so by the messiness with which flawed people seek God.

We yield to fear of the weighty significance of this life, if we throw that feeling over in favor of a lightness of being that must either reject the momentous claims of religion, or sanitize it to something psychologically more manageable. If we mentally reduce the Lion of Judah to a comfy plush toy we are then tempted to a vision of reality which excludes hard choices more generally. It is not necessarily true that rejection of God also means rejection of objective truth. But it is always true that rejection of objective truth means rejecting God.

Truth is "objective" because it is out there to be discovered, not in here to be invented. Good and evil, likewise. They are unchanging and eternal, not fitted by people to their various desires. They are not to be invented from what "works" (pragmatism) or what we internally generate (existentialism) or what we find congenial to existing beliefs (coherentism).

Just as truth is an external feature of the universe, so numbers and mathematical relationships are real features of the universe, and not something we invent and project onto it. When we do mathematics, we are engaged in discovery, not merely playing a game. If mathematical principles are not real out there, but are merely constructs here in my mind, then in what sense are they "true?" The number 2 is not real then, and neither is the relationship $2+2=4$.

Just as truth and mathematics are real features of the universe, so are other transcendent ideals, like beauty and goodness. They exist in the universe that we did not create, but which we came to inhabit. And so we find these transcendent ideals there or we do not. We don't invent them and project them onto reality. Just as truth and mathematics and binary oppositions and transcendent ideals are real features of the universe, so with meaning, derived literally from the semantic content of the universe, the logos. We find meaning, and therefore purpose, in existence. We don't create it.

These are all ways of describing ideals stacked on values stacked on meaning stacked on facts, stacked on like-with-like differentiation, stacked on binary oppositions of things and concepts, and at the pinnacle of this system of human cognition resides not just truth, and mathematics, and transcendent ideals, and meaning, but the pinnacle of all those things: the origin of truth, and all ideals, and all meaning; that is, God.

Whether God is properly understood to reside at the pinnacle of these abstractions or not, however, we should understand that the hierarchy of value is necessary to guide our understanding of everything. Without this hierarchy of value, there is a collapse into undifferentiated facts from which we can derive no meaning at all. This is a collapse or denial of foundational and oppositional binary dualisms, which frustrates our effort to differentiate in order to find meaning. There is an inability to transcend oppositions progressively with new avenues of understanding, so we are left with ongoing uncomfortable dissonance and tension that never gets resolved.

What has happened over the course of many generations is that we have mentally removed the pinnacle of value and for a time imagined the hierarchy of value to remain in place. But it is collapsing. In society at large, the time-frame for this collapse involves generations, and yet is unmistakable if we have some reckoning of history and especially the history of secular ideas. Today, the sources of truth and beauty and morality and meaning are subject to endless disputation—a sure sign of this collapse. If they're not "out there" phenomena to be discovered, they're internal phenomena to be generated, and that's what many believe. It is no surprise, given this evolution, that truth is supposedly whatever one groups says it is; there is no metanarrative that is authoritative, because all metanarratives are suspect. Metanarratives constitute the hierarchy of values that has now been overthrown. Beauty, too, is an essentially subjective matter, ever in the eye of the beholder, and on this thinking a toilet can be beautiful if arranged as an ironic statement of meaning. Meaning itself, however, is reduced to polemical force only; we are unwilling to find it independently in the universe. Morality is an endless battlefield, in these Stygian ruins of civilization.

Just as we can tear down, we can build up. For an ideal to be an ideal, it must be representative of something that is true. To be representative of something that is true is to be intangibly real itself. The good, the true, and the beautiful exist in tangible things. Those values are not merely suggested by them, nor do they reside in our minds to be imputed to tangible things. For the beautiful mountainscape, for example, beauty has to reside in the thing itself, it is not just something in my mind. If beauty is not a feature of physical things (or mental, like with theorems; or representations, like with paintings), then there is no such thing as an ideal of beauty, it is only a word we use for something that originates with us. Similarly with respect to goodness. Goodness is a product of physical action to some unexplained goal. Similarly with respect to truth. Things are true or they are not in absolute terms, truth is not just something we impute to a state of affairs of our choosing.

What did Pontius Pilate ask? "What is truth?" If truth is only what "works," then it's not an "out there" transcendent truth. As with mathematics, so with any other ideal, like beauty, goodness, and truth itself. If these ideals are not in any sense real, then neither are principles for which we use metaphor and analogy and myth. If you take the Jesus story as only a metaphor, for what is it a metaphor? It can't be true if the ideals for which it is a metaphor are not true. What's in play here, besides all the detailed stuff you already know about Christianity, is the idea of transcendent idealism in the abstract. Nothing is true. The number 2 is not real, and doubling it might yield 5.

Myths are stories to illustrate truths, by way of extended analogy or illustration through hypothetical. They don't create truth, however. They have no meaning if the truth being described is not in fact true. And for the truth to be true, truth in the abstract must exist. And it must exist objectively, not in a way manufactured in the mind. Myths are metanarratives. Metanarratives are the stories we tell to explain ourselves to ourselves, and to explain the world around us. If we reject metanarratives, we reject the hierarchical connectedness of all their elements. Postmodernism does not just reject a metanarrative in order to replace it with another, unless that other be Marxist social engineering, which, though a metanarrative, serves the postmodern deconstruction project. Ultimately, postmodernism rejects all hierarchical values. No mythology, no stories with a "moral," no religion. The entire superstructure of understanding is thus eliminated. The entire hierarchy of value is eliminated. Our recognition of God is a casualty, of course, but so is our recognition of layered moral awareness, and differentiation of profane and sacred, and discernment of like with like and against unlike, in ever-finer shades of meaning, building that hierarchy of values. We worship science, but that metanarrative, too, must fall in time, as we decline to mediocrity and then engage in the all-against-all battle among the ruins of a civilization that was built on hierarchical values, the ruins of the metanarratives that postmodernism destroyed.

It doesn't have to be this way. We can reclaim what our ancestors knew to be true. We can start with the simplest thing: the oppositions by which we make sense of anything. They are fundamental. They provide meaning. All abstractions like mathematics similarly have meaning, and so do abstractions more directly related to physical things and events, like beauty, truth, and goodness. And meaning in the abstract, flooding the world in which we live and move and have our being, building beautiful and intricate towers of hierarchical meaning, metanarratives which populate the plain of our existence, not built from the ground up by us, but pulled upward at the pinnacle by the Hand that brought all into being and who let there be light and who spoke truth into the world.

The opposition of God's justice and mercy cannot be canceled or collapsed. It can be transcended, however, in the death and resurrection of Christ. The opposition of God to me cannot be eliminated, but it can be transcended in how I respond to the offer of reconciliation. The certainty of death would seem to enhance the tension this situation creates in this life, but for most of us, it doesn't seem to. We carry on as if the fact of death is an unfortunate certainty for everyone else—I am the lone exception.

We might instead think of it the way Leo Tolstoy suggested. Imagine you set out in a boat on a river. You are pushed off from shore, and you begin to row to get to the other side. But the current is strong. You tire. You rest and float with the current. Your boat becomes intermingled with the boats of many others. A few struggle against the current, to achieve the other side, but most yield to it. Along the way, you forget your goal, you relax at the oars, you join in the merry-making and revelry of your fellow boaters floating downstream. And then you hear, dimly at first but with increasing clarity, the roar of cataracts ahead, which will destroy you and your boat if you do not wrench yourself free of the current and pull, pull for the other side. Tolstoy: "That shore was God; that direction was tradition; the oars were the freedom given me to pull for the shore and unite with God. And so the force of life was renewed in me and I again began to live."[5]

---

5 Tolstoy, Leo, *Confessions*, 1882.

Life in the body, the span from birth to animal death, is like an airplane runway. The runway ends, so we must either take off or crash. The runway is short, compared to the flight. Its sole purpose is to get us to lift-off. We don't race down the runway unaware of its purpose. It takes some effort to concentrate on a frivolous magazine while the plane hurtles toward the end of the finite runway. God finds us on this short runway, and we either acknowledge him or we don't. It's too late when we get to the end of the runway. If we understand our life as being like this runway, it takes on extra significance. People die all the time, but when it's someone close to us, we have a little sense, vicariously, of this important transition to the air or to the crash. It's why the Bible says: "The heart of the wise is in the house of mourning; but the heart of fools is in the house of mirth."[6]

It is a good thing that we want to build. It is in our nature as image-bearers of God to do so. But on our own, we build futility. We should build on the civilizational metanarrative we have inherited from faithful forbears, being guided by the One who spoke truth into the world, paring away falsehood and distraction and delusion as we go. Let us do our best, as our prophets have admonished, to present ourselves to God as workers approved by him, without shame, rightly handling the word of truth.

---

6 Ecclesiastes 7:4.

Bibliography

Abbott, Edwin Abbott. *Flatland: A Romance of Many Dimensions*. London: Seeley & Co., 1884.

Albert, David. *On the Origin of Everything*, New York Times, March 23, 2012.

Armstrong, Karen. *The Case for God*. New York: Anchor Books, 2009.

Augros, Michael. *Who Designed the Designer?/A Rediscovered Path to God's Existence*. San Francisco: Ignatius, 2015.

Augros, Robert and George Stanciu. *The New Story of Science*. New York: Bantam, 1984.

Ayer, Alfred Jules. *Language, Truth, and Logic*, New York: Dover, 1952 (second edition published 1946).

Baer, Mark. "When Binary Thinking is Involved, Polarization Follows," *Psychology Today* online, January 27, 2017.

Baker, Hunter. *The End of Secularism*. Wheaton, IL: Crossway, 2009.

Baldwin, J.F. *The Deadliest Monster/An Introduction to Worldviews*. New Brunfels, TX: Fishermen, 2005 (4th ed.).

Boethius, Ancius. *Consolation of Philosophy*. New York: McMillan, 1962. (Originally published c. 524).

Bloom, Harold. *The American Religion*. New York: Chu Hartley, 2006 (2nd ed.).

Budziszewski, J. "This Time Will Not Be the Same," *First Things*, March 2014.

_____. *Written on the Heart/The Case for Natural Law*. Downers Grove, IL: Intervarsity, 1997.

Camus, Albert. *The Myth of Sisyphus and Other Essays*. London: H. Hamilton, 1965.

Carroll, Sean. *The Big Picture/On the Origin of Life, Meaning, and the Universe Itself*. New York: Dutton, 2016.

Casanova, Jose. *Public Religions in the Modern World*, Chicago: University of Chicago Press, 1994.

Chopra, Deepak, MD and Anoop Kumar, MD. "As We Evolve, Do We Need God?" Blog at deepakchopra.com, April 16, 2018.

Clegg, Brian. *The God Effect/Quantum Entanglement, Science's Strongest Phenomenon*. New York: St. Martin's Press, 2006.

Clouser, Roy A. *The Myth of Religious Neutrality/An Essay on the Hidden Role of Religious Belief in Theories*. Notre Dame: University of Notre Dame Press, 2006.

Cox, Harvey. *The Secular City*. Princeton, NJ: Princeton University Press, 2013 (first edition 1965).

Crick, Francis. *The Astonishing Hypothesis*. New York: Touchstone, 1994.

Darwin, Charles. *On the Origin of Species*. London: John Murray, 1859.

Davies, Paul. *The Mind of God/The Scientific Basis for a Rational World*. New York: Simon & Schuster, 1992.

_____. *The Demon in the Machine*. New York: Penguin, 2019.

Dawkins, Richard. *The God Delusion*. New York: Houghton Mifflin, 2006.

_____. *The Greatest Show on Earth/The Evidence for Evolution*. New York: Free Press, 2009.

_____. *The Selfish Gene*. New York: Oxford University Press, 1989.

Dennett, Daniel C. *Breaking the Spell/Religion as a Natural Phenomenon*. New York: Penguin, 2006.

_____. *Darwin's Dangerous Idea/Evolution and the Meanings of Life*. New York: Simon & Schuster, 1995.

Dewey, John. *A Common Faith*. New Haven, CT: Yale University Press, 1934.

Dooley, Patrick Kiaran. *Pragmatism as Humanism/The Philosophy of William James*. Chicago: Nelson Hall, 1974.

Douthat, Ross. *Bad Religion/How We Became a Nation of Heretics*. New York: Free Press, 2012.

Durkheim, Emile. *The Elementary Forms of the Religious Life*. New York: Macmillan, 1915.

Dworkin, Ronald. *Religion Without God*. Cambridge, MA: Harvard University Press, 2013.

Dyson, Freeman. *Disturbing the Universe*. New York: Harper & Row, 1979.

Eliot, George. *Scenes from a Clerical Life*, 1857.

Feser, Edward. *Five Proofs of the Existence of God*. San Francisco: Ignatius, 2017.

_____. *The Last Supersititon/A Refutation of the New Atheism*. South Bend, IN: St. Augustine's Press, 2008.

_____. *Philosophy of Mind*. London: Oneworld, 2005.

_____. "Scientists Should Tell Lawrence Krauss to Shut Up Already," *Public Discourse* (Witherspoon Institute) September 28, 2015.

Flew, Anthony. *There is a God/How the World's Most Notorious Atheist Changed His Mind*. New York: Harperone, 2007.

Gabriel, Markus. *I Am Not a Brain*. Medford, MA: Polity Press, 2017.

Geisler, Norman L. and Frank Turek. *I Don't Have Enough Faith to be an Atheist*. Wheaton, IL: Crossway, 2004.

Geisler, Norman L. and Patrick Zukeran. *Christian Apologetics*. Grand Rapids, MI: Baker, 2009.

Gilbert, Alan D. *The Making of Post-Christian Britain/A History of the Secularization of Modern Society*. New York: Longman, 1980.

Girard, René. *I See Satan Fall Like Lightning*. Maryknoll, NY: Orbis, 2001.

_____. *Things Hidden Since the Foundation of the World*. Stanford, CA: Stanford University Press, 1987.

Giridharadas, Anand. "How Elites Lost Their Grip in 2019," *Time Magazine*, Nov. 21, 2019.

Goldstein, Rebecca. *Incompleteness/The Proof and Paradox of Kurt Gödel*. New York: W.W. Norton, 2005.

Grayling, A.C. *The God Argument/The Case Against Religion and for Humanism*. New York: Bloomsbury USA, 2013.

Grenz, Stanley J. *A Primer on Postmodernism*. Grand Rapids, MI: Eerdmans, 1996.

Groothius, Douglas. *Truth Decay/Defending Christianity Against the Challenges of Postmodernism*. Downer's Grove, IL: Intervarsity, 2000.

Gurri, Martin. "Everything Explained," *City Journal*, Summer 2020, see https://www.city-journal.org/2020-riots-protests?

Harris, Sam. *The End of Faith*. New York: W.W. Norton, 2004.

Hägglund, Martin. *This Life/Secular Faith and Spiritual Freedom*. New York: Anchor Books, 2019.

Hall, Kirsten A. "Crusoe at the Crossroads/On Robinson Crusoe, Lost, and Why We Keep Returning to Mysterious Islands Where Science Blurs with the Supernatural," *The New Atlantis*, Summer 2019.

Hardy, G.H. *A Mathematician's Apology*. Cambridge, MA: Cambridge University Press, 1992 (originally published 1940).

Harris, Sam. *Letter to A Christian Nation*. New York: Vintage, 2006.

Hart, David Bentley. *Atheist Delusions/The Christian Revolution and Its Fashionable Enemies*. New Haven: Yale University Press, 2009.

_____. *The Experience of God/Being, Consciousness, Bliss*. New Haven, CT: Yale University Press, 2013.

_____. *The Story of Christianity/A History of 2000 Years of the Christian Faith*. London: Quercus Editions, 2009.

Hasker, William. *The Emergent Self*. Ithaca, NY: Cornell University Press, 1999.

Hemon, Aleksandar. "Fascism is Not an Idea to Be Debated, It's a Set of Actions to Fight," *Literary Hub*, November 1, 2018.

Hicks, Stephen R.C. *Explaining Postmodernism/Skepticism and Socialism From Rousseau to Foucault*. Ockam's Razor, 2017 (3rd ed.).

Hitchens, Christopher. *God is Not Great/How Religion Poisons Everything*. New York: Twelve, 2009.

Hitchens, Peter. *The Rage Against God*. London: Continuum, 2010.

Hobbes, Thomas. *Leviathan.* 1651.

James, William. *Pragmatism.* Cambridge, NH: Hackett, 1981. (originally published 1907).

_____. *Will to Believe.* New York: Dover, 1956 (originally published 1897).

Jacoby, Susan. *Freethinkers.* New York: Metropolitan Books, 2004.

Johnson, Dru. *The Universal Story/Genesis 1-11.* Bellingham, WA: Lexham Press, 2018.

Johnson, Paul. *The Birth of the Modern/World Society 1815-1830.* New York: Harper Collins, 1991.

_____. *Modern Times.* London: Weidenfield & Nicolsen, 1983.

Keller, Timothy. *The Reason for God/Belief in an Age of Skepticism.* New York: Dutton, 2008.

Kierkegaard, Søren. *Fear and Trembling,* translated by Howard V. Hong and Edna H. Hong. Princeton, NJ: Princeton University Press, 1983 (originally published 1843).

_____. *The Lily of the Field and the Bird of the Air,* translated by and introduction by Bruce H. Kirmmse. Princeton, NJ: Princeton University Press, 2016 (originally published 1849).

_____. *The Sickness Unto Death.* Milwaukee, WI: Wiseblood Books, 2013 (originally published 1849).

_____. *Either/Or.* New York: Doubleday, 1959 (originally published 1843).

Konner, Melvin. *Believers/Faith in Human Nature.* New York: W.W. Norton, 2019.

Koukl, Gregory. *The Story of Reality.* Grand Rapids, MI: Zondervan, 2017.

Krauss, Lawrence. "All Scientists Should be Militant Atheists," *The New Yorker*, Sept. 8, 2015.

_____. *A Universe from Nothing/Why There is Something Rather than Nothing*. New York: Atria, 2012.

Lacan, Jacques. *The Four Fundamental Concepts of Psychoanalysis*. Editions du Seuil, 1973 (translated to English 1978 by Alan Sheridan).

Lande, Daniel R. "Development of the Binary Number System and the Foundations of Computer Science," *The Mathematics Enthusiast*: Vol. 11: No. 3, Article 6, 2014. Available at: https://scholarworks.umt.edu/tme/vol11/iss3/6.

Levi, Carlo. *Christ Stopped at Eboli,* translated by Frances Frenaye. New York: Farrar, Straus and Giroux, 1945.

Levinas, Emmanuel. *Totality and Infinity*. Pennsylvania: Duquesne University Press, 1969.

_____. *Alterity and Transcendence*. New York: Columbia University Press, 1999.

Lewis, C.S. *The Abolition of Man*. New York: HarperOne, 2000.

_____. *God in the Dock*. Grand Rapids, MI: Eerdmans, 2002.

_____. *Mere Christianity*. New York: Macmillan, 1960.

Lewis, C.S. and Joy Davidman. *Miracles: A Preliminary Study*. New York: Macmillan Co., 1947.

Lyotard, Jean-Francois. *The Postmodern Condition/A Report on Knowledge*. Manchester, UK: Manchester University Press, 1979.

MacLeod, Adam. "Essences or Intersectionality: Understanding Why We Can't Understand Each Other," *Witherspoon Institute* March 1, 2020.

Mahoney, Daniel. *The Idol of Our Age: How the Religion of Humanity Subverts Christianity*. New York: Encounter Books, 2018.

Mayr, Ernest. *What Evolution Is*. New York: Perseus, 2001.

Merricks, Trenton. *Truth and Ontology*. Oxford: Oxford University Press, 2009.

Mill, John Stuart. *On Liberty*. 1859.

Milosz, Czeslaw. *The Captive Mind*. New York: Vintage International, 1990 (originally published 1951).

Moyers, Bill and Joseph Campbell. *Joseph Campbell and the Power of Myth*, Interview with Bill Moyers, Episode 2: 'The Message of the Myth,' at billmoyers.com.

Murray, Abdu. *Saving Truth/Finding Meaning & Clarity in a Post-Truth World*. Grand Rapids, MI: Zondervan, 2018.

Mussolini, Benito. *The Fundamentals of Fascism*. 1935.

Von Neumann, John. *The Computer and the Brain*. New Haven, CT: Yale University Press, 2012.

Nietzsche, Friedrich. *On the Genealogy of Morals*, translated by Walter Kaufmann and RJ Hollingdale, NY: Vintage Books, 1989 (originally published 1887).

_____. *Twilight of the Idols*. Oxford: Oxford University Press, 1998 (originally published 1889).

Noble, Alan. *Disruptive Witness/Speaking Truth in a Distracted Age*. Downer's Grove, IL: Intervarsity, 2018.

Noll, Mark A. *The Scandal of the Evangelical Mind*. Grand Rapids, MI: Eerdmans, 1994.

Norton, Albert. *Another Like Me*. Dallas: eLectio Publishing, 2016.

_____. *Intuition of Significance/Evidence Against Materialism and for God*. Eugene, OR: Resource Publications, 2020.

O'Grady, Selina. *And Man Created God*. New York: St. Martin's, 2013.

Otto, Rudolf. *The Idea of the Holy*. London: Oxford University Press, 1950 (2nd ed.)

Plantinga, Alvin. *Knowledge and Christian Belief*. Grand Rapids, MI: Eerdmans, 2015.

_____. *Where the Conflict Really Lies/Science, Religion, & Naturalism*. New York: Oxford University Press, 2011.

Rawls, John. *The Law of Peoples/The Idea of Public Reason Revisited*. Cambridge, MA: Harvard University Press, 1999.

Rée, Jonathan. *Witcraft/The Invention of Philosophy in English*. London: Penguin/Random House, 2019.

Derrida, Jacques. "Violence and Metaphysics and Writing and Difference," as cited by Jack Reynolds of LaTrobe University Australia, in his contribution on Derrida to the *Internet Encyclopedia of Philosophy*, iep.utm.edu/derrida (section 5).

Rorty, Richard and Gianni Vattimo. *The Future of Religion*. New York: Columbia University Press, 2004.

Rousseau, Jean-Jacques. *On the Social Contract*, translated by G.D.H. Cole, Mineola, NY: Cosimo Classics, 2003 (originally published 1762).

Rutherford, Adam. *A Brief History of Everyone Who Ever Lived*. New York: The Experiment, 2016.

Schaeffer, Francis A. *The Complete Works of Francis A. Schaeffer*. Wheaton, IL: Crossway, 1985 (2nd ed).

Schrift, Alan D. *Nietzsche and the Critique of Oppositional Thinking, History of European Ideas*, Volume 11. 1989, pp. 783-790.

Schwartz, Barry. *The Paradox of Choice*. New York: Harper, 2004.

Scruton, Roger. *Beauty/A Very Short Introduction*. New York: Oxford University Press, 2011.

_____. *Modern Philosophy/An Introduction and Survey*. New York: Penguin, 1994.

_____. *The Soul of the World*. Princeton, NJ: Princeton University Press, 2014.

_____. "The Turing Machine Speaks," *City Journal* online blog, Summer 2019.

Scruton, Roger and Peter Singer and Christopher Ganaway and Michael Tanner. *German Philosophers*, Kant, Hegel, Schopenhauer, and Nietzche. New York: Oxford University Press, 1997.

Smith, James K.A. *How (Not) to be Secular/Reading Charles Taylor*. Grand Rapids, MI: Eerdmans, 2014.

_____. *Who's Afraid of Postmodernism/Taking Derrida, Lyotard, and Foucault to Church*. Grand Rapids, MI: Baker, 2006.

Smith, R. Scott. *Truth & The New Kind of Christian/The Emerging Effects of Postmodernism in the Church*. Wheaton, IL: Crossway, 2005.

Smith, Steven D. *The Disenchantment of Secular Discourse*. Cambridge, MA: Harvard University Press, 2010.

_____. *Foreordained Failure/The Quest for a Constitutional Principle of Religious Freedom*. New York: Oxford University Press, 1995.

_____. *Pagans & Christians in the City/Culture Wars from the Tiber to the Potomac*. Grand Rapids, MI: Eerdmans, 2018.

Stanciu, George. "Physics, Beauty, & the Divine Mind," *The Imaginative Conservative* (on-line journal), September 28, 2016.

Stenger, Victor J. *God/The Failed Hypothesis/How Science Shows That God Does Not Exist*. Amherst, NY: Prometheus, 2007.

Trueman, Carl. *The Rise and Triumph of the Modern Self/Cultural Amnesia, Expressive Individualism, and the Road to Sexual Revolution.* Wheaton, IL: Crossway, 2020.

Taylor, Charles. *A Secular Age.* Cambridge, MA: Belknap 2007.

Thoreau, Henry Walden. *The Variorium Walden.* New York: Washington Square Press, 1962. (Originally published 1854).

Thornton, Sharon G. "Beyond Oppositional Thinking: Radical Respect," paper for 2007 Ohio Valley Philosophy of Education Society, files.eric.ed.gov/fulltext/EJ1072476.pdf.

Tolstoy, Leo. *A Confession.* 1882.

Vardy, Peter. *An Introduction to Kierkegaard.* Peabody, MA: Penguin, 2008.

Weaver, Richard. *Ideas Have Consequences.* Chicago: University of Chicago Press, 2013 (originally published 1948).

Weber, Max. *The Sociology of Religion.* Boston, MA: 1922 (2nd ed.).

White, Heath. *Postmodernism 101.* Grand Rapids, MI: Brazos, 2006.

Wood, Jack Denfeld and Gianpiero Petriglieri. "Transcending Polarization: Beyond Binary Thinking," *Transactional Analysis Journal,* Vol. 35, No. 1, January, 2005, p. 33.

Zacharias, Ravi. *The End of Reason/A Response to the New Atheists.* Grand Rapids, MI: Zondervan, 2008.

Zuckerman, Phil. *Living the Secular Life/New Answers to Old Questions.* New York: Penguin, 2014.

Index

V

value(s) 12, 14, 21-23, 38, 39, 41, 43,
          48, 50, 58, 59, 108, 112, 134,
          140, 144-146 148, 171, 183-
          186, 209, 238-240
  hierarchical 38, 48, 145, 146

W

Weber, Max 169, 253
weight of meaning 93
will-to-power 86, 104, 132
worldview 9, 10, 29, 150, 154, 157,
          199, 201
  atheism/atheist 10, 12, 79, 80, 81,
          89, 93, 94, 106, 114, 115, 123,
          124, 128, 130, 137, 142, 143,
          144, 147, 152, 154, 155, 156,
          160, 170, 177, 180, 187, 189,
          190, 193, 194, 198, 199, 200,
          201, 203, 208, 237
  theism/theist 10, 76, 80, 87, 88, 91,
          94, 124, 127, 147, 151, 153,
          154, 155, 177, 178, 187, 189,
          190, 192, 193, 199, 202

Y

yin and yang 19

Z

ziggurat 56, 132

CPSIA information can be obtained
at www.ICGtesting.com
Printed in the USA
BVHW080457150521
607367BV00003B/371